基礎から学ぶ

貿易実務

日英対訳

【改訂版】

Learn International Trade from Basics
(in Japanese & English)
Revised Edition

曽我しのぶ 著
Shinobu Soga

参考訳：㈱アースリンク
Translated by Earth Link Co., Ltd.
(for Reference Purposes Only)

公益財団法人 日本関税協会
Japan Tariff Association

本書について

- 本英訳は参考訳であり、日本語版と英訳に齟齬がある場合、日本語版が優先されます。
- 本書は著者・発行者が実際に調査した結果を慎重に検討し著述・編集しています。ただし、本書の記述内容に従って行った結果により発生するあらゆる損害・障害につきましては、責任を負いませんのであらかじめご了承ください。
- 本書は2023年9月現在の情報にもとづいて記述されております。
- 本書で紹介している各種のサンプル書式は、その様式が会社ごとに異なる場合があります。予めご了承ください。詳細については書類を提供する会社等にお問い合わせください。特に売買契約書は、参考契約書であり、個別の案件につきましては、弁護士等各専門家にご相談ください。
- サンプル書式を利用した結果にまつわるあらゆる損害・障害については、責任を負いませんのであらかじめご了承ください。
- サンプル書式の著作権は、著者及び公益財団法人日本関税協会が所有します。許可なく配布・販売することは固く禁止致します。

About This Book

- This English translation is for reference purposes only. If there is any discrepancy between the Japanese version and the English translation, the Japanese version shall prevail.
- This book has been written and edited by careful review of the study the author and the publisher have actually conducted. However, please note that neither the author nor the publisher assumes any responsibility and shall be liable for any loss or damage incurred as a result of performance based on the descriptions in this book.
- This book provides the information as of September 2023.
- Please note that the sample forms introduced in this book may differ among companies. For details, please contact the company etc., providing the relevant form.
  In particular, the sales contract is provided for reference purposes only. You should consult with your legal adviser etc., regarding your particular situation.
- Please note that neither the author nor the publisher assumes any responsibility and shall be liable for any loss or damage arising from the use of the sample forms.
- The author and Japan Tariff Association hold a copyright of the sample forms. Any distribution or sale of the sample forms without permission is strictly prohibited.

はじめに

　現在、わが国の生産活動には多くの国々との関わりがあり、原材料を直接的間接的に海外から仕入れたり、日本で生産した物を海外に販売したりして成り立っています。

　自社が直接海外と取引しているのでなくても、組み込んでいる部品の一部に海外からの輸入品が含まれていたりしますので、今やこのような海外との商取引は、大企業のみならず、どんな企業にも少なからず関わりがあるといえます。

　私たちの身の回りにある商品も、その多くがこれらの海外との輸出取引や輸入取引を経て、私たちの手元に届いています。

　ところが、海外との商取引をするには商品が必ず国境を越えることになり、国内の商取引とは異なる手続が必要となってくるため、同じ商取引でも国内の場合よりも関係機関や業務が増え、複雑化しています。その全貌をとらえたり、複雑な手続きを遅滞なく進めていくことは初心者の方には高いハードルとなっているのが現状です。

　筆者は長い間、初めて貿易業務を担当する、あるいはこれから海外展開を検討しているという方のために、貿易実務の基礎知識についてのセミナーを担当したり、コンサルタントをしたりして参りましたが、せっかくの事業拡大のチャンスをその高いハードルのためにつかめないでいる企業や、日常業務をこなしきれずに悩んでいらっしゃる方を多くお見掛けしました。

　本書はそのような方々のために、独学ではなかなかつかみきれない取引の全体像と、業務に必要な知識を体系的に整理し、学べることを目的に執筆しました。

　また、海外との取引を進めていくにあたり、最近は日本人スタッフだけではなく、外国人スタッフとも緊密な連携を図っていくことが不可欠となってきています。

　このため本書は、貿易取引の基礎知識についてわかりやすく体系立てて説明するとともに、英語による対訳をつけました（弊社による参考訳）。同じ内容を日本人だけでなく様々な国のスタッフと共有し、仲間として共に学んで頂ければと思っております。

　本書は、筆者が多くの企業様からのご質問、ご相談を通し、海外との取引においてここをしっかり理解しておかないとトラブルやリスクにつながると経験的に学んだポイントを、わかりやすくまとめることを心掛けました。

　ご相談頂きました多くの企業様の事例が普遍的に読者の皆様に還元され、共有して頂けて、多くの方の海外取引の一助になりましたら幸甚です。

　本書の発刊にあたり、筆者の伝えたいという思いに共感して頂き、公益財団法人日本関税協会の皆様に多大なご支援を頂戴致しました。発刊のお声がけを頂戴し、筆者の執筆目的に細やかに寄り添い編集して下さいましたご担当者の皆様へ心からの感謝と賛辞を捧げます。

　本書の英訳は、弊社に過去在籍したスタッフ、現在おりますスタッフによる参考訳であり、筆者を含め、気の遠くなるような時間をかけて膨大な作業を致しました。こうして一つの形になりましたことにスタッフにあらためて心から感謝したいと思います。

　本書が、貿易取引をめざす、あるいは貿易実務を担う多くの方へ向けたエールとなり、少しでもお役に立てましたら心からうれしく思います。

2023年9月

（株）アースリンク　代表取締役

曽我　しのぶ

Introduction

Currently, our production activities involve many countries and depend on purchasing raw materials directly or indirectly from overseas and selling goods produced in Japan overseas.

Even if no direct overseas transaction is conducted, imported goods may be contained in built-in components. Therefore, overseas transactions are now significantly relevant to not only large companies but also any company.

Most of our personal belongings also reach us through export or import transactions.

However, overseas transactions involve more authorities and operations and are more complicated than domestic transactions because goods are definitely transported across national borders and the procedures different from those of domestic transactions are required. At present, there is a high bar for beginners to understand the whole process and conduct complicated procedures without delay.

For a long time, the author has been conducting seminars on basic knowledge of international trade and consultations for persons assigned to international trade for the first time or considering overseas expansion. At such times, the author saw many companies that let an opportunity for business expansion go by due to this high bar and many persons who were suffering from difficulty in performing routine tasks.

The author has written this book so that such persons can organize systematically and learn the whole picture of transaction and the required knowledge, which are difficult to be obtained by learning on their own.

In addition, it is absolutely necessary that both Japanese staff and non-

Japanese staff closely cooperate in order to proceed overseas transactions.

For this reason, the English translation (by our company for reference purposes only) is also included. The author hopes the contents can be shared among staff from various nations and learned together.

The author has endeavored to clearly sort out the points the author learned through the experiences of questions from or consultations with many companies that any trouble or risk may arise without a full understanding of such points.

It would be my pleasure if such questions and consultations could be universally utilized by and shared among you readers, and help your overseas transactions.

On the occasion of publication of this book, Japan Tariff Association shared my idea and provided me with great support. I would like to express my sincere gratitude and appreciation to the members of Editorial Department for their offer of publication and the editing with meticulous care to achieve our goals.

The English translation was conducted by former and current staff in our company for reference purposes only. All of them, myself included, did a huge amount of work over an incredibly long period of time. I am deeply grateful to all the staff.

I would be very pleased if this book would send hearty cheers and be of some help to many persons who start overseas transactions or are assigned to international trade.

Shinobu Soga
Earth Link Co., Ltd.
September 2023

【目次】

はじめに.. iii

目次 viii

第1章　マーケティングと取引交渉

1. 貿易取引開始までの流れ **002**

2. 市場調査と取引先の発見 **002**

(1) 輸入の市場と輸出の市場.. 002

(2) 市場調査の調査項目 004

(3) 市場調査の方法 006

(4) 輸出戦略.. 008

(5) 取引先発見の方法 008

3. 取引交渉..**010**

(1) 取引交渉の流れ 010

(2) 申込み 012

4. 信用調査..**014**

(1) 信用調査の重要性 014

(2) 信用調査の方法 016

第2章　売買契約の成立

1. 売買契約の成立.......................................**020**

(1) 契約書の作成... 020

(2) 契約書の書式... 020

(3) 簡略書式の売買契約書 020

(4) タイプ条項と印刷条項 (裏面約款) 022

(5) タイプ条項の具体例 022

(6) 印刷条項 (裏面約款) の例 028

2. ウィーン売買条約 (CISG) **030**

(1) ウィーン売買条約とは 030

(2) わが国の加入と条約の発効.. 032

【Contents】

Introduction v

Contents ix

Chapter 1　Marketing and Trade Negotiation

❚ 1. Flow to Conclude Trade Contract 003

❚ 2. Market Research and Finding Trading Partner 003

(1) Import Market and Export Market 003

(2) Items for Market Research 005

(3) Methods of Market Research 007

(4) Export Strategy..009

(5) Methods of Finding Trading Partners 009

❚ 3. Trade Negotiation. 011

(1) Flow of Trade Negotiation...011

(2) Offer 013

❚ 4. Credit Investigation 015

(1) Items for Credit Investigation..015

(2) Methods of Credit Investigation 017

Chapter 2　Conclusion of a Sales Contract

❚ 1. Conclusion of a Sales Contract 021

(1) Drawing up a Contract 021

(2) Documentary Forms of a Contract..021

(3) Simplified Contract Forms...021

(4) Typed and Printed Terms and Conditions..................................023

(5) Example of Typed Clause 023

(6) Example of Printed Clause (Terms and Conditions on Reverse Side).......029

❚ 2. United Nations Convention on Contracts for the
International Sale of Goods (Vienna, 1980) (CISG) 031

(1) What is CISG?...031

(2) Japan's Accession and Entry into Force 033

(3) CISGの適用要件 032

(4) CISGの適用排除 034

| 3. 契約の当事者 **036**

(1) 本人と代理人 036

(2) 販売店契約と代理店契約 038

(3) 独占的販売権、代理権 038

第3章　貿易実務の流れ

| 1. 貿易取引と国内取引との相違点 **042**

(1) 貿易取引は売買取引 042

(2) 国内取引との相違点 042

(3) 貿易取引のリスク 044

| 2. 輸出実務の流れ **046**

| 3. 為替変動リスクの回避 **050**

(1) 為替変動リスクとは 050

(2) 為替先物予約によるリスクの回避 050

(3) 先物相場の受け渡し時期の決め方 052

(4) 為替予約の手続 054

| 4. 主要貿易書類 **054**

(1) Commercial Invoice (商業送り状) 054

(2) Packing List (梱包明細書) 054

(3) Bill of Lading (B/L) (船荷証券) 054

(4) Insurance Policy (保険証券) 056

第4章　貿易条件とインコタームズ

| 1. 貿易条件とインコタームズ **060**

(1) 貿易条件とは 060

(2) インコタームズ (Incoterms) とは 060

| 2. 定型取引条件の示すもの **062**

(1) 定型取引条件で示される負担の範囲 062

(2) FOB、CFR、CIFと書類 064

（3）Applicable Requirements for CISG 033

（4）Exclusion from Application of CISG 035

| 3. Party to a Contract 037

（1）Principal and Agent 037

（2）Distributorship Agreement and Agency Agreement 039

（3）Exclusive Distributorship, Exclusive Agency. 039

Chapter 3   Flow of Trade Practice

| 1 Differences between Trade Transactions and
Domestic Transactions 043

（1）Trade means Transactions between Different Countries 043

（2）Differences from Domestic Transactions. 043

（3）Risks Involved in Trade Transactions 045

| 2. Flow of Export Practice 047

| 3. Averting Foreign Currency Exchange Risks 051

（1）Currency Exchange Risks 051

（2）Averting Foreign Currency Exchange Risks by Forward Exchange
Contract 051

（3）How to Decide Delivery Date/Period 053

（4）Procedures for Forward Exchange Contract 055

| 4. Major Trade Documents 055

（1）Commercial Invoice 055

（2）Packing List 055

（3）Bill of Lading (B/L) 055

（4）Insurance Policy 057

Chapter 4   Trade Terms and Incoterms

| 1. Trade Terms and Incoterms 061

（1）Trade Terms 061

（2）Incoterms 061

| 2. Interpretation of Trade Terms. 063

（1）Responsibilities Indicated by Trade Terms 063

（2）FOB, CFR, CIF, and the Documents. 065

┃ 3. 貨物の危険の移転時点と保険 066
　(1) FOB、CFR規則の場合の保険 068
　(2) CIF規則の場合の保険 068
┃ 4. インコタームズ2020の11規則 070
┃ 5. 輸送方法とインコタームズ 076
　(1) 輸送方法とインコタームズの不一致 076
　(2) 輸送方法に適したインコタームズ 078
┃ 6. 見積価格の算出 080

第5章　貿易取引の運送

┃ 1. 主な貿易運送の種類 086
┃ 2. 海上輸送 088
　(1) 定期船と不定期船 088
　(2) 定期船の運賃 088
　(3) 傭船契約の運賃 090
　(4) 船荷証券 (B/L) 092
┃ 3. 航空輸送 100
　(1) 直接貨物輸送契約と混載貨物輸送契約 100
　(2) 航空運送状 (Air Waybill) 104
┃ 4. 国際複合輸送 106
　(1) 国際複合輸送とは 106
　(2) 複合運送人 106
　(3) 国際複合輸送の運送書類 108

第6章　貨物海上保険

┃ 1. 英文貨物海上保険証券 112
┃ 2. 協会貨物約款 (ICC) 112
┃ 3. 旧ICCと新ICC 112
┃ 4. 損害の種類 114
　(1) 全損 (Total Loss) 114
　(2) 分損 (Partial Loss) 114
　(3) その他の費用損害 114

3. Transfer of Risks and Insurance 067
　(1) Insurance under FOB and CFR Rules 069
　(2) Insurance under CIF Rule 069
4. 11 Rules in Incoterms 2020 071
5. Incoterms and Modes of Transportation............................077
　(1) Inconsistency between the Modes of Transportation and Incoterms......077
　(2) Incoterms Appropriate for the Modes of Transportation..................079
6. Preparation for a Quotation 081

Chapter 5　Transportation for International Trade

1. Major Modes of Transportation 087
2. Ocean Transportation 089
　(1) Liner and Tramper..089
　(2) Freight of Liners..089
　(3) Freight of Charter Party...091
　(4) Bill of Lading 093
3. Air Transportation 101
　(1) Transportation Contract with Airline and Transportation Contract
　　　with Consolidator..101
　(2) Air Waybill...105
4. International Combined Transportation............................107
　(1) Combined Transportation...107
　(2) Combined Transport Operators 107
　(3) Transport Document of International Combined Transportation..........109

Chapter 6　Marine Cargo Insurance

1. Marine Cargo Insurance Policy...................................113
2. Institute Cargo Clauses (ICC)...................................113
3. ICC (1963) / ICC (1982) 113
4. Covered Loss / Damage 115
　(1) Total Loss 115
　(2) Partial Loss 115
　(3) Other Damage of Cost..115

| | 5．保険金額 | 116 |

| | 6．各種の約款（新ICCバージョン） | 116 |

	7．新ICCにおける基本条件	116
	(1) ICC (A)	118
	(2) ICC (B)	118
	(3) ICC (C)	120

| | 8．戦争危険とストライキ危険 | 124 |

| | 9．付加危険 | 124 |

| | 10．新旧ICCの担保条件の比較 | 126 |

	11．旧ICCにおける基本条件	130
	(1) ICC (1963) における基本条件	130
	(2) 戦争危険およびストライキ、暴動危険のてん補	134

| | 12．保険でてん補されないもの | 134 |

	13．確定保険と予定保険	136
	(1) 個別予定保険 (Provisional Insurance)	136
	(2) 包括予定保険 (Open Cover)	138

第7章　代金決済方法

	1．外国との決済手段の種類	142
	2．荷為替手形による代金決済	142
	(1) 信用状取引	142
	(2) 一覧払手形と期限付手形	150
	(3) 信用状にもとづかない荷為替手形の決済	154

	3．送金による代金決済	158
	(1) 前払い送金と後払い送金	158
	(2) 送金方法	158

第8章　輸出の通関・船積み

	1．輸出実務の流れ	164
	2．輸出通関の流れ	168
	(1) 輸出通関の流れ	168
	(2) 保税地域	168

5. Amount Insured 117
6. Various Clauses (ICC (2009)) 117
7. Basic Conditions in ICC(2009)....................................117
   (1) ICC(A) 119
   (2) ICC(B)..119
   (3) ICC(C) 121
8. Coverage against the Risk of War & Strikes 125
9. Extraneous Risk 125
10. Comparisons of Conditions between ICC (1963) and ICC(2009) ..127
11. Basic Conditions in ICC...131
   (1) Three Basic Conditions in ICC (1963)........................131
   (2) Coverage against the Risk of War & S.R.C.C.
      (Strikes, Riots and Civil Commotions)......................135
12. Uncovered Loss / Damage.......................................135
13. Definite Insurance Contract and Provisional Insurance Contract. ..137
   (1) Provisional Insurance Contract for Individual Shipment..................137
   (2) Open Cover Contract 139

Chapter 7   Methods of Settlement

1. Methods of Settlement in International Trade 143
2. Settlement of Documentary Bill.................................143
   (1) Transactions under Letter of Credit........................143
   (2) Sight Bill and Usance Bill..................................151
   (3) Settlement of Bill of Exchange Without L/C.................155
3. Settlement by Remittance.......................................159
   (1) Advance Payment and Deferred Payment 159
   (2) Methods of Remittance 159

Chapter 8   Export Clearance and Shipment

1. Flow of Export Practice 165
2. Export Clearance...169
   (1) Flow of Export Clearance 169
   (2) Bonded Area 169

┃ 3．法令による輸出規制．．．．．．．．．．．．．．．．．．．．．．．．．．．．．．．．．．．．．168
┃ 4．輸出通関・船積み．．．．．．．．．．．．．．．．．．．．．．．．．．．．．．．．．．．．．．170
　（1）コンテナ・ターミナル．．．．．．．．．．．．．．．．．．．．．．．．．．．．．．．．．．．170
　（2）FCL貨物とLCL貨物．．．．．．．．．．．．．．．．．．．．．．．．．．．．．．．．．．．174
　（3）コンテナ船への船積み．．．．．．．．．．．．．．．．．．．．．．．．．．．．．．．．．176
　（4）船積通知．．178

第9章　輸入の通関・荷受け

┃ 1．輸入実務の流れ．．．．．．．．．．．．．．．．．．．．．．．．．．．．．．．．．．．．．．．182
┃ 2．輸入通関の流れ．．．．．．．．．．．．．．．．．．．．．．．．．．．．．．．．．．．．．．．186
┃ 3．輸入の法規制．．186
┃ 4．関税制度．．186
　（1）関税の算出方法．．．．．．．．．．．．．．．．．．．．．．．．．．．．．．．．．．．．．186
　（2）特恵関税制度．．．．．．．．．．．．．．．．．．．．．．．．．．．．．．．．．．．．．．188
　（3）経済連携協定（EPA）等にもとづく税率．．．．．．．．．．．．．．．．．．．．188
　（4）減免税、戻し税制度．．．．．．．．．．．．．．．．．．．．．．．．．．．．．．．．．188
┃ 5．貨物の荷受け．．．．．．．．．．．．．．．．．．．．．．．．．．．．．．．．．．．．．．．190
　（1）コンテナ船の貨物の荷受け．．．．．．．．．．．．．．．．．．．．．．．．．．．．．190
　（2）B/Lなしでの貨物の引取り．．．．．．．．．．．．．．．．．．．．．．．．．．．．．192

第10章　クレーム

┃ 1．貨物の点検．．．200
┃ 2．発生の確認．．．200
┃ 3．事故通知（予備クレーム）．．．．．．．．．．．．．．．．．．．．．．．．．．．．．．200
┃ 4．保険会社への通知とサーベイ．．．．．．．．．．．．．．．．．．．．．．．．．．．202
　（1）保険会社への通知．．．．．．．．．．．．．．．．．．．．．．．．．．．．．．．．．．202
　（2）サーベイ（損害検査）による責任所在の究明．．．．．．．．．．．．．．．．204
┃ 5．保険金の請求．．．．．．．．．．．．．．．．．．．．．．．．．．．．．．．．．．．．．．204
┃ 6．保険金の支払いと保険会社の代位請求．．．．．．．．．．．．．．．．．．．．204

3. Laws and Regulations of Export....................................169
4. Export Clearance and Shipment 171
(1) Container Terminal..171
(2) FCL Cargo and LCL Cargo..175
(3) Making Shipment by Container Ship 177
(4) Shipping Advice..179

Chapter 9   Import Clearance and Receiving Cargo

1. Flow of Import Practice...183
2. Flow of Import Clearance..187
3. Laws and Regulations of Import 187
4. Tariff System...187
(1) Calculation Method of Customs Duties....................................187
(2) Outline of Generalized System of Preferences (GSP) 189
(3) Duty Rates under Economic Partnership Agreements (EPAs).............189
(4) Reduction and Exemption of Customs Duties 189
5. Receiving a Cargo...191
(1) Receiving a Cargo from a Container Ship 191
(2) Receiving a Cargo without a B/L..193

Chapter 10   Claims

1. Examination of Cargo 201
2. Finding Damages 201
3. Notice of Loss or Damage (Preliminary Claims) 201
4. Notice to Insurance Company and Survey 203
(1) Notice to Insurance Company..203
(2) Survey..205
5. Insurance Claims...205
6. Insurance Money Payment and Subrogation 205

第11章　製造物責任（P/L）

1．製造物責任...208
 （1）製造物責任（P/L）とは 208
 （2）無過失責任.. 208
2．製造物責任への対応策...................................208
 （1）PL対応策の重要性.. 208
 （2）製品安全対策... 208
 （3）PL予防対策 210
 （4）PL訴訟対策 212
3．PL保険...212
 （1）輸出PL保険 212
 （2）輸入PL保険 216

第12章　紛争の解決方法

1．売手へのクレーム......................................220
2．紛争の解決手段.......................................220
 （1）解決方法... 222
 （2）裁判と仲裁.. 222
 （3）仲裁 224

付録　各種帳票集

印刷条項（裏面約款）の例 228
Commercial Invoice（商業送り状）（送金用）................................ 229
Packing List（梱包明細書）（送金用）...................................... 230
Bill of Lading（B/L）（船荷証券）（送金用）................................ 231
貨物海上保険証券（ICC2009）... 232
貨物海上保険証券（ICC2009）裏面... 233
貨物海上保険証券（S.G.フォーム）.. 234
貨物海上保険証券（S.G.フォーム）裏面.................................... 235
受取船荷証券（Received B/L）... 236

Chapter 11　Product Liability (P/L)

1. Product Liability 209
　(1) Product Liability (P/L)..209
　(2) Strict Liability...209
2. Protection against Product Liability Claim........................209
　(1) Importance of Protection against PL......................................209
　(2) Product Safety...209
　(3) Product Liability Prevention 211
　(4) Product Liability Defense..213
3. Product Liability Insurance 213
　(1) Export PL Insurance 213
　(2) Import PL Insurance...217

Chapter 12　Settlement of Disputes

1. Claim against Seller 221
2. Dispute Resolution Method......................................221
　(1) Settlement of Dispute..223
　(2) Lawsuit and Arbitration 223
　(3) Arbitration 225

Appendix　Trade Documents

Example of Printed Clause (Terms and Conditions on Reverse Side)...........228
Commercial Invoice (for T.T. Remittance) 229
Packing List (for T.T. Remittance)...230
Bill of Lading (B/L) (for T.T. Remittance) 231
Marine Insurance Policy (ICC2009)...232
Reverse Side of Marine Insurance Policy (ICC2009)............................233
Marine Insurance Policy (S.G. Form)...234
Reverse Side of Marine Insurance Policy (S.G. Form)...........................235
Received B/L..236

船積船荷証券（Shipped B/L）... 237

House Air Waybill 238

複合運送証券（Combined Transport B/L）............................... 239

信用状（郵送）... 240

信用状（電信）... 241

荷為替手形 242

荷為替手形（記載項目の説明）... 243

Commercial Invoice（商業送り状）（L/C用）.............................. 244

Packing List（梱包明細書）（L/C用）...................................... 245

Bill of Lading (B/L)（船荷証券）（L/C用）................................ 246

B/L Instructions.. 247

Shipping Instruction 248

Shipping Instruction（記載項目の説明）................................... 249

輸出申告書 250

輸入（納税）申告書 252

輸入許可通知書（NACCS見本　空欄）..................................... 254

実行関税率表（一部）.. 256

Letter of Guarantee 258

海上運送状（Sea Waybill）... 259

事故通知 260

保険金請求書 261

‖索引 263

Shipped B/L 237

House Air Waybill. 238

Combined Transport B/L. 239

Letter of Credit (Mail) 240

Letter of Credit (Cable). 241

Bill of Exchange. 242

Bill of Exchange (Instructions in Japanese) 243

Commercial Invoice (for L/C) 244

Packing List (for L/C) 245

Bill of Lading (B/L) (for L/C) 246

B/L Instructions. 247

Shipping Instruction. 248

Shipping Instruction (Instructions in Japanese) 249

Export Declaration Form in Japan. 250

Import (Customs Duty Payment) Declaration Form in Japan 252

Import Declaration (NACCS Sample Blank Copy) 254

An Excerpt from Customs Tariff Schedules of Japan. 256

Letter of Guarantee. 258

Sea Waybill 259

Notice of Damage 260

Insurance Claim Form 261

Index. **263**

第1章
マーケティングと取引交渉

Chapter 1
Marketing and Trade Negotiation

1．貿易取引開始までの流れ

　輸出入者が取引相手を発見し、具体的な取引交渉に入り、契約を締結するまでのおおまかな流れは次のようになっている。

図表1−1　取引成立までの流れ

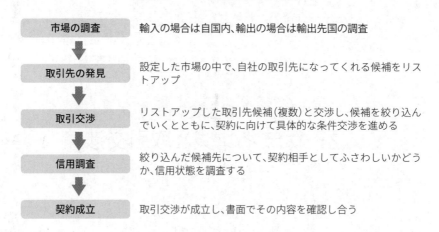

市場の調査	輸入の場合は自国内、輸出の場合は輸出先国の調査
取引先の発見	設定した市場の中で、自社の取引先になってくれる候補をリストアップ
取引交渉	リストアップした取引先候補（複数）と交渉し、候補を絞り込んでいくとともに、契約に向けて具体的な条件交渉を進める
信用調査	絞り込んだ候補先について、契約相手としてふさわしいかどうか、信用状態を調査する
契約成立	取引交渉が成立し、書面でその内容を確認し合う

2．市場調査と取引先の発見

(1) 輸入の市場と輸出の市場

　商品を輸入する場合の市場とは、自国内となり、その場合の市場調査とは基本的には国産品の市場調査と大差ない。

　ただし、外国の商品をそのまま自国に持ち込めないケースもあるので、その場合には、自国の市場に合うように商品に変更を加える市場への適合化が必要となる。外国の商品をそのまま自国に持ち込めないケースとは、例えば次のようなケースである。

　①　輸入国（自国）の法律で規制されている場合
　②　外国商品のままだと輸入国市場の趣味、嗜好に合わない場合
　　（色、サイズなど）

1. Flow to Conclude Trade Contract

Following chart shows a business practice to conclude a trade contract, starting from finding trading partners, then negotiating the details of the transaction and concluding the contract.

Fig.1-1　Flow to Conclude Trade Contract

Market Research	Import Business: Domestic Market Export Business: Market in a country to export to
Finding Business Partner	Listing companies to be a candidate for a trading partner in the targeted market
Trade Negotiation	Starting negotiation with the listed companies Screening them Negotiating the terms and conditions of the contract
Credit Investigation	Investigating financial status of the prospective companies
Conclusion of a Contract	After negotiation, confirming the terms and conditions of the contract

2. Market Research and Finding Trading Partner

(1) Import Market and Export Market

From a perspective of importers, "market" means their own domestic market. Their market research is usually conducted in the same way as the domestic one.

However, some foreign goods are not suitable to be imported as they are produced for the market of its origin country, so they need to be adjusted to meet the demand of the market in an importing country.

Listed below are examples of the cases in which foreign goods are not suitable to be imported without adjustments.

> ①　Goods are restricted to be imported by laws of an importing country.
> ②　Goods do not fit the market in an importing country in terms of likes and dislikes. (e.g. color, size, etc.)

　自国市場へ適合させるためには、手直しをした商品を別途用意したりするなどそれだけコストがかかるため、そのコストをかけてまで輸入する価値があるのか、採算を検討する必要がある。

　一方、輸出の場合の市場とはつまり外国になるので、以下の方法で相手国の市場調査をしていく必要がある。

(2) 市場調査の調査項目

　商品の市場性は商品がもっている特性によって決まるが、それはまた、相手国の経済力や貿易政策、あるいは計画経済の実態等によって影響を受けている。貿易戦略をたてる場合には、まず第一に商品の特性を把握し、その特性に適した貿易相手国を選択することが重要である。

　市場調査の項目としては、次のようなものがある。

> ・　その国が市場として適しているか
> ・　輸出に際して相手国に法的規制はないか
> ・　輸出しようとする商品の需要はあるか、その需要を今後も伸ばしていく方策はあるか

　このような情報を十分検討し、その結果輸出することにメリットがあるということになったら、取引先候補を探すなど、具体的な実行計画に移していくことになる。

Adjusting goods to meet the demands of the market often results in increasing cost. Importers must consider whether it is still worth to import the goods at the expense of increased costs.

For exporters, as the markets are in foreign countries, it is necessary to conduct market research in a targeted country described as follows.

(2) Items for Market Research

How well the goods can sell in a certain market depends on their characteristics. It is also determined by economic power and trading policy of the importing country as well as by economic plan of the country. The key to successful trading strategies is understanding the characteristics of the goods and selecting suitable countries to export to.

Items for Market Research are shown as follows.

It is necessary to analyze the marketability in the targeted country, that is;

- whether the country is suitable for an export market
- whether the country has legal restriction
- whether there is demand for the goods and possibility to expand the demand

After such thorough studies, when an exporter finds enough benefit to export the goods, the exporter moves on to the practical steps like looking for trading partners.

図表1－2　市場調査の項目

一般的情報		商品特有の情報	
地理・文化・社会	気候、風俗習慣、所得水準、社会構造等	消費者・供給者	消費者数、供給者数、購入意欲、信頼性等
政治・経済	政治形態、外国政策、国民総生産、成長率等	市　場	販売方法、流通機構、競争力、宣伝活動等
法制度	民法、商法、税法等	需要情報	輸出入量、生産量、販売量、販売額等
金融・為替	金融機関、為替管理、国際収支等	製　品	品質、スタイル、サイズ等
通商政策	貿易管理、貿易統計、関税、通関規則等	価　格	製造原価、小売価格、目標価格
流通・物流・通信	流通制度、港湾設備、道路交通等	競合製品	競合品の有無、品質、価格、特性等
その他	リスクの生じる可能性等	その他	購入、販売条件等

（3）市場調査の方法

　次に、どのようにしてこれらの情報を入手するかであるが、例えば次のような方法がある。

① 関係業界や業者あるいは専門商社などから情報を収集する
② 貿易や生産統計資料などを使って比較分析する
③ 専門紙誌や業界紙誌あるいはカタログ等を収集して情報分析する
④ 大使館商務部や日本貿易振興機構（ジェトロ）などの貿易関係機関に助言を求め、情報と資料を入手する
⑤ 調査機関に市場調査を委託する

Fig. 1-2 Items for Market Research

General Information		Information of the Goods	
Geography / Culture / Sociality	Climate, Customs, Income Level, Community Structure, etc.	Consumer / Supplier	Numbers of Consumers and Suppliers, Purchasing Motivation, Reliability, etc.
Politics / Economy	Political Form, Foreign Policy, GNP, Economic Growth Rate, etc.	Market	Sales Style, Distribution System, Competitiveness, Promotion, etc.
Legal System	Civil Law, Commercial Law, Tax Law, etc.	Demand	Amount of Import, Export and Production, Volume of Sales, etc.
Financial System / Foreign Exchange	Banking Establishment, Exchange Control, Balance of International Payment, etc.	Product	Quality, Style, Size, etc.
Trade Restriction	Trade Control, Trade Statistics, Customs Duty, Customs Restriction, etc.	Price	Production Cost, Retail Price, Target Price, etc.
Distribution / Communication System	Distribution System, Port Facility, Road Traffic, etc.	Competing Product	Competitors, Quality, Price, Characteristics, etc.
Others	Risks, etc.	Others	Purchasing and Sales Terms, etc.

(3) Methods of Market Research

The followings are examples of methods to acquire marketing information.

① Gather information from related industries or trading companies specialized in the goods
② Analyze trade/product statistics, etc.
③ Analyze market information using business magazines/catalogues, etc.
④ Acquire information from a trading organization like commercial departments of Embassies, etc.
⑤ Outsource marketing research companies
⑥ Conduct feasibility studies by visiting overseas

⑥　海外渡航で実態調査をする
⑦　海外見本市などに出品し、反響を調べる

（4）輸出戦略

　以上の方法で市場調査を行ったら、輸出者は相手国側の市場ニーズに合わせて具体的に商品を設定し、更にその市場を今後も成長させ維持するためのマーケティング戦略を立てることになる。
　マーケティング戦略は、次の4つの要素を市場に合わせて効果的に組み合わせることにより行われる。これらの4つの要素はそれぞれPで始まることから4Pと呼ばれ、これを効果的に組み合わせることを マーケティング・ミックス という。

①　商品計画（Product）
②　価格設定（Price）
③　流通システム（Place）
④　販売促進（Promotion）

（5）取引先発見の方法

　輸出戦略の構想が練られたところで、輸出者は、相手国で取引相手となってくれる企業を探すことになる。相手企業の見つけ方には例えば次の方法がある。

①　取引関係業者、同業者、知人から紹介を受ける
②　在日外国機関（大使館商務部、貿易関係機関）を利用する
③　商工会議所やジェトロ（日本貿易振興機構）、あるいは貿易関係団体に寄せられる引合い等を利用する
④　海外の商工会議所や貿易関係団体に直接照会状を送付し、紹介を依頼する
⑤　海外のダイレクトリー（Trade Directory：業者名簿）を利用する
⑥　海外の業界紙誌や専門紙誌等の記事や広告を活用する
⑦　海外の見本市を活用する

⑦ Participate in and receive feedbacks at international exhibitions, etc.

(4) Export Strategy

After market researches, an exporter decides which products to sell according to the market's needs in the importing countries. Then, the exporter develops marketing strategy in order to grow and keep their market share.

Following 4 elements are especially important to develop marketing strategy: "Product", "Price", "Place" and "Promotion". Since words of these elements start with a "P", they are called "4Ps". Using combinations of 4Ps effectively is called "Marketing Mix".

<4Ps>
① Product
② Price
③ Place
④ Promotion

(5) Methods of Finding Trading Partners

Once an export strategy is developed, exporters move on to the step to find trading partners in the countries to export to.

The followings are examples of methods to find business partners.

① Get an introduction from business related circle, other companies in the same business and acquaintance
② Utilize foreign organization like commercial departments of Embassies, etc.
③ Utilize business inquiries sent to a Chamber of Commerce and Industry, etc.
④ Send a letter of inquiry to a Chamber of Commerce and Industry, etc. and ask to introduce trading partners
⑤ Utilize a foreign trade directory
⑥ Utilize foreign business magazines, articles and advertisements in specialized magazines
⑦ Participate in international exhibitions

　⑧　海外渡航をして企業訪問する
　⑨　海外市場調査を委託する

3．取引交渉

(1) 取引交渉の流れ

　市場調査を行い、取引先候補が見つかると、輸出者はその候補先に勧誘の手紙を出すなどして、取引交渉を働きかけることになる。取引交渉の大まかな流れは次のとおりである。

図表1－3　取引交渉の流れ

通常、相手の提示した申込みを一度で承諾することはあまりないので、申込みと反対申込みとを繰り返して、お互いの条件を歩み寄らせていく。また、必ず勧誘から取引交渉がスタートするわけではなく、たとえば展示会で商品を見たといって、直接引合いがくることもある。

⑧ Visit overseas companies
⑨ Outsource foreign marketing research companies

3. Trade Negotiation

(1) Flow of Trade Negotiation

After conducting a market research and finding candidates of trading partners, an exporter starts negotiating with them by sending proposal, etc. The following is a flow of trade negotiations.

Fig. 1-3 Flow of Trade Negotiation

Proposal	**Aggressive Action for Trade** Make requests to a foreign Chambers of Commerce and Industry for introductions of appropriate companies to trade with, Send catalogues to candidates of business partners
Inquiry	**Making Inquiries for Details** price, estimation, sample, amount of supply, earliest possible time of shipping, etc.
Offer	**Offer of Detailed Terms and Conditions** quality, specification, quantity, price, delivery date, payment terms, etc.
Counter Offer	Reject the Terms Proposed and Make a Counter-offer with New Terms
Acceptance	Accept the Terms Proposed and Conclude a Contract

As Offers are not usually accepted at a time, negotiations become a series of offers and counteroffers bouncing back and forth between sellers and buyers until the terms and conditions satisfy the both sides. Business negotiations do not necessarily start from proposal. Sometimes, for example, exporters receive inquiries directly for the goods exhibited at trade shows, etc.

(2) 申込み

A．ファーム・オファー（Firm Offer　確定申込み）

　もしオファーをしてからかなり期間が過ぎてから承諾回答をもらった場合、その時点では市況が変わっていて、オファー内容が時勢に合わなくなってしまうことがある。そこで通常、貿易取引では、承諾回答の到着期限を定めたファーム・オファーを行う。

　ファーム・オファーは取引条件提示の際に、"subject to your acceptance reaching us by December 15, 20XX"（貴社のご回答が当社に20XX年12月15日までに到着することを条件に）などといった文言を入れることにより行われる。

図表1－4　Firm Offerの文例

We offer you firm the following, subject to your acceptance reaching us by December 15, 20XX: 1,000 sets of Personal Computers at US$1,200.00/set, CIP Hong Kong, for shipment on January, 20XX.

20XX年12月15日を承諾回答の到着期限として、以下の条件で取引を申し込みます― パソコン1,000セット、単価CIP（輸送費保険料込みの運送人渡し）香港 1,200米ドル、船積は20XX年の1月中

　このように承諾回答の到着期限が限定された場合、期限までに相手から承諾回答がくればその場で契約が成立し、承諾回答が来なかったらオファーは失効する。また、わが国の商法では、回答期限内はオファーの撤回も変更もできない。

B．反対申込み（Counter Offer）

　一方のオファーを他方が無条件に承諾すれば契約が成立するが、実際には条件の一部に修正や変更を求めてくることが普通である。この場合、最初のオファーは拒絶され、他方からあらためて新規の申込みをしたことになる。このようなオファーを**反対申込み（Counter Offer）**という。

　ファーム・オファーに対してこの反対申込みが行われると、それがファーム・オファーの有効期限内であってもその取引条件は拒絶されたことになり、その時点でファーム・オファーは失効する。

　通常はこの反対申込みをお互いが繰り返すことで、条件を歩み寄らせていく。

(2) Offer

A. Firm Offer

If an acceptance was received after a long time since an offer was made, contents of the offer sometimes can not meet the requirements due to the changes in market conditions.

In trading business, therefore, a firm offer is often used to limit the period of validity of the offer. The date by which acceptance must be received is fixed in a firm offer.

The firm offer includes a phrase like "subject to your acceptance reaching us by December 15, 20XX".

Fig.1-4   Example of Firm Offer

We offer you firm the following, subject to your acceptance reaching us by December 15, 20XX: 1,000 sets of Personal Computers at US$1,200.00/set, CIP Hong Kong, for shipment on January, 20XX.

In this case, a contract comes into effect if an acceptance reaches within the duration. The offer, on the other hand, expires if an acceptance does not reach by the due date. In some countries like Japan, once an offer is made, the offer can not be cancelled or amended until the due date.

B. Counter Offer

Once either of the parties accepts the other's offer, the contract is concluded. In actual negotiations, however, the parties involved have to revise and change the conditions. If the initial offer is rejected and a new proposal is offered from the other party, this new offer is called "Counter Offer".

The counter offer means rejection to the firm offer and invalidates the firm offer regardless of the period of validity.

Both parties make a series of counteroffers until the conditions satisfy the both sides.

C．サブ・コン・オファー（Offer subject to Seller's Final Confirmation）

　相手の承諾があっても直ちに契約が成立するのではなく、オファーした側の最終的な確認があって初めて契約が成立するというオファーである。したがって、正確にはサブ・コン・オファーは申込みではなく、申込みの誘引と考えられている。

D．先売りごめんオファー（Offer subject to Prior Sale）

　供給する商品数に限りがある場合に使用される、相手の承諾前に商品が売り切れた場合には、オファーの効力は消滅するという条件付きのオファーのことである。商品が売り切れてからもなお、承諾がくるたびに商品を供給しなければならないのでは、売り手側はその需要に応えきれない。そこで、商品が売り切れてしまったら、そのオファーの効力もその時点で終わり、たとえその後他の者から承諾回答が届いてもそれは無効とするというオファーである。

4．信用調査

(1) 信用調査の重要性

　取引交渉において取引先候補が絞られ、具体的な引合いがあったり、申込みをしたり受けたりする時点で、今後本当にその取引先候補と契約を交わしてもいいのか、相手の信用調査をすることになる。

　取引相手の信用調査項目としては、次の項目をチェックすることが重要であるといわれており、これらは①〜③が**3Cs**、①〜④が**4Cs**と呼ばれている。

> ①　Capital（資産、財政状態）
> ②　Capacity（営業能力、経験、取引量）
> ③　Character（品格、誠実性）
> ④　Conditions（政治・経済的事情）

　信用調査の結果をもとに、信用度に応じて取引条件を設定し、無理のない取引をすることは、リスクを回避できるだけでなく、相手業者との取引を長期的に継続させ安定取引に導くことになる。

C. Offer subject to Seller's or Buyer's Final Confirmation

This is a type of offer which requires not only an acceptance but also a final confirmation of the offerer in order to close a deal.

Therefore, this type of offer is not an exact offer but regarded as an inducible factor for an offer.

D. Offer subject to Prior Sale

This is a type of offer which is used for goods with limited supply.

This offer loses its validity if the goods are sold out before a seller receives an acceptance from a buyer.

The seller usually has responsibility to supply the goods if the seller receives an acceptance from the buyer during the period of validity.

If the goods are sold out before the expiry date, the seller can not respond to the demands.

The seller, therefore, makes an offer which loses its validity if the goods are sold out.

4. Credit Investigation

(1) Items for Credit Investigation

In the process of selecting trading partners by trade negotiations, receiving inquiries and making offers, credit standing of the candidates should be investigated to determine whether to start business with them or not.

The followings are items to be investigated: ① - ③ is called "3Cs", and ① - ④ is called "4Cs"

> ① Capital (Assets, Financial Condition)
> ② Capacity (Business Capability, Experience, Business Volume)
> ③ Character (Dignity, Conscientiousness of the Managements)
> ④ Conditions (Political and Economical Environments)

In order to establish a long term and stable business, it is essential to conduct a credit investigation. Trade conditions should be determined depending on the partner's reliability based on the result of the investigation.

（2）信用調査の方法

信用調査の方法としては、次のようなものがある。

Ａ．銀行に照会して行う方法（Bank Reference）

相手から知らされた銀行信用照会先（Bank Reference）に直接手紙で照会するか、あるいは日本の取引銀行を経由して照会する。

Ｂ．信用調査機関に調査を依頼する方法

特に重要な取引相手と判断される場合には、経費がかかっても信用調査機関を利用する方が望ましい。有名な所に次のようなものがある。

ダン社（Dun & Bradstreet Corp.）は国際的に有名な商業興信所で、ニュージャージー州に本拠をおき、世界各国に組織をもっている。ダン社の報告書は特に「ダン・レポート」と呼ばれ、国際的な信用度が高く有名である。

(2) Methods of Credit Investigation

Followings are methods of credit Investigation.

A. Bank Reference

Bank reference is a reference for credit standing of negotiating partners in trade negotiation to their banks. The bank names are usually given by the negotiating partners.

B. Credit Agency

It is advisable to use a credit agency when a negotiating partner is expected to be an important trading partner even though it takes additional expense.

Dun & Bradstreet Corp. (D&B) headquartered in New Jersey is one of the leading international credit agencies all over the world. D&B's report called "Dun Report" is enjoying good international reputation and regarded as being reliable.

第2章
売買契約の成立

Chapter 2
Conclusion of a Sales Contract

1. 売買契約の成立

(1) 契約書の作成

　貿易取引は売買契約であり、その契約は一方のオファーに他方が承諾すると成立する諾成契約である。したがって契約は口頭でも成立するが、法制度や商習慣が異なる者の間での合意だけに、合意内容を明確にし契約の履行を円滑に行うため、実務上は書面で契約書を作成することになる。

(2) 契約書の書式

　契約書の書式には、次のようなものがある。

> ①　両者が合意した条件を全て1つの契約書中に記載する場合
> ②　基本的取引条件をあらかじめ協定しておき、個々の売買取引のつどその売買取引についての条件を個別に規定していく場合
> ③　注文書や注文請書を簡略化された売買契約書として使用する場合

　一回限りの輸出入契約では①、②のような正式の契約書は作成されず、③のように注文書や注文請書を売買契約書に使用する場合がほとんどである。一方、プラント輸出や継続的取引では、契約条件を1つずつ挙げて輸出入者が相互に確認し、取決め事項を全て文書にした基本契約書を作成し、個々の船積みに関しては簡単な書式とする②が使われることが多くなる。①、②は通常、代理店契約、買付委託契約、受託販売契約等の場合に作成される。

(3) 簡略書式の売買契約書

　通常、輸出入契約が成立すると、輸出入者はそれぞれが自社の書式による確認書を相手方に送付し、署名を求めるのが一般的である。これらの確認書の名

1. Conclusion of a Sales Contract

(1) Drawing up a Contract

A trade transaction is based on a sales (or purchase) contract, which is a consensual contract made by mutual agreement between a seller and a buyer.

The contract comes into effect when the seller or the buyer accepts an offer made by the other even though the contract is completed by a verbal agreement. However, as it is an agreement between the seller and the buyer with different trade customs and legal systems, a written contract is usually made to confirm the contents of the agreement and to perform the contract smoothly.

(2) Documentary Forms of a Contract

The following shows types of documentary form of a contract.

> ① All terms and conditions agreed by the seller and the buyer are stated in one contract.
> ② Basic terms and conditions are set in advance, and specific terms for each transaction are individually set at the time of the transaction.
> ③ A simplified form such as a purchase order and a confirmation of sales is used as a form of the contract.

In a one-time, not continuous, export/import transaction, ③ is often chosen. Unlike ① or ②, ③ is not a formal form. Only major terms are filled in ③. On the other hand, in the case of plant exports or continuous transactions, both the exporter and the importer negotiate each of the terms and conditions of the contract in detail. In the case of ②, after an agreement, the seller and the buyer draw up a basic contract stipulating all contents both agreed, and a simple form of contract is made for each shipment. For agency agreement, purchase consignment contract, and sales consignment contract, etc. ① or ② is usually made.

(3) Simplified Contract Forms

Usually, upon conclusion of an import/export contract, an exporter and an importer send a confirmation in their own contract form to their trading partner for signature.

称はまちまちであるが、通常、輸出者は「販売確認書」や「プロ・フォーマ・インボイス（仮送り状）」の書式を、輸入者は「注文書」を契約書書式として利用することが多い。これらの書式は自社製のため形式は異なっているが、記載項目欄には大差はない。

　輸出入者いずれかの書式に双方が署名すれば、その書式が契約書となるが、いずれか一方の署名がなければ、注文書、または注文請書のままである。

(4) タイプ条項と印刷条項（裏面約款）

　簡略化書式の売買契約書は、表裏の条項で構成されており、表面は取引交渉において成立した契約条件を整理して、所定の条件欄にタイプしたもので、**タイプ条項**と呼ばれる。裏面には、その企業のすべての取引に共通な一般取引条件があらかじめ印刷されており、**印刷条項**（または**裏面約款**）と呼ばれている。

　通常表面の頭書に、裏面条件も合わせて確認のうえ署名するように求める書式となっているのが一般的である。これは、オファー段階で、裏面に記載された条件を１つ１つ取引条件として取り上げていたのでは契約交渉が進展しないため、交渉段階では主要条件のみを取り決め、契約書の作成段階で印刷条項も加え、これも契約条件の一部であることを相手企業に認めさせようとする戦略の１つといえる。

(5) タイプ条項の具体例

　注文書型、注文請書型の契約書において、表面のタイプ条項に記載する取引条件としては、たとえば次のようなものがある（図表２－１）。

① 　頭書
② 　日付（Date）
③ 　荷印（Marking, Case Mark）
④ 　商品名および品質
⑤ 　数量（Quantity）
⑥ 　単価（Unit Price）

As a simplified contract form, the seller (the exporter) often uses a confirmation of sales or a pro-forma invoice and the buyer (the importer) often uses a purchase order. Although each exporting or importing company usually has their own forms of confirmation, the contents are not much different.

When both the seller and the buyer sign the form, regardless of which of them made it, the form turns into the contract agreement. Without obtaining the signature of their trading partner, the confirmation of sales or the purchase order does not have an effect of a contract.

(4) Typed and Printed Terms and Conditions

At a conclusion of contract, exporting/importing companies use a simplified contract form in which the terms and conditions are stated on the face and the reverse side.

The terms mutually agreed in a trade negotiation are typed in the appropriate space on the face side. This is called "Typed Clause". On the reverse side, the companies' general terms and conditions are printed in advance. This is called "Printed Clause" (or terms and conditions on the reverse side). The companies apply their printed clause to every type of transactions.

The heading on the face side usually requests signatures from both the seller and the buyer after confirming the terms and conditions printed on the reverse side. This is a strategy to make a trade negotiation go smoothly. As it takes long time to negotiate all terms and conditions respectively in detail, the seller and the buyer determine only major terms in trade negotiations. The other terms are printed on the reverse side in advance. When both the seller and the buyer sign on the contract, the terms and conditions including printed clauses are regarded to be agreed with.

(5) Example of Typed Clause

Following are examples of the terms and conditions typed on the face side of the simplified form (See Fig. 2-1).

① Heading
② Date
③ Marking (Case Mark)
④ Commodity and Quality
⑤ Quantity
⑥ Unit Price

⑦　金額（Amount）

⑧　貨物の引渡し条件（Terms of Delivery）

　　貨物をいつ、どこで引き渡すかについての条件。FCA、CPT、CIPなどの「貿易条件」によって決まってくる（後述）。

　　また、

　　ⅰ）契約の商品について数回に分けて船積みすること（分割船積み）

　　ⅱ）貨物を途中で他の船に積み替えること（積替え）

　　についても、許容するのかしないのかを明確にしておく。

⑨　積出し港（仕出港）（Port of Shipment）

⑩　揚げ港（仕向港）（Port of Destination）

⑪　船積み時期（Time of Shipment）

⑫　検査（Inspection）

⑬　梱包（Packing）

⑭　保険（Insurance）

⑮　支払い条件（Payment Terms）

⑯　その他特別条件（Special Terms and Conditions）

⑰　買主の署名欄

⑱　売主の署名欄

⑲　契約日

⑦ Amount
⑧ Terms of Delivery
Specify the date and the place of the delivery, which is decided depending on the "Trade Terms" such as FCA, CPT, CIP, etc. (As described later)
Also, following permission or prohibition must be clearly stated:
i) the contracted goods being shipped partially (Partial Shipment)
ii) the cargo being transshipped to other vessels (Transshipment)
⑨ Port of Shipment
⑩ Port of Destination
⑪ Time of Shipment
⑫ Inspection
⑬ Packing
⑭ Insurance
⑮ Payment Terms
⑯ Special Terms and Conditions
⑰ Buyer's Signature
⑱ Seller's Signature
⑲ Contract Date

図表2－1　売買契約書の書式（タイプ条項の例）

CONFIRMATION OF SALE

①ABC Corporation as Seller hereby confirms the sale to undermentioned Buyer of the following goods (the "**Goods**") on the terms and conditions given below **INCLUDING ALL THOSE PRINTED ON THE REVERSE SIDE HEREOF,** which are expressly agreed to, understood and made a part of this Contract:

BUYER'S NAME AND ADDRESS			SELLER'S DEPT.	DATE ②	
			SELLER'S CONTRACT NO.	BUYER'S REFERENCE NO.	
MARKING	COMMODITY & QUALITY	QUANTITY	UNIT PRICE	AMOUNT	
③	④	⑤	⑥	⑦	
TERMS OF DELIVERY ⑧		TIME OF SHIPMENT			
PORT OF SHIPMENT ⑨		⑪			
PORT OF DESTINATION ⑩					
INSPECTION ⑫		PACKING ⑬			
INSURANCE ⑭		SPECIAL TERMS & CONDITIONS ⑯			
PAYMENT ⑮					

Accepted and confirmed by
(BUYER)　　　　　　　　　　　　　　　　(SELLER)
　　　　　⑰　　　　　　　　　　　　　　　　　　⑱
_____　　　　_____

ON　　　　　　　　20XX
　　　　⑲
....

Fig.2-1   Example of Typed Clause (Confirmation of Sale)

CONFIRMATION OF SALE

①ABC Corporation as Seller hereby confirms the sale to undermentioned Buyer of the following goods (the "**Goods**") on the terms and conditions given below **INCLUDING ALL THOSE PRINTED ON THE REVERSE SIDE HEREOF,** which are expressly agreed to, understood and made a part of this Contract:

BUYER'S NAME AND ADDRESS			SELLER'S DEPT.	DATE ②
			SELLER'S CONTRACT NO.	BUYER'S REFERENCE NO.
MARKING	COMMODITY & QUALITY	QUANTITY	UNIT PRICE	AMOUNT
③	④	⑤	⑥	⑦
TERMS OF DELIVERY ⑧		TIME OF SHIPMENT		
PORT OF SHIPMENT ⑨				
PORT OF DESTINATION ⑩		⑪		
INSPECTION ⑫		PACKING ⑬		
INSURANCE ⑭		SPECIAL TERMS & CONDITIONS ⑯		
PAYMENT ⑮				

Accepted and confirmed by
(BUYER)   (SELLER)
           ⑰   ⑱

_____   _____

ON   20XX
          ⑲

(6) 印刷条項（裏面約款）の例

図表2－2　印刷条項（裏面約款）の例（売契約書の場合）

GENERAL TERMS AND CONDITIONS

1. **TRADE TERMS** -- Seller and Buyer shall be governed by the provisions of INCOTERMS 20　, as amended, with regard to the trade terms, such as FCA, CPT, CIP, used herein, unless otherwise provided for herein.

2. **SHIPMENT** -- Partial shipment or delivery and/or transshipment shall be permitted. Each lot of partial shipment or delivery shall be regarded as a separate and independent contract.

   Date of bill of lading or air waybill shall be accepted as conclusive evidence of the date of shipment or delivery.

   If the vessel is not provided or nominated by Buyer in time for the shipment or delivery of the Goods under the terms of FCA, FAS or FOB or within any extension of time for such shipment or delivery granted by Seller, Seller may, at its option, extend the time of shipment or delivery of the Goods, or cancel this Contract or any part of thereof, without prejudice to any other rights and remedies Seller may have.

   In case of the mode of transportation for which the trade terms of FCA, CPT or CIP under which the Goods shall be handed over to the carrier should be used, for example, air transportation, transportation by container ships, or combined transportation, when trade terms such as FOB, CFR or CIF shall be applied, risk of loss of the Goods shall pass from Seller to Buyer upon delivery of the Goods to the carrier or its agent for transportation.

   In the event Seller shall charter a vessel for ocean transportation of the Goods, all charges and expenses for discharge of the Goods, including demurrage and other damages, which are to be for the account of the charterer against the shipowner or the chartered owner under the relevant charter party, shall be borne and paid by Buyer.

3. **PAYMENT** -- In case payment for the Goods shall be made by a letter of credit under this Contract, Buyer shall, unless otherwise provided for herein, establish in favor of Seller an irrevocable and confirmed letter of credit negotiable on sight draft through a prime bank of good international repute and satisfactory to Seller immediately after the conclusion of this Contract with validity of at least 20 days after the last day of the period of relative shipment or delivery. Such letter of credit shall be in a form and upon terms satisfactory to Seller and shall authorize reimbursement to Seller for such sums, if any, as may be advanced by Seller for consular invoices, inspection fees and other expenditures for the account of Buyer. Should payment under such letter of credit not be duly effected, Buyer shall, upon notice thereof from Seller, immediately make payment in cash to Seller directly and unconditionally.

   If payment for the Goods is not effected fully by Buyer when due under terms of payment, or, in case of payment to be made by a letter of credit, such letter of credit is not established in accordance with the terms of this Contract, Seller may cancel all or any part of this Contract at any time without prejudice to the rights of Seller to recover any damages incurred thereby and/or to enforce any other rights or remedies under applicable laws, and all accounts payable by Buyer to Seller for the Goods delivered under this Contract shall, upon Seller's declaration, become immediately due and payable in cash in full.

   If Buyer's failure to make payment or otherwise perform its obligations hereunder is reasonably anticipated, Seller may demand adequate assurance, satisfactory to Seller, of the due performance of this Contract by Buyer and withhold shipment or delivery of the undelivered Goods. Unless Buyer gives Seller such assurance within a reasonable time, Seller may, without prejudice to any other remedies it may have, cancel the portion of this Contract which relates to the undelivered Goods, and all accounts payable by Buyer to Seller for the Goods delivered under this Contract shall, upon Seller's declaration, become immediately due and payable in cash in full.

   All bank charges outside Japan, including collection charges and stamp duties, if any, shall be for the account of Buyer, provided that confirming commissions shall be for the account of Buyer, regardless of being charged within or outside Japan.

4. **INSURANCE** -- If this Contract is on a CIP or CIF basis, 110% of the invoice amount shall be insured by Seller, unless otherwise agreed herein.

5. **INCREASED COSTS** -- Any new, additional or increased freight rates, surcharges (bunker, currency, congestion or other surcharges), taxes, customs duties, export or import surcharges or other governmental charges, or insurance premiums, including those for war and strikes risks, which may be incurred by Seller with respect to the Goods after conclusion of this Contract, shall be for the account of Buyer and shall be reimbursed to Seller by Buyer.

6. **WARRANTY** -- UNLESS OTHERWISE EXPRESSLY STIPULATED ON THE FACE OF THIS CONTRACT, SELLER MAKES NO WARRANTY OF FITNESS OR SUITABLITY OF THE GOODS FOR ANY PARTICULAR PURPOSE OR SPECIAL CIRCUMSTANCE.

7. **CLAIM** -- No claim may be raised by Buyer against Seller with regard to the Goods unless Buyer notifies Seller of its claim by registered airmail, containing full particulars of the claim and accompanied by evidence thereof certified by an authorized surveyor within thirty (30) days after the arrival of the Goods at the port of destination, or within six (6) months after the arrival of the Goods at the port of destination in the event of a latent defect.

   Seller shall not be responsible to Buyer for any incidental, consequential or special damages. Seller's total liability on any or all claims from Buyer shall in no event exceed the price of the Goods with respect to which such claim or claims are made.

8. **PATENT, TRADEMARK, ETC.** -- Seller shall not be responsible to Buyer, and Buyer waives any claim against Seller, for any alleged infringement of patent, utility model, design, trademark or other industrial property right or copyright, in connection with the Goods except that infringement of any Japanese patent, utility model, design, trademark, or copyright.

   Buyer shall hold Seller harmless from any such alleged infringement on said Japanese rights arising from or in connection with any instruction given by Buyer to Seller regarding patent, utility model, design, trademark, copyright, pattern and specification.

9. **FORCE MAJEURE** -- In the event the performance by Seller of its obligations hereunder is prevented by force majeure, directly or indirectly affecting the activities of Seller or any other person, firm or corporation connected with the sale, manufacture, supply, shipment or delivery of the Goods, including but not limited to, act of God, flood, typhoon, earthquake, tidal wave, landslide, fire, plague, epidemic, quarantine restriction, perils of sea; war or serious threat of the same, civil commotion, blockade, arrest or restraint of government, rulers or people, requisition of vessel or aircraft; strike, lockout, sabotage, other labor dispute; explosion, accident or breakdown in whole or in part of machinery, plant, transportation or loading facility; governmental request, guidance, order or regulation; unavailability of transportation or loading facility; curtailment, shortage or failure in the supply of fuel, water, electric current, other public utility, or raw material including crude oil, petroleum or petroleum products; bankruptcy or insolvency of the manufacturer or supplier of the Goods; boycotting of Japanese goods; substantial change of the present international monetary system; or any other causes or circumstances whatsoever beyond the reasonable control of Seller, then, Seller shall not be liable for loss or damage, or failure or delay in performing its obligations under this Contract and may, at its option, extend the time of shipment or delivery of the Goods or cancel unconditionally and without liability the unfulfilled portion of this Contract to the extent so affected.

10. **SETTLEMENT OF DISPUTE** -- Any legal action taken by Buyer against Seller shall be brought in a Japanese court having competent jurisdiction over Seller, provided, however, that Buyer may submit any dispute between itself and Seller to arbitration in Japan in accordance with the rules of the Japan Commercial Arbitration Association in which case the award shall be final and binding on both parties.

    Any legal action by Seller against Buyer shall be brought in a court having competent jurisdiction over Buyer.

    Subsequent to the bringing of such legal action by either party or submission of dispute to arbitration by Buyer, the other party shall submit any claim it may have in connection with said action or arbitration to the court in which jurisdiction has first been established or in the case of such arbitration to the arbitrator or arbitrators appointed in accordance with such rules.

11. **LAW APPLICABLE** -- This contract shall be governed by and construed in all respects in accordance with the laws of Japan.

12. **WAIVER** -- No claim or right of Seller under this Contract shall be deemed to be waived or renounced in whole or in part unless the waiver or renunciation of such claim or right is acknowledged and confirmed in writing by Seller.

13. **ENTIRE AGREEMENT** -- This Contract is based on the terms and conditions expressly set forth herein and no other terms and conditions are binding on Seller without its agreement in writing to such other terms and conditions.

14. **HEADINGS** -- The headings are for convenience only and shall not affect the construction of this Contract.

（6）Example of Printed Clause (Terms and Conditions on Reverse Side)

Fig.2-2 Example of Printed Clause (Seller's Form)

GENERAL TERMS AND CONDITIONS

1. **TRADE TERMS** -- Seller and Buyer shall be governed by the provisions of INCOTERMS 20 , as amended, with regard to the trade terms, such as FCA, CPT, CIP, used herein, unless otherwise provided for herein.

2. **SHIPMENT** -- Partial shipment or delivery and/or transshipment shall be permitted. Each lot of partial shipment or delivery shall be regarded as a separate and independent contract.

   Date of bill of lading or air waybill shall be accepted as conclusive evidence of the date of shipment or delivery.

   If the vessel is not provided or nominated by Buyer in time for the shipment or delivery of the Goods under the terms of FCA, FAS or FOB or within any extension of time for such shipment or delivery granted by Seller, Seller may, at its option, extend the time of shipment or delivery of the Goods, or cancel this Contract or any part of thereof, without prejudice to any other rights and remedies Seller may have.

   In case of the mode of transportation for which the trade terms of FCA, CPT or CIP under which the Goods shall be handed over to the carrier should be used, for example, air transportation, transportation by container ships, or combined transportation, when trade terms such as FOB, CFR or CIF shall be applied, risk of loss of the Goods shall pass from Seller to Buyer upon delivery of the Goods to the carrier or its agent for transportation.

   In the event Seller shall charter a vessel for ocean transportation of the Goods, all charges and expenses for discharge of the Goods, including demurrage and other damages, which are to be for the account of the charterer against the shipowner or the chartered owner under the relevant charter party, shall be borne and paid by Buyer.

3. **PAYMENT** -- In case payment for the Goods shall be made by a letter of credit under this Contract, Buyer shall, unless otherwise provided for herein, establish in favor of Seller an irrevocable and confirmed letter of credit negotiable on sight draft through a prime bank of good international repute and satisfactory to Seller immediately after the conclusion of this Contract with validity of at least 20 days after the last day of the period of relative shipment or delivery. Such letter of credit shall be in a form and upon terms satisfactory to Seller and shall authorize reimbursement to Seller for such sums, if any, as may be advanced by Seller for consular invoices, inspection fees and other expenditures for the account of Buyer. Should payment under such letter of credit not be duly effected, Buyer shall, upon notice thereof from Seller, immediately make payment in cash to Seller directly and unconditionally.

   If payment for the Goods is not effected fully by Buyer when due under terms of payment, or, in case of payment to be made by a letter of credit, such letter of credit is not established in accordance with the terms of this Contract, Seller may cancel all or any part of this Contract at any time without prejudice to the rights of Seller to recover any damages incurred thereby and/or to enforce any other rights or remedies under applicable laws, and all accounts payable by Buyer to Seller for the Goods delivered under this Contract shall, upon Seller's declaration, become immediately due and payable in cash in full.

   If Buyer's failure to make payment or otherwise perform its obligations hereunder is reasonably anticipated, Seller may demand adequate assurance, satisfactory to Seller, of the due performance of this Contract by Buyer and withhold shipment or delivery of the undelivered Goods. Unless Buyer gives Seller such assurance within a reasonable time, Seller may, without prejudice to any other remedies it may have, cancel the portion of this Contract which relates to the undelivered Goods, and all accounts payable by Buyer to Seller for the Goods delivered under this Contract shall, upon Seller's declaration, become immediately due and payable in cash in full.

   All bank charges outside Japan, including collection charges and stamp duties, if any, shall be for the account of Buyer, provided that confirming commissions shall be for the account of Buyer, regardless of being charged within or outside Japan.

4. **INSURANCE** -- If this Contract is on a CIP or CIF basis, 110% of the invoice amount shall be insured by Seller, unless otherwise agreed herein.

5. **INCREASED COSTS** -- Any new, additional or increased freight rates, surcharges (bunker, currency, congestion or other surcharges), taxes, customs duties, export or import surcharges or other governmental charges, or insurance premiums, including those for war and strikes risks, which may be incurred by Seller with respect to the Goods after conclusion of this Contract, shall be for the account of Buyer and shall be reimbursed to Seller by Buyer.

6. **WARRANTY** -- UNLESS OTHERWISE EXPRESSLY STIPULATED ON THE FACE OF THIS CONTRACT, SELLER MAKES NO WARRANTY OF FITNESS OR SUITABLITY OF THE GOODS FOR ANY PARTICULAR PURPOSE OR SPECIAL CIRCUMSTANCE.

7. **CLAIM** -- No claim may be raised by Buyer against Seller with regard to the Goods unless Buyer notifies Seller of its claim by registered airmail, containing full particulars of the claim and accompanied by evidence thereof certified by an authorized surveyor within thirty (30) days after the arrival of the Goods at the port of destination, or within six (6) months after the arrival of the Goods at the port of destination in the event of a latent defect.

   Seller shall not be responsible to Buyer for any incidental, consequential or special damages. Seller's total liability on any or all claims from Buyer in no event exceed the price of the Goods with respect to which such claim or claims are made.

8. **PATENT, TRADEMARK, ETC.** -- Seller shall not be responsible to Buyer, and Buyer waives any claim against Seller, for any alleged infringement of patent, utility model, design, trademark or other industrial property right or copyright, in connection with the Goods except that infringement of any Japanese patent, utility model, design, trademark, or copyright.

   Buyer shall hold Seller harmless from any such alleged infringement on said Japanese rights arising from or in connection with any instruction given by Buyer to Seller regarding patent, utility model, design, trademark, copyright, pattern and specification.

9. **FORCE MAJEURE** -- In the event the performance by Seller of its obligations hereunder is prevented by force majeure, directly or indirectly affecting the activities of Seller or any other person, firm or corporation connected with the sale, manufacture, supply, shipment or delivery of the Goods, including but not limited to, act of God, flood, typhoon, earthquake, tidal wave, landslide, fire, plague, epidemic, quarantine restriction, perils of sea; war or serious threat of the same, civil commotion, blockade, arrest or restraint of government, rulers or people, requisition of vessel or aircraft; strike, lockout, sabotage, other labor dispute; explosion, accident or breakdown in whole or in part of machinery, plant, transportation or loading facility; governmental request, guidance, order or regulation; unavailability of transportation or loading facility; curtailment, shortage or failure in the supply of fuel, water, electric current, other public utility, or raw material including crude oil, petroleum or petroleum products; bankruptcy or insolvency of the manufacturer or supplier of the Goods; boycotting of Japanese goods; substantial change of the present international monetary system; or any other causes or circumstances whatsoever beyond the reasonable control of Seller, then, Seller shall not be liable for loss or damage, or failure or delay in performing its obligations under this Contract and may, at its option, extend the time of shipment or delivery of the Goods or cancel unconditionally and without liability the unfulfilled portion of this Contract to the extent so affected.

10. **SETTLEMENT OF DISPUTE** -- Any legal action taken by Buyer against Seller shall be brought in a Japanese court having competent jurisdiction over Seller, provided, however, that Buyer may submit any dispute between itself and Seller to arbitration in Japan in accordance with the rules of the Japan Commercial Arbitration Association in which case the award shall be final and binding on both parties.

    Any legal action by Seller against Buyer shall be brought in a court having competent jurisdiction over Buyer.

    Subsequent to the bringing of such legal action by either party or submission of dispute to arbitration by Buyer, the other party shall submit any claim it may have in connection with said action or arbitration to the court in which jurisdiction has first been established or in the case of such arbitration to the arbitrator or arbitrators appointed in accordance with such rules.

11. **LAW APPLICABLE** -- This contract shall be governed by and construed in all respects in accordance with the laws of Japan.

12. **WAIVER** -- No claim or right of Seller under this Contract shall be deemed to be waived or renounced in whole or in part unless the waiver or renunciation of such claim or right is acknowledged and confirmed in writing by Seller.

13. **ENTIRE AGREEMENT** -- This Contract is based on the terms and conditions expressly set forth herein and no other terms and conditions are binding on Seller without its agreement in writing to such other terms and conditions.

14. **HEADINGS** -- The headings are for convenience only and shall not affect the construction of this Contract.

① 貿易条件 (Trade Terms)
② 船積条件 (Shipment Terms)
③ 支払条件 (Payment Terms)
④ 保険 (Insurance)
⑤ 追加費用 (Increased Costs)
⑥ 保証 (Warranty)
⑦ クレーム (Claim)
⑧ 特許、商標等 (Patent, Trademark, etc.)
⑨ 不可抗力 (Force Majeure)
⑩ 紛争の解決 (Settlement of Dispute)
⑪ 準拠法 (Law Applicable)
⑫ 権利放棄 (Waiver)
⑬ 完全なる合意 (Entire Agreement)（完全合意条項）
　　「完全合意条項」「統合条項」「最終条項」とも呼ばれる。本契約締結以前のすべての約束や合意事項を排除し、契約書に書かれたものがすべてであり、最終であるとする条項で、もし、本契約以外の合意を有効とする場合には、書面でこれを残すこととしている。
⑭ 見出し (Headings)
　　見出しは便宜上のものであって、本契約の解釈には何の効力もないことが規定されている。

　以上、裏面の印刷条項（裏面約款）の内容について、例を挙げてみてきたが、未合意の裏面の一般取引条件は無効と解釈するのが主流であるとはいえ、紛争を避けるためにも、自社にとって譲れない条項は、契約条件として具体的に交渉し、表のタイプ約款の特別条件として取り決めることが大切である。

2. ウィーン売買条約 (CISG)

(1) ウィーン売買条約とは

　一般的な輸出入取引では、準拠法について取り決めがない場合には、通常は、紛争解決地（裁判を行う地）における国際私法によって、どの国の売買法が適用されるかが決定される。

① Trade Terms
② Shipment Terms
③ Payment Terms
④ Insurance
⑤ Increased Costs
⑥ Warranty
⑦ Claim
⑧ Patent, Trademark, etc.
⑨ Force Majeure
⑩ Settlement of Dispute
⑪ Law Applicable
⑫ Waiver
⑬ Entire Agreement

It is also called "Complete Agreement Clause", "Integration Clause", or "Merger Clause".

This is a clause to eliminate any other agreements or promises made prior to the conclusion of the contract, stipulating that those in the contract are the final. If some agreement other than those stipulated in the contract is required to be effective, such other agreements should be put in writing with the date and signature.

⑭ Headings

Headings are just for convenience and have no legal bindings for the interpretation of the clauses in the contract.

Although it is considered that general terms and conditions on the reverse side should be invalid if not agreed, it is significant to put forward important terms during the negotiation, and state them on the typed clauses on the face side of the contract in order to avoid any dispute.

2. United Nations Convention on Contracts for the International Sale of Goods (Vienna, 1980) (CISG)

(1) What is CISG?

Unless the governing law is otherwise stipulated, the laws applicable to international trade shall usually be subject to the private international law in the place of dispute settlement (or venue).

　このため、相手国側の売買法が適用されることになった場合、その紛争の結末について予測ができないという大きな不安を抱えることになる。

　そこで、国際間の売買取引に適用される統一的な売買法が必要であるとの認識から生まれてきたのが、ウィーン売買条約である。

　国際的な物品売買契約を規律する統一ルールとして採択された国連条約であり、正式名称は「国際物品売買契約に関する国際連合条約」（United Nations Convention on Contracts for the International Sale of Goods、以下「CISG」）という。

　1987年末までに発効に必要な批准国（10カ国）がそろったため、1988年1月1日に発効している。日本の主要貿易相手国である米国、オーストラリア、中国、フランス、ドイツなどもこの条約に加盟している。

> ＜成立経緯＞
> 1966年：国連国際商取引法委員会（UNCITRAL）にて作成作業開始
> 1980年4月：採択
> 1988年1月1日：発効
> 2009年8月1日：日本でも効力発生

（2）わが国の加入と条約の発効

　わが国はイギリスとともにずっと未加入だったが、国会が2008年6月に同条約を承認し、政府が加入書を7月1日に国連事務総長に寄託したので、この寄託日から12カ月を経過した日の翌月初日、つまり2009年8月1日から発効することとなった。

　したがって、日本でも本条約発効を受け、2009年8月1日以降に成立するわが国とCISG締約国間の国際物品売買契約には、CISGが自動的に適用されることになった。

（3）CISGの適用要件

　「国際」、「物品」、「売買契約」、に適用されるとされており（本条約第1条1項）、以下の3つの要件全てを満たす契約であるか否かが判断基準となる。

For this reason, when the laws of the counterpart's country are applied, the other party becomes uncertain about a result of disputes.

Thus, CISG has been established from the necessity for a uniform regime applicable to contracts for the international sale of goods.

CISG is the UN Convention adopted as a uniform legislation which governs contracts for international sale of goods and it is formally called "United Nations Convention on Contracts for the International Sale of Goods (Vienna, 1980) (CISG)".

CISG entered into force on January 1, 1988, since the ratifying states reached 10 by the end of 1987 as required. Japan's top trading partners such the US, Australia, China, France and Germany are also contracting states of this convention.

<History>
1966:Commencement of work by United Nations Commission
   on International Trade Law (UNCITRAL)
April 1980:Adoption
January 1, 1988:Entry into force
August 1, 2009:Entry into force in Japan

(2) Japan's Accession and Entry into Force

Japan as well as the UK had not been contracting states of CISG. However, Japanese Diet approved the convention in June 2008, and the government deposited the instruments of accession with the Secretary-General of the United Nations on July 1, 2008. Then, on the first day of the month following the expiration of twelve (12) months after the date of deposit, that is, on August 1, 2009, CISG entered into force in Japan.

Therefore, the contracts for international sale of goods between Japan and a CISG contracting state concluded on and after August 1, 2009 shall be governed by CISG automatically.

(3) Applicable Requirements for CISG

CISG applies to "contracts of sale" of "goods" between parties in "different states" (Paragraph (1) of Article 1).

The criteria for application of CISG are whether all three (3) requirements listed below are satisfied.

図表2－3　CISGの適用要件

「国際性」	①当事者の営業所（place of business）が異なる国にあること（営業所：恒久性・独立性を備えている施設） ※両当事者の営業の場所が同一国内にある場合には、本条約は適用されず、国内の売買法が適用される <u>且つ</u> ②(a)契約当事者の営業所が共に異なるCISG締結国に所在すること <u>又は</u> (b) CISG締約国の法が契約準拠法として適用されること。
「物品」	可動性ある有体物に関する売買契約であること。 有価証券、船舶・航空機、電気の売買はこれに当たらない。
「売買契約」	売買を本質とするものであること。 労働その他のサービスの提供が本質とされるものはこれに該当しない（材料注文者負担による製造物供給契約や役務提供を主とするプラント契約等）。 ＊消費者売買や強制執行その他法令に基づく売買には適用されない。

（4）CISGの適用排除

　したがって、完全な国内商取引以外で、前述3要件の全てを満たす国際売買契約は自動的にCISG適用を受けることになる。

　しかし、当事者間の合意でCISGの適用は排除可能（第6条）である。

　CISG適用を排除する場合には、契約書中に、明確にCISG適用排除文言を規定する必要がある（「日本法を契約準拠法にする」との規定だけでは、前述「国際性」②（ｂ）のルールに従い、CISGが自動的に適用されてしまうので要注意）。

Fig.2-3 Applicable Requirements for CISG

International Transaction	①Parties' place of business in different states (place of business: a facility with permanency and independence) ※In case parties have their place of business in a same state, this convention shall not apply and their domestic sales act shall apply. <u>and</u> ②(a)Parties' place of business in different CISG contracting states, <u>or</u> (b) Application of the law of CISG contracting state as a governing law
Goods	Contracts of sale regarding tangible objects with mobility Sales of negotiable instruments, vessels or aircraft, or electricity are not applied.
Contracts of Sale	Sales as the essential part CISG does not apply to contracts in which the preponderant part consists in the supply of labor or other services (including contracts in which the party who orders the goods undertakes to supply a substantial part of the materials necessary for such manufacture or production or contracts for plant in which the services are preponderantly provided). ＊Sales to consumers or sales on execution or otherwise by authority of law are not applied.

(4) Exclusion from Application of CISG

Except for complete domestic transactions, international contracts of sale which meet above three requirements are subject to CISG automatically.

However, the parties may agree to exclude the application of CISG (Article 6).

When the application of CISG is excluded, the wording to exclude the application of CISG is required to be expressly included in a contract (Please be advised that CISG automatically applies in accordance with the above "international" ②(b) requirement, if only the provision "This contract shall be governed by the laws of Japan" is included).

図表2－4　CISGの適用排除

×（CISG適用）	「日本法を契約準拠法とする」（←日本は締約国）
○（CISG排除）	「英国法を契約準拠法とする」（←英国は非締約国）
○（CISG排除）	「日本法を契約準拠法とし、且つCISGの適用を排除する」

＜CISG適用排除のための英文契約文言例＞

The United Nations Convention on Contracts for the International Sale of Goods shall not apply to this Contract.

　実際の契約書中には、「準拠法」条項に、日本法を準拠法とする旨と上記の文言とを併記することが望ましい。

> Article _ Governing Law
> _.1 This Contract shall be governed and construed in accordance with the laws of Japan.
> _.2 The United Nations Convention on Contracts for the International Sale of Goods shall not apply to this Contract.

3．契約の当事者

（1）本人と代理人

　取引の相手方が**本人**（**Principal**）なのか**代理人**（**Agent**）なのかについて、留意する必要がある。

　本人（**Principal**）とは、自己の名と計算で取引し、その結果生じるリスクを負担するものをいい、**代理人**（**Agent**）とは本人に代わって第三者との契約その他の法律行為および商行為を代行して行う権限を持つものをいう。

　いずれの場合でも、その責任の範囲、権限、義務、手数料について、本人として自己が全責任を負担するのか、あるいは代理人として手数料収入範囲の責任しか取らないのか、その資格を明確にし、その業務の範囲と責任を明記しなければならない。

Fig. 2-4   Sample Wording for Contracts

× (CISG applies)	This contract shall be governed by the laws of Japan. (Japan is a contracting state.)
○ (CISG is excluded)	This contract shall be governed by the laws of the UK. (The UK is not a contracting state.)
○ (CISG is excluded)	This contract shall be governed by the laws of Japan and CISG shall not apply to this contract.

<Governing Law Sample Clause>

"The United Nations Convention on Contracts for the International Sale of Goods shall not apply to this Contract."

It is recommended to include the laws of Japan as the governing law and above wording in a "Governing Law" clause.

> Article _ Governing Law
> _.1 This Contract shall be governed and construed in accordance with the laws of Japan.
> _.2 The United Nations Convention on Contracts for the International Sale of Goods shall not apply to this Contract.

3. Party to a Contract

(1) Principal and Agent

It is important to clarify whether a trading partner is a principal or an agent.

A "Principal" does business in its own name and for its own account, while an "Agent" has the right to conclude a contract or to do any legal and business actions with third parties on behalf of the principal.

It is necessary to clearly state its position as either, a principal or an agent, as well as the limit of responsibility, authority, obligation, and commission fee. A principal takes all of the responsibilities, while an agent takes limited responsibility according to the commission.

（2）販売店契約と代理店契約

輸出者が海外の販売業者や輸入業者と**販売店契約**（Distributorship Agreement）を締結する場合には、その輸出者と海外の販売店（Distributor）との関係は、輸出者がVender（売主）、販売店がVendee（買主）であると契約書上に明記されており、対等な関係、つまり本人対本人の契約となる。

したがって、自社がこれらの販売店に輸出する契約をする場合、あるいは自社がこれらの販売店となって輸入する場合には、契約当事者は全て本人となるので、販売店の在庫や輸入地での販売価格などは全て販売店の責任となる。

一方、その市場の有力な商社や販売会社に自社の代理権を与えて、海外の支店または出張所で行う行為を契約によって代理させ、営業活動を行わせるための拠点を代理店という。

この場合には、輸出者と代理店とは**代理店契約**（Agency Agreement）を締結し、契約当事者は本人（Principal）と代理人（Agent）との関係となる。代理人は本人に代わって第三者との契約その他の法律行為および商行為を代行して行う権限を与えられている。

したがって、代理店の商行為はすべて代理人として行われ、商行為の結果生ずる利潤または損失は本人に帰属する。そして代理人は代理行為に対して、本人との契約に基づき、一定のコミッションを受け取る。

この代理店契約にもとづいて行われる売買取引は、本人と売買取引相手（輸入国でのエンドユーザー）との契約となり、取引商品は直接本人から取引相手に送付される。代金決済もまた直接決済され、代理店は売買契約の取次にすぎない。

代理店は売込先の支払いについて法律上はそれを保証する義務はないが、代理店にその支払いを保証させる特約を結んで、代理店手数料(コミッション)に支払保証手数料を加算して、支払保証代理店として代理店契約を結ぶ場合もある。

（3）独占的販売権、代理権

海外の販売店や代理店と契約する際に、ある地域における一手販売権（独占的販売権）や一手代理権（独占的代理権）を与える場合がある。

この場合には、**Exclusive Distributorship Agreement**あるいは**Excusive Agency Agreement**となり、決められた地域内での独占的販売権や代理権を持つ。**Sole Distributorship Agreement**あるいは**Sole Agency Agreement**ともいわれる。

(2) Distributorship Agreement and Agency Agreement

When an exporter concludes a "Distributorship Agreement" with a distributor or an importer in foreign country, the relationship between the exporter and the overseas distributor is stated in the contract as a Vendor (Seller) and a Vendee (Buyer). They are on an equal footing, and the contract is considered to be made between principals.

For example, in the cases to export goods to overseas distributors or to import goods as a distributor, as the distributors are principals in the contract, they are responsible for the inventory and setting up the sales price in their country.

On the other hand, sales agents undertake sales activities on behalf of a principal based on a contract. Leading trading companies or dealers in the market often take a role of a sales agent.

The exporter and the sales agent conclude an "Agency Agreement" and establish a relationship as a principal and an agent. The agent is granted the right to conclude a contract or to do legal and business activities with third parties on behalf of the principal.

As the sales agent undertakes the commercial activities as an agent, any profit or loss belongs to the principal. For such agency activities, the agent receives a certain amount of commission based upon the contract with the principal.

A transaction based upon the agency agreement is conducted between the exporter and a buyer (an end user) in the importing country under their sales agreement.

The goods are delivered directly to the buyer from the exporter. The exporter receives the payment directly as the principal, and the role of the agent is limited to selling on commission.

Although the agent usually has no legal obligation to guarantee the collection of payment, the exporter (the principal) can require them to guarantee the payment by adding a special clause to the agency agreement. Payment guarantee fee is to be added to the agent commission.

(3) Exclusive Distributorship, Exclusive Agency

Sometimes, an exclusive distributorship or an exclusive agency in a certain territory is given to a distributor or an agent overseas at the time of a contract.

In this case, the contract to be concluded is an "Exclusive Distributorship Agreement" or an "Excusive Agency Agreement". It is also called "Sole Distributorship Agreement" or "Sole Agency Agreement".

第3章
貿易実務の流れ

Chapter 3
Flow of Trade Practice

1. 貿易取引と国内取引との相違点

(1) 貿易取引は売買取引

　貿易取引では、国境を越えて商品が売買されるが、そのことを除けば基本的にはその取引は「売買取引」である。つまり、

> 貿易とは　＝　異なる国の間の売買取引

といえる。

(2) 国内取引との相違点

　売買取引は日本国内にもあるが、貿易の場合は国内取引といったいどこが異なるのだろうか。

　国内で私たちが例えば本を買う場面を想定してみると、本を買うという売買契約の成立と、商品の引渡し、代金の支払いがすべて同時に行われ、その場ですぐに契約が履行される形となっている。

　ところが貿易取引の場合には、売主と買主とが異なる国のため通常遠く離れており、売買契約がまず成立し、その後時期をずらして、売主の商品引渡し（具体的には商品の船積み）や、買主の代金支払いが行われることになる。

　つまり、貿易取引の場合は、国内取引のように売買契約の締結と同時に契約の履行が行われるのではなく、後日、売主は輸出商品の製造や仕入れ、船積み手配その他の義務を果たし、買主は代金支払いその他の義務を果たすことになり、そこで初めて売買が完了する。

　したがって、貿易取引の場合には後日の契約履行になるため、売買契約を結ぶにあたっては、船積みの時期や代金決済方法などを契約の条件として前もって一つひとつ取決め、売主および買主は自己の義務をきちんと果たすことを約束するのである。

1. Differences between Trade Transactions and Domestic Transactions

(1) Trade means Transactions between Different Countries

In trade transactions, goods are sold or bought across national borders. Apart from such aspect, sale and purchase are basically conducted in trade transactions.

Trade Transaction = Transaction between Different Countries

(2) Differences from Domestic Transactions

How are trade transactions different from domestic transactions?

For example, when we buy a book in our own country, conclusion of a sales contract, delivery of the book, and payment for the book are made simultaneously. In short, the contract is immediately performed on the spot.

On the other hand, in a trade transaction, firstly, a sales contract is concluded between a seller and a buyer, since they are located in different countries which are usually far apart from each other. After a while, the seller delivers the goods to the buyer (specifically, the seller makes shipment of the goods), and the buyer makes the payment.

In other words, in a trade transaction, unlike a domestic transaction, after conclusion of the contract, a seller manufactures or purchases the goods, and carries out its obligations including shipping arrangements. A buyer also carries out its obligations including making payment. The transaction is completed only after fulfillment of the contract.

Therefore, in case of trade transactions, for conclusion of a sales contract, a seller and a buyer negotiate terms and conditions including time of shipment and payment terms and agree to faithfully fulfill their respective obligations in accordance with each of the terms and conditions determined in advance.

（3）貿易取引のリスク

　貿易取引と国内取引の相違点は、同時に貿易取引のリスクでもある。貿易取引の特徴を挙げながら、それがなぜリスクになるのかを考えてみよう。

① 　国が異なるため、売主（輸出者）と買主（輸入者）とが互いについての情報をあまり持っていないことが多い
　　→ 　取引相手の信用に不安がある（**信用リスク**）
　　→ 　とりわけ、輸出者側から見たときに、代金回収がきちんと行われるか不安がある（**代金回収リスク**）

② 　国が異なるため、商品の輸送距離が長く、時間がかかる
　　→ 　輸送途上の貨物の変質・損傷や、事故に対する不安がある（**貨物の事故リスク**）

③ 　通貨が異なるため、代金決済が複雑
　　→ 　通貨の交換が必要となり、その際為替相場を利用する（**為替変動リスク**）

　このように、貿易取引の場合には、国内取引と比べより多くのリスクを抱えている。これらのリスクをカバーするために商人達はさまざまな工夫を生み出し、それが商習慣として長い歴史の中で定着してきた。また、一見複雑に見える貿易取引のしくみや手続も、これらのリスクをできるだけ軽減し、回避するために生まれてきたものといえる。

　したがって、貿易取引の手続やしくみを理解するためには、それらの手続やしくみがどのようにして貿易取引のリスクをカバーしているのかと考えれば、その必然性が非常によく理解できることになる。これから各種の手続を学んでいくことになるが、常に「なぜその手続が必要なのか」、「その手続はどんなリスクをカバーしているのか」と考えてみることにより、正しい手続きを理解することができる。

(3) Risks Involved in Trade Transactions

The differences between trade transactions and domestic transactions are risks at the same time. By describing characteristics of trade transactions, let us consider why there are those risks.

① In many cases, neither a seller (an exporter) nor a buyer (an importer) has much information about its counterpart.
→ Concerns about Counterpart's Credit Standing (Credit Risk)
→ Especially an Exporter's Concerns about Collection (Collection Risk)

② It takes longer to transport goods.
→ Concerns about Deterioration of or Loss or Damage to Goods during Transportation (Damage Risk)

③ Settlement is complicated due to different currencies.
→ Requirement for Currency Exchange by using Currency Exchange Rate (Currency Exchange Risk)

As seen above, trade transactions bear more risks compared to domestic transactions. To avert these risks, merchants have made all kinds of efforts and those efforts have been established as trading practices over a long period of history. Besides, the system and procedures of trade transactions, which are seemingly complicated, have been made to minimize or avert these risks.

Therefore, in order to understand the system and procedures of trade transactions, the necessity of them can be very well-understood by consideration about the way to avert the risks of trade transactions. The followings show each procedure. Proper procedures can be understood by always thinking about "why those procedures are needed" and "what type of risks can be averted by those procedures".

2．輸出実務の流れ

図表3－1　輸出実務の流れ（コンテナ船、CIP建て送金取引の場合）

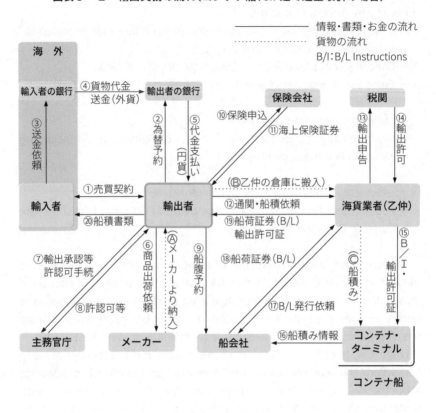

① 海外の輸入者と売買契約を締結する。

② 契約上の取引通貨が外貨の場合には、海外からの送金（④）は契約通貨どおりとなるので外貨となる。このとき、外貨ではなく、外貨を円に換えて受け取りたい（⑤）場合には、④⑤の時点で外国為替相場を使用する必要がある。

　　もし外国為替相場が④⑤の時点で円高に動いていたら、輸出者にとっては不利になってしまうので、為替変動リスクを回避するために、輸出者は売買契約を締結した時点で将来④⑤の時点で使用する相場を銀行に予約しておく。

2. Flow of Export Practice

Fig.3-1 Flow of Export Practice
(by Container Ship, on CIP Basis, by T.T. Remittance)

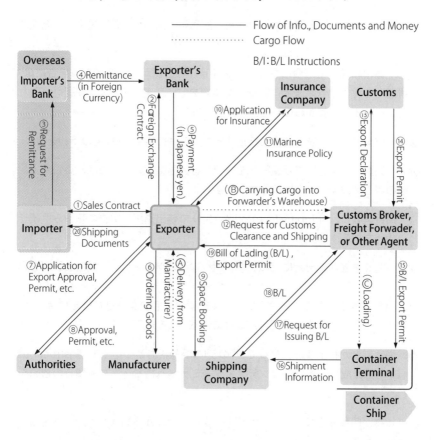

① An exporter concludes a sales contract with an overseas importer.

② When foreign currency is agreed as transaction currency under the contract, the remittance from overseas (④) is made in such foreign currency as agreed. However, if the exporter prefers to receive Japanese yen (⑤), currency exchange rate is required to be applied at the time of ④ and ⑤.

   If Japanese yen appreciates at the time of ④ and ⑤, the exporter would be disadvantaged. To avert currency exchange risks, at the time of conclusion of the sales contract, the exporter and its bank agree to exchange currencies at

③　契約上の支払期限までに輸入者が輸入地の銀行へ送金依頼を行う。

④　輸入地の仕向銀行から、輸出地の被仕向銀行へ外貨で送金されてくる。

⑤　②で予約された相場を適用し、円で輸出者に送金が支払われる。

⑥　国内メーカーから商品や、原材料、部品等の調達が必要な場合には発注する。

⑦⑧　輸出に際して法令にもとづき関係省庁の許認可が必要となる場合には、税関への輸出申告時までに許認可の申請をし、取得しておく（許認可が取れていないと、税関からの輸出許可がおりない）。

⑨　売買契約で輸出者が運賃を負担する貿易条件の場合には、船の予約を行う。

⑩⑪　売買契約で輸出者が保険料を負担する貿易条件の場合には、貨物海上保険の申し込みをし、保険証券を入手する。

⑫　海貨業者に、Shipping Instruction（S/I）で輸出通関と貨物の船積み手続きの代行を依頼する。

⑬⑭　海貨業者が輸出者に代わり、税関へ輸出の申告を行い、輸出の許可を得る。
　貨物が輸出に際して法令にもとづく許認可の必要な貨物だった場合には、申告時に税関に必要な許認可が取れていることを証明する。

⑮　海貨業者が輸出者に代わって、⑫のS/Iの情報にもとづいてB/L Instructions（B/I）を作成し、貨物をコンテナ・ターミナルへ持ち込んで船積みの依頼を行う。

⑯　貨物が船積みされたら、コンテナ・ターミナルから船会社へ船積み情報が通知される。

⑰⑱　貨物の船積み確認後、海貨業者が船会社にB/Lの発行依頼をし、B/Lの発行を受ける。

⑲　海貨業者が税関から受領した輸出の許可証（Export Permit：E/P）と、船会社から受領したB/Lを輸出者に渡す。

⑳　輸出者は、契約時に輸入者が必要書類として指定したものを、直接輸入者

a specified foreign exchange rate applied to the time of ④ and ⑤.

③   The importer applies for remittance with its bank by the due date agreed under the contract.

④   The foreign currency remittance is made from the sending bank in the importing country to the paying bank in the exporting country.

⑤   The exporter receives the remittance in Japanese yen at the foreign exchange rate agreed in ②.

⑥   If necessary, the exporter places an order for goods, materials or parts with a domestic manufacturer.

⑦⑧   In case that the goods for export are subject to permits and/or approvals from relevant authorities under the laws and regulations of the exporting country, the exporter is required to apply for and obtain such permits and/or approvals. (Unless such permits and/or approvals are obtained, the customs will not issue an export permit.)

⑨   In accordance with the trade terms agreed, if the exporter must pay the costs of carriage, the exporter books shipping space with a shipping company.

⑩⑪   In accordance with the trade terms agreed, if the exporter must pay the insurance premium, the exporter concludes an insurance contract with an insurance company and obtains the insurance policy.

⑫   The exporter issues a shipping instruction requesting its customs broker, freight forwarder or other agent to clear export customs and arrange a shipment of the goods on behalf of the exporter.

⑬⑭   The customs broker, freight forwarder or other agent files an Export Declaration with the customs on behalf of the exporter and an Export Permit (E/P) is issued. If the goods are subject to permits and/or approvals under the laws and regulations of the exporting country, the exporter proves at the time of filing that it has already obtained such permits and/or approvals required in accordance with the laws and regulations of the exporting country.

⑮   The customs broker, freight forwarder or other agent prepares a B/L Instructions (B/I) based on the information provided by the exporter's shipping instruction and brings the goods into the container terminal for loading.

⑯   After the shipment has been completed, the shipping company is advised of the shipment information from the container terminal.

⑰⑱   When the shipment has been confirmed, the customs broker, freight forwarder or other agent requests the shipping company to issue the B/L and the B/L is issued.

⑲   The customs broker, freight forwarder or other agent delivers the E/P and

へ送付する。このとき、保険証券裏面に、輸出者が白地裏書を行う。

3．為替変動リスクの回避

(1) 為替変動リスクとは

　海外の輸入者と売買契約を交わすとき、輸出者は当然採算を検討するが、このとき売買価格が外貨（ドルなど）の場合にはそれを円貨に換算したときの価格で検討することになる。

　ところが外貨と円貨との交換比率である外国為替相場は、市場で常時変動するため、場合によっては代金を円貨で受取ったときに採算割れを引き起こすことになる。

　相場が変動することにより、為替差損を被るかもしれないリスクのことを「為替変動リスク」という。相場の変動の状況によっては、売り上げ利益が相殺されてしまうほどの差損を被ることもあるので、為替変動リスクへの対策は、貿易に関わる企業の経営上の最重要課題となっている。

　いかに売買価格を慎重に見積もっても、為替相場の変動が大きければ採算は確定せず、貿易取引は不安定になってしまう。そのようなリスクへの対策はいろいろあるが、最も一般的で広く利用されているのが、「**為替先物予約**」である。

(2) 為替先物予約によるリスクの回避

　為替先物予約とは、将来使う予定の外国為替相場を、事前に銀行に「予約」しておくことをいう。

　「予約」とは、銀行と1ドル何円で交換するかをあらかじめ決めて契約しておくことをいい、予約することで、当日の相場がいくらに動いても予約（契約）した相場で外貨を円に交換してもらうことができる。

　将来の相場のことを「先物相場」ということから、先物相場を予約するので「先物予約」という。

　たとえば、売買契約の金額がUS$10,000で、1ドル100円で予約した場合、送金を受領した当日の相場がいくらに変動していても、必ず1ドル100円で交換してもらえることになるので、予約した時点で輸出者は、将来自分が円貨で受け

the B/L to the exporter.

⑳   The exporter sends the required documents designated by the importer at the time of conclusion of the contract directly to the importer. At this time, the exporter blank endorses on the back of the insurance policy.

3. Averting Foreign Currency Exchange Risks

(1) Currency Exchange Risks

When an exporter concludes a sales contract with an overseas importer, the exporter naturally considers whether the transaction is profitable or not. If the price is quoted in foreign currency such as US dollar, the exporter considers the profit by converting such foreign currency to its own currency.

However, the foreign exchange rate is fluctuating in the markets all the time. So, in some cases, the transaction becomes unprofitable when the exporter receives the payment in its own currency.

This risk is called "Foreign Currency Exchange Risk". In some circumstances, sales profit may be offset by exchange loss caused by fluctuation in exchange rate. Therefore, the measures against the foreign currency exchange risk are one of the most crucial business issues for trade-related companies.

No matter how carefully the prices are quoted, if the exchange rate fluctuates significantly, the profit is not fixed and trade transactions become at risk. To avert such risk, various measures are taken. The most common and widely-used measure is "Forward Exchange Contract".

(2) Averting Foreign Currency Exchange Risks by Forward Exchange Contract

A forward exchange contract is an agreement between a bank and an exporter/importer to exchange currencies at a specified foreign exchange rate on a future date/period.

Under this contract, the foreign exchange rate between two currencies is agreed in advance. In accordance with this agreement, regardless of the spot rate, foreign currency can be exchanged to another currency at the agreed rate.

As the rate for future transaction is called "Forward Rate", the contract for agreement on the forward rate is called "Forward Exchange Contract".

For example, when the sales contract amount is USD 10,000.00, if one US

取れる金額が必ず1,000,000円になることが確定したことになる。

　仮に送金受領時の当日の相場が円高で1ドル80円に変動したとしても、円貨での受取額が800,000円に目減りすることはなく、必ず1,000,000円受け取れる。

　このように、為替予約の最大のメリットは、円貨に換算した受取り金額があらかじめ確定することにある。受取り金額が確定することで採算が確定するので、為替が変動したことによる為替差損を防ぐことができる。

（3）先物相場の受け渡し時期の決め方

　先物相場による為替の受け渡しの時期の決め方には、次のような種類がある。

Ａ．順月確定日渡し

　直物為替の引渡し日から１ヵ月目、２ヵ月目などの応答日に受け渡しを約束するものをいう。

　たとえば１月10日に３ヵ月の順月確定日渡しの為替予約をした場合には、翌々営業日が起算日となる。つまり、１月12日を起算日として、引渡しはその３ヵ月後、つまり４月12日になる。

　これは、日本の外国為替市場では、銀行間直物為替の引渡しが翌々営業日となっているからである。

Ｂ．確定日渡し

　将来の特定の日を引渡し日とする方法をいう。

Ｃ．暦月オプション渡し

　たとえば５月渡しとか６月渡しなど、特定の月を決めておき、その月を引渡し期間とする方法をいう。その月の銀行営業日であれば、予約者が自由に為替の受け渡し時期を決定できる。

Ｄ．順月オプション渡し

　これは各月の応答日までの間であれば、予約者がいつでも自由に為替予約の実行を決定できるというものである。

dollar is agreed to be converted to 100 Japanese yen, regardless of the spot rate, the exporter will be able to receive JPY1,000,000 in the future and the amount is fixed at the time of conclusion of the forward exchange contract.

Even if the spot rate becomes JPY 80 against one US dollar, the exporter can surely receive JPY1,000,000, not JPY800,000.

As seen above, the greatest benefit of forward exchange contracts is the amount of receipt converted to an exporter's own currency is fixed in advance. At the same time the prospect of profit is also fixed. Therefore, exchange loss caused by currency fluctuation can be avoided.

(3) How to Decide Delivery Date/Period

A. Delivery on a Date after Fixed Period from the Contract Date

Delivery of currency is to be executed at the fixed rate on the date after a fixed period of time from exchange contract date. The period is decided in the contract like one month or two months.

For example, when an exchange contract for delivery in three months is concluded on Jan. 10th, the delivery date is calculated starting from the two bank business days (Jan. 12th) after the contract is concluded. The delivery will be executed on Apr. 12th, three months later from the starting date, Jan. 12th.

It is because the delivery under the interbank spot rate is executed in two bank business days.

B. Delivery on a Fixed Date

Delivery is executed on a specified date in the future.

C. Delivery on a Date within a Specified Month

Delivery is executed within a specified month (e.g. May or June) agreed in advance. In other words, the exporter or the importer can decide the delivery date from any bank business days in a specified month.

D. Delivery on a Date within Fixed Period

The exporter or the importer can decide the delivery date within a fixed period of time based on a fixed day of each month corresponding to the forward exchange contract day.

（4）為替予約の手続

　為替予約は外国為替を取り扱う銀行ならばどこでもできる。ただし、初めて海外と取引する場合には、あらかじめ銀行に「外国為替取引約定書」などの差し入れが必要である。

　取引が恒常的になれば、銀行とも電話による為替予約の申し込みが可能となるが、この場合にもあとから必ず書面で予約内容を確認することが大切である。通常は**予約スリップ**（**為替予約票：Exchange Contract Slip**）に必要事項を記載して、銀行に差し入れる。

■ 4．主要貿易書類

（1）Commercial Invoice（商業送り状）

　貨物を出荷する輸出者が作成する書類で、商品の送り状にあたり、通常インボイスと呼ばれている。インボイスには商品の明細、金額が記載され、輸出者から輸入者への請求書の役割を持つ書類である。

　その取引が実際にあったことを証明する書類なので、輸出でも輸入でも税関手続（通関手続）に欠かせない書類である。わが国だけでなく、どこの国の通関手続でも税関へのインボイス情報の申告が義務付けられている。

（2）Packing List（梱包明細書）

　輸出や輸入の通関手続の際、税関がインボイスに加えてPacking List（パッキング・リスト　梱包明細書）情報の申告を求めることがある。

　Packing Listは、貨物の梱包の数、重量、容積、段ボール・木箱などいった梱包の種類、各梱包ごとの内容物が記載された書類である。

（3）Bill of Lading（B/L）（船荷証券）

　貨物を船積みすると、船会社が発行する書類である。船積みしないと発行されないので、貨物の出荷の証拠となる。B/L上には貨物の船積み日が記載され、その日付は売買契約上の輸出者が守るべき納期を示している。

　またB/Lは、各種の船積書類の中で唯一、現金と同じ価値を持つ有価証券で

(4) Procedures for Forward Exchange Contract

Forward exchange contracts can be concluded with any bank engaging in foreign exchange business. However, in the case of an initial overseas transaction, documents such as "Foreign Exchange Transaction Agreement" are required to be submitted.

When transactions are conducted regularly, it is possible to conclude a forward exchange contract by phone. Even in this case, it is important to confirm the agreement in writing afterward. Usually an exporter or an importer fills in necessary information on an "Exchange Contract Slip" and submits it to its bank.

4. Major Trade Documents

(1) Commercial Invoice

A "Commercial Invoice" is a document prepared by the exporter that ships goods. It contains the description and amount of the goods and serves as a bill for the goods from the exporter to the importer.

As this is a document showing the transaction has actually conducted, it is crucial to customs clearance both for export and import. Not only in Japan but also in any country the information on the commercial invoice shall be declared in the process of customs clearance.

(2) Packing List

In the process of export or import clearance, the customs may request to declare the information on the packing list.

A "Packing List" is a document containing number of packages, weight, measurement, kind of package such as carton or wooden box, and description of the goods in each package.

(3) Bill of Lading (B/L)

A "Bill of Lading (B/L)" is a document issued by a shipping company after the shipment has been completed. As the B/L is issued only after the shipment has been completed, it is the evidence for shipment of the cargo. The date of shipment is entered on the B/L and shows the delivery date the exporter shall meet in accordance with the contract.

ある。貨物を引取る権利（貨物の引渡し請求権）が証券化された書類なので、輸入地に到着した貨物を引き取るには、原則として船会社にB/Lの呈示が必要となる。

（4）Insurance Policy（保険証券）

　輸送中に発生した貨物の損傷や変質、盗難などをカバーするには、通常、保険をかけるが、そのとき保険会社が発行する書類が保険証券である。

　保険証券は保険契約をした者に対して発行されるので、もし輸出者が保険をかける契約条件だった場合、保険証券は輸出者に宛てて発行される。

　輸入者が貨物引取り後損傷を発見して保険金請求する際には、この保険証券が必要となるため、輸出者が保険付保した場合には、その保険証券を輸入者に送付する必要がある。

Besides, among shipping documents, only the B/L is "Negotiable Securities" equivalent to cash. As a B/L embodies the right to receive the cargo, the B/L is generally required to be presented to the shipping company to receive the cargo arrived in the importing country.

(4) Insurance Policy

An "Insurance Policy" is a document issued by an insurance company when an insurance contract covering deterioration of or loss or damage to goods in transit is concluded.

An insurance policy is issued to the party that has concluded an insurance contract. If an exporter is obliged to conclude an insurance contract in accordance with the sales contract, the insurance policy is issued to the exporter.

When an importer files an insurance claim for the damage after receipt of the cargo, this insurance policy is required. Therefore, in case an exporter obtains insurance, the exporter needs to send the insurance policy to the importer.

第4章
貿易条件とインコタームズ

Chapter 4
Trade Terms and Incoterms

1. 貿易条件とインコタームズ

(1) 貿易条件とは

　売買契約を締結するときに、輸出入者双方にとって最も重要な条件が貿易条件である。**FOB**、**CIF**などと称される貿易条件は、英語ではTrade Termsといい、取引条件、交易条件、あるいは建値(たてね)ともいわれている。貿易条件は価格算定の基礎となり、貨物の受渡時期を示し、また同時に保険条件にも関わっている。

　異なる国の間での売買契約では、輸出者と輸入者の負担の範囲が明確に規定されていないと、それぞれの解釈が異なり紛争の原因となってしまう。そのような紛争を避けるために、長年の取引慣習として、共通の了解事項や合意事項を略語で表現する定型的な貿易条件が生まれてきた。

(2) インコタームズ (Incoterms) とは

　インコタームズ (Incoterms) とは、**International** の **In** と、**Commerce** の **Co** に、条件を意味する **Terms** を組み合わせた造語であり、国際商業会議所 (ICC：International Chamber of Commerce) が、定型的な貿易条件の解釈に関する国際規則として制定した解釈規準である。

　定型的な貿易条件の国際ルールとして統一解釈を行うことで、貿易取引上の紛争や摩擦を避けることを目的に、1936年に国際商業会議所(ICC) によって定められた。

　その後時代の要求に合わせて何度か修正、改正、追加、削除などが行われ、現在は2010年版を改正した2020年版が最新版となっている。インコタームズでは、定型的な貿易条件のことを「定型取引条件」と称している (国際貿易だけでなく国内取引にも適用可能となってきたため)。

　各定型取引条件の解釈基準がインコタームズとして明確に規定されたことで、インコタームズの11規則から選定した定型取引条件を表記することで、インコタームズにもとづき輸出者と輸入者の義務と責任が明確に規定されることになり、取引交渉時にこれらをあらためて取り決める必要がなくなる。

　ただし、インコタームズは規制でも法律でもないため、これを契約条件として使用するためには、契約書上に、その契約当事者間における貿易取引では、定型取引条件についての解釈はインコタームズにもとづく旨を明記しなければならない。その場合、インコタームズは上記のように何回か改正がされ、その度に義務と責任の範囲が変更されているので、何年版のインコタームズにもとづくのかを併せて規定することが重要である。

1. Trade Terms and Incoterms

(1) Trade Terms

Trade terms like "FOB" and "CIF" are the most important conditions in a trade transaction and also called business conditions, trade conditions and pricing terms. Trade terms are a basis to determine a price of goods to be imported or exported. Trade terms indicate not only the time of delivery of goods but also insurance terms.

Obligations of an exporter and an importer must be clearly defined in international transactions in order to avoid disputes. As a result of a long time practice of trade, some typical terms and conditions, which exporters and importers commonly use, have been established. Those terms and conditions represent mutual agreement between the exporter and the importer in simple abbreviation.

(2) Incoterms

"Incoterms" is a combination of words which consists of "In" for "International" and "Co" for "Commerce", and "Terms" as the meaning of trade conditions.

International Chamber of Commerce (ICC) established the Incoterms as a set of international rules for the interpretation of trade terms in 1936.

The purpose of Incoterms is to avoid disputes and frictions in trade business.

Incoterms has been revised to keep up with changes in the international trade needs. The latest version is the "Incoterms 2020" (revision of year 2020), which is updated from the 2010 version. The trade terms in Incoterms can be applied to both international and domestic transactions.

When the trade terms chosen from among 11 Incoterms rules which stipulate interpretation and definition of each trade term are specified, the obligations and responsibilities of an exporter and an importer are clarified. Thus, there is no need to negotiate each obligation and responsibility at the time of trade negotiations.

As Incoterms is neither regulations nor legislation, when it is used as trade conditions under sales contracts, the exporter and the importer need to make it clear in the contracts that the interpretation of trade terms shall be based on Incoterms. As the obligations and responsibilities of the exporter and the importer vary by the version of Inctoterms, it is advisable to stipulate the version to be followed.

2．定型取引条件の示すもの

(1) 定型取引条件で示される負担の範囲

　インコタームズ2020による定型取引条件は11規則あるが、その中でも最もよく利用されているのがFOB、CFR、CIFの3種類で、その使用頻度はきわめて高い。
　インコタームズ2020では、11規則それぞれについて、売主の義務10項目と買主の義務10項目とを規定しているが、その骨子は、①費用負担の範囲と、②貨物の危険の移転時点であり、所有権の移転については特に規定していない。インコタームズで使用頻度の高い定型取引条件であるFOB、CFR、CIFの3つの規則は、それぞれこの①②についてはどのような条件になっているだろうか。

A．費用負担の範囲

　FOB（Free On Board）は「本船渡し」の価格のことをいう。つまり、輸出港の本船上で貨物を引き渡すまでにかかった費用を示しているといえる。これをCostという。

図表4－1　「Cost」に含まれる費用

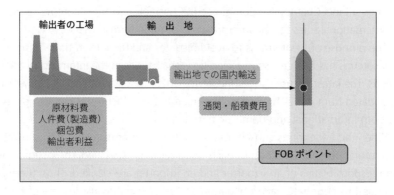

　CFRは、**Cost＋Freight**（運賃）のことで、FOBに運賃が加わった「運賃込み」の価格である。
　CIFは、**Cost＋Insurance Premium**（保険料）**＋Freight**（運賃）のことで、FOBに運賃と保険料とが加わった「運賃保険料込み」の価格である。
　この関係を図示してみると、次のようになる。

2. Interpretation of Trade Terms

(1) Responsibilities Indicated by Trade Terms

There are 11 rules in Incoterms 2020. Among them, FOB, CFR, and CIF are most frequently used. They are used in actual trade transactions very often.

Under all 11 rules, respective obligations of a seller and a buyer are stipulated under 10 articles. The major points are ① allocation of costs and ② transfer of risks. Incoterms does not stipulate anything about transfer of title to the goods. Under FOB, CFR, and CIF, the rules relating to above ① and ② are stipulated as follows.

A. Allocation of Costs

FOB is an abbreviation of "Free On Board". The seller delivers when the goods are placed on board the vessel at the named port of export. FOB indicates the "Cost". The "Cost" in Incoterms includes all the costs required until the point where the seller delivers the goods on board the vessel.

Fig. 4-1   Factors of "Cost"

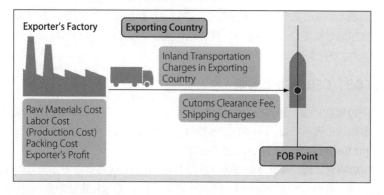

CFR means "Cost and Freight", which is above-mentioned "Cost" plus "Freight".

CIF means "Cost Insurance and Freight", which is "Cost", "Freight" plus "Insurance Premium".

The following figure shows the difference between FOB, CFR, and CIF.

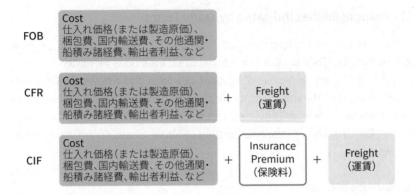

図表4－2　FOB、CFR、CIFの価格構成

B．貨物の危険の移転時点

FOB、CFR、CIFの３つの規則とも、輸出者から輸入者への貨物の危険の移転は、図表4－3のように、「**本船の船上に物品が置かれたとき**」とインコタームズでは規定されている。つまり、貨物の危険の移転時点については、３つとも同じなのである。

(2) FOB、CFR、CIFと書類

FOBの場合には、運賃・保険料は輸入者負担ということになる。このため、各種書類への表示では「FOB 指定船積港」と表示され、一般には運賃について**Freight Collect**（運賃着払い）と表示される。

CFRの場合には、運賃は輸出者負担のため、CFRの後ろにはそこまでの運賃は支払済みということで指定仕向港名が表記され、「**CFR指定仕向港**」と表示される。運賃については**Freight Prepaid**（運賃前払い）と表示される。

CIFの場合も運賃は輸出者負担のため、CFRの場合と同様、CIFの後ろにはそこまでの運賃は支払済みということで指定仕向港名が表記され、「**CIF指定仕向港**」と表示される。運賃については**Freight Prepaid**（運賃前払い）と表示される。保険料を輸出者が負担するのは、この３つの規則の中ではCIFだけなので、この場合のみ輸出者側に保険証券があることになる。

Fig.4-2   Composition of FOB, CFR, and CIF

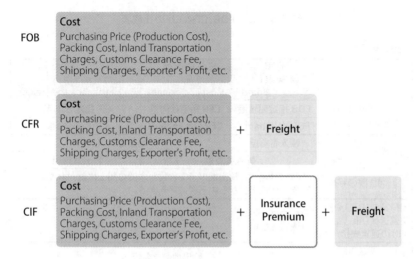

B.   Transfer of Risks

Under FOB, CFR, and CIF, it is stated that all risks of loss of or damage to the goods are transferred from the seller to the buyer when the goods are placed on board the vessel in the port of shipment as shown in the Fig. 4-3.

(2) FOB, CFR, CIF, and the Documents

As the importer pays the freight and the insurance premium under FOB, a description of "FOB named port of shipment" is stated in the shipping documents. Regarding the payment of the freight, a description of "Freight Collect" is shown on the shipping documents.

Under CFR, the exporter pays the freight. Descriptions of "CFR named port of destination" and "Freight Prepaid" are stated in the shipping documents as the freight to the port of destination has already been paid by the exporter.

Under CIF, the exporter pays the freight. Descriptions of "CIF named port of destination" and "Freight Prepaid" are stated in the shipping documents as the freight to the port of destination has already been paid by the exporter. Only under CIF in these three rules, the exporter pays the insurance premium and receives the insurance policy from the insurance company.

これらの相違点をまとめてみると、次のようになる。

図表4-3　FOB、CFR、CIFの比較表

＜2020年版＞

			FOB （本船渡し） Free On Board	CFR （運賃込み） Cost and Freight	CIF （運賃保険料込み） Cost Insurance and Freight
Rules（規則）の 表示方法と例示			**FOB 指定船積港** FOB Yokohama	**CFR 指定仕向港** CFR Los Angeles	**CIF 指定仕向港** CIF New York
負担の範囲	①費用	運賃	輸入者負担	輸出者負担	
		保険料	輸入者負担		輸出者負担
	②危険の移転		いずれの規則も、輸出地の港で貨物が本船の船上に置かれた時点で、危険が輸出者から輸入者に移転する。		
船荷証券（B/L）や航空運送状（Air Way-bill）の運賃表示			Freight Collect （運賃着払い）	Freight Prepaid （運賃前払い）	
書類	運送書類 （B/L、AWBなど）		輸出地側で発行		
	保険証券		輸入地側で発行	輸出地側で発行	

3．貨物の危険の移転時点と保険

　保険付保は輸出入者のいずれが行い、保険料を支払うのか、またどのように保険を付保するのかは、インコタームズによる「貨物の危険の移転時点」と密接な関係がある。

　保険を付保した貨物に事故が発生し、保険金が支払われる場合、保険金はその貨物の危険を負担する者に対して支払われる（これを「被保険利益」という）。

　また、保険期間は原則として、「貨物が保険証券に記載された地の倉庫または保管場所を出てから、保険証券記載の仕向地の、荷受人のまたはその他の最終倉庫または保管場所に引き渡されたとき」終了する。

　これを図示すると次のようになる。

Fig.4-3　Differences among FOB, CFR, and CIF

\<Incoterms 2020\>

		FOB Free On Board	CFR Cost and Freight	CIF Cost Insurance and Freight
Indications of Incoterms Rules and Examples		FOB named port of shipment	CFR named port of destination	CIF named port of destination
		FOB Yokohama	CFR Los Angeles	CIF New York
Costs and Risks	①Costs — Freight	Paid by Importer	Paid by Exporter	
	Insurance Premium	Paid by Importer		Paid by Exporter
	②Transfer of Risks	All risks transfer from the exporter to the importer when the cargo is loaded at the exporting port (**when the goods are placed on board the vessel in the port of shipment**)		
Documentations	Indication of Freight Payment on Bill of Lading (B/L) or Air Waybill(AWB)	FREIGHT COLLECT	FREIGHT PREPAID	
	Transport Document (B/L, AWB, etc.)	Issued in Exporting Country		
	Insurance Policy	Issued in Importing Country		Issued in Exporting Country

3. Transfer of Risks and Insurance

Which party obtains insurance and pays the insurance premium and how such party obtains insurance are closely related to the "point where risk transfer takes place" under the Incoterms.

In the event of any loss of or damage to the goods covered by insurance, the party who bears all risks of loss of or damage to the goods can file a claim. (The party has an "insurable interest".)

Moreover, in principle, the insurance attaches "from the time the goods leave the warehouse or the place of storage at the place named in the insurance policy", and terminates "on delivery to the final warehouse or place of storage at the destination named in the insurance policy".

The following figure shows above.

図表4-4 保険期間と被保険利益

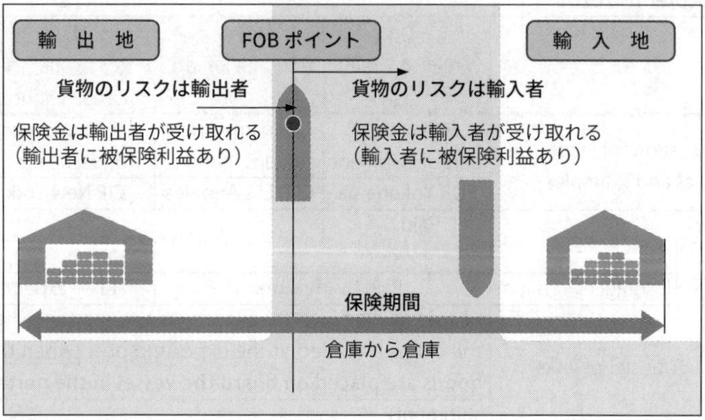

(1) FOB、CFR規則の場合の保険

FOB、CFR規則の場合の保険付保時には、次のようなポイントがある。
① 保険料は輸入者負担（保険を付保するかどうかは輸入者の任意）
② 輸入者は自分のリスクに対してだけ保険をかければいいので、自身が保険金を受け取ることができない区間（輸出地の倉庫からFOBポイントまで）を保険期間から外してしまうことができる。

　輸入者のリスク開始時である船積み時から保険期間を開始させるためには、「FOB Attachment」と呼ばれる保険特約をつけることができる（この特約をつけると、輸出者の倉庫からFOBポイントまではカバーされなくなる）。
③ 輸出者の危険負担区間は、輸出者自身で**輸出FOB保険**と呼ばれる保険をかけてカバーすることになる。輸出FOB保険とは、輸出国内の陸上輸送用に加え、港湾荷役による損害もカバーする保険のことである。

(2) CIF規則の場合の保険

CIF規則の場合の保険付保時には、次のようなポイントがある。
① 保険料は輸出者負担（保険付保は売買契約上の輸出者の義務）
② 輸出者は特約なしの倉庫から倉庫までの保険期間で保険付保する。
③ １つの保険で、貨物船積み時に保険金の受取人（Assured：被保険者）が輸

Fig. 4-4 Coverage Period and Insurable Interest

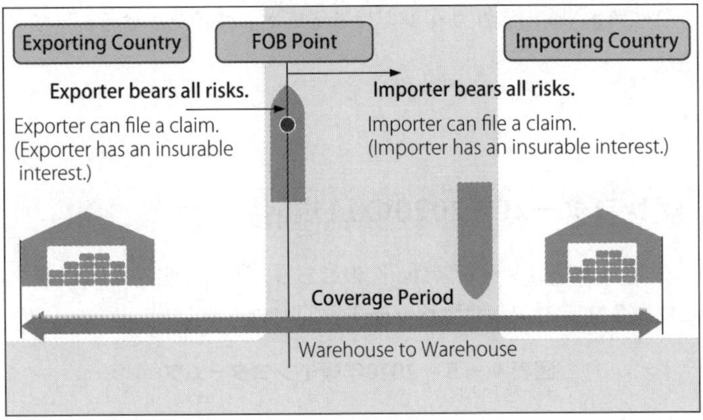

(1) Insurance under FOB and CFR Rules

The followings are points to obtain insurance under FOB and CFR rules.

① The importer pays the insurance premium. (The importer has no obligation to conclude an insurance contract.)

② The importer can conclude an insurance contract only against its own risks and exclude the period when the importer cannot file a claim (from the warehouse in the exporting country to the FOB point).

In order to commence the insurance coverage from the time of loading when the importer bears all risks, the importer can apply a clause called "FOB Attachment Clause". (Under this clause, any loss of or damage to the goods from the warehouse in the exporting country to the FOB point is not covered by insurance.)

③ The exporter, at its own expense, obtains insurance covering land transport and cargo handling from the time the goods leave the warehouse of the exporting country to the FOB point.

(2) Insurance under CIF Rule

The followings are points to obtain insurance under CIF rule.

① The exporter must pay the insurance premium. (The exporter has an obligation to obtain insurance under the terms and conditions of the sales contract.)

② The exporter must conclude an insurance contract that covers any loss of

出者から輸入者へと変わるので、発行時に輸出者が被保険者となっている保険証券で輸入者が保険金を受け取れるようにするために、保険証券裏面に輸出者の白地裏書（輸出者がサインだけすること）が必要となる。

4．インコタームズ2020の11規則

　2020年改定のインコタームズは、次のとおり、運送形態ごとに11規則に分類されており、3文字のアルファベットで表記されている。

図表4－5　2020年版インコタームズ

2020年版規則
＊いかなる単一または複数の運送手段にも適した規則
①EXW「工場渡し（指定引渡地）」 　Ex Works (--- named place of delivery)
②FCA「運送人渡し（指定引渡地）」 　Free Carrier (--- named place of delivery)
③CPT「輸送費込み（指定仕向地）」 　Carriage Paid To (--- named place of destination)
④CIP「輸送費保険料込み（指定仕向地）」 　Carriage and Insurance Paid To (--- named place of destination)
⑤DAP「仕向地持込渡し（指定仕向地）」 　Delivered at Place (--- named place of destination)
⑥DPU「荷卸込持込渡し（指定仕向地）」 　Delivered at Place Unloaded (--- named place of destination)
⑦DDP「関税込持込渡し（指定仕向地）」 　Delivered Duty Paid (--- named place of destination)
＊海上および内陸水路運送のための規則
⑧FAS「船側渡し（指定船積港）」 　Free Alongside Ship (--- named port of shipment)
⑨FOB「本船渡し（指定船積港）」 　Free On Board (--- named port of shipment)
⑩CFR「運賃込み（指定仕向港）」 　Cost and Freight (-- named port of destination)
⑪CIF「運賃保険料込み（指定仕向港）」 　Cost Insurance and Freight (--- named port of destination)

これらを図にすると次のようになる。

or damage to the goods from the warehouse to the warehouse.

③   A single contract of insurance covers the entire period of insurance. However, as the assured is transferred from the exporter to the importer at the time of loading, in order that the importer can file a claim by using the insurance policy on which the name of the exporter is initially stated as the assured, the insurance policy should be endorsed in blank by the exporter. ("Blank Endorsement" means the exporter endorses the reverse side of insurance policy without designating the next assured.)

4. 11 Rules in Incoterms 2020

Incoterms 2020 rules are classified into 11 rules according to modes of transport, as shown in Fig. 4-5.

All of them are abbreviated to 3 alphabetic characters.

Fig. 4-5   Incoterms 2020

Incoterms 2020 Rules
＊Rules for Any Mode or Modes of Transport
①EXW   Ex Works (--- named place of delivery)
②FCA   Free Carrier (--- named place of delivery)
③CPT   Carriage Paid To (--- named place of destination)
④CIP   Carriage and Insurance Paid To (--- named place of destination)
⑤DAP   Delivered at Place (--- named place of destination)
⑥DPU   Delivered at Place Unloaded (--- named place of destination)
⑦DDP   Delivered Duty Paid (--- named place of destination)
＊Rules for Sea and Inland Waterway Transport
⑧FAS   Free Alongside Ship (--- named port of shipment)
⑨FOB   Free On Board (--- named port of shipment)
⑩CFR   Cost and Freight (-- named port of destination)
⑪CIF   Cost Insurance and Freight (--- named port of destination)

図表4−6　2020年版インコタームズの11規則

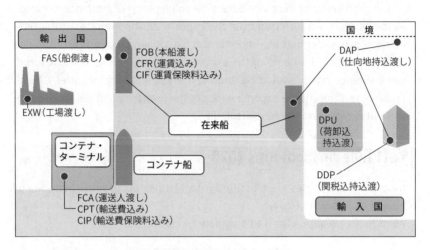

＜いかなる単一または複数の運送手段にも適した規則＞
①　EXW（工場渡し（指定引渡地））

　輸出地（積み地）の工場で貨物を引き渡す規則で、この時点で貨物の危険、費用負担は売主から買主に移る。輸出通関の義務も買主側にある。

②　FCA（運送人渡し（指定引渡地））

　売主の指定した場所等で買主の指定した運送人に貨物を引き渡し、このときに貨物の危険、費用負担が売主から買主に移転する規則である。

　具体的には、コンテナ船による貨物をコンテナ・ターミナルのCY（Container Yard：コンテナ・ヤード）やCFS（Container Freight Station：コンテナ・フレート・ステーション）で引き渡した場合や、航空貨物を航空会社または代理店に引き渡した場合、国際複合輸送の場合に貨物を複合運送人に引き渡した場合が該当する。

③　CPT（輸送費込み（指定仕向地））

　貨物の危険の移転時点はFCAと同様であるが、費用負担については輸入地までの輸送費を含んだ（売主側が負担する）規則である。FCA同様コンテナ船等の場合に使われ、在来船の場合のCFRに対応している。

Fig. 4-6   11 Rules in Incoterms 2020

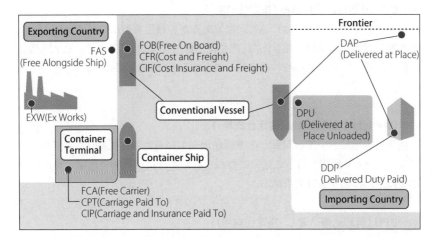

< Rules for Any Mode or Modes of Transport >
① **EXW (Ex Works (---- named place of delivery))**
The seller delivers when they place the goods at the disposal of the buyer at the seller's premises such as their factory or another named place, which is at the exporting (shipping) location. The buyer has to bear all costs and risks involved in taking the goods from the seller's premises. The buyer is responsible for the export customs clearance.
② **FCA (Free Carrier (---- named place of delivery))**
The seller delivers the goods cleared for export to the carrier nominated by the buyer at the named place. The buyer has to bear all costs and risks of loss of or damage to the goods from that moment.
For example, costs and risks transfer from the seller to the buyer;
-when the seller releases the goods to be carried by a container ship at a container yard (CY) or a container freight station (CFS)
-when the seller delivers the air cargo to an airline company or its agent
-when the seller delivers the goods to a combined transport operator.
③ **CPT (Carriage Paid To (---- named place of destination))**
The seller delivers the goods to the carrier contracted by the seller. The seller must pay the cost of carriage necessary to bring the goods to the named destination. The buyer has to bear all risks and any other costs occurring after the goods have been delivered. CPT is equivalent to CFR, which is used for transportation by a conventional vessel. For transportation by a container ship,

④　CIP（輸送費保険料込み（指定仕向地））

　貨物の危険の移転時点はFCAと同様であるが、費用負担については輸入地までの輸送費および保険料を含んだ（売主側が負担する）規則である。FCA同様コンテナ船等の場合に使われ、在来船の場合のCIFに対応している。

⑤　DAP（仕向地持込渡し（指定仕向地））

　指定仕向地において、荷卸しの準備が出来ている到着した輸送手段（トラックなど）の上で貨物が買主の処分に委ねられたときに、貨物の危険と費用負担とが買主に移転する規則である。

⑥　DPU（荷卸込持込渡し（指定仕向地））

　指定仕向地、または指定仕向地内の合意された地点において、貨物が到着した輸送手段（船、航空機など）から荷卸しされ買主の処分に委ねられたとき、貨物の危険と費用負担とが買主に移転する規則である。

⑦　DDP（関税込持込渡し（指定仕向地））

　指定仕向地において、荷卸しの準備が出来ている到着した輸送手段（トラックなど）の上で、輸入通関を済ませ、貨物が買主の処分に委ねられたときに、貨物の危険と費用負担とが買主に移転する規則である。

　売主が輸入通関義務を負い、かつ、輸入のための関税を支払う。

＜海上および内陸水路運送のための規則＞

⑧　FAS（船側渡し（指定船積港））

　指定された船積港において、貨物が埠頭上または艀（はしけ）に積み込まれて本船船側に置かれたときに貨物の危険、費用負担が売主から買主に移転する規則である。

　一般的な規則ではなく、木材等の特別な貨物の場合に適用される規則である。

⑨　FOB（本船渡し（指定船積港））

　貨物を輸出港に停泊中の本船に積み込んだとき、貨物の危険、費用負担が売主から買主に移転する規則で、積み込んだときとは、具体的には本船の船上に物品が置かれたときとされている。古くからある規則で、コンテナ船でない在

CPT should be used like FCA.

④ **CIP (Carriage and Insurance Paid To (---- named place of destination))**

The seller delivers the goods to the carrier contracted by the seller. The seller must pay the cost of carriage necessary to bring the goods to the named destination. The seller also has to obtain cargo insurance. The buyer has to bear all risks and any additional costs occurring after the goods have been delivered like FCA. CIP is equivalent to CIF, which is used for transportation by a conventional vessel. For transportation by a container ship, CIP should be used like FCA.

⑤ **DAP (Delivered at Place (---- named place of destination))**

The seller delivers when the goods are placed at the disposal of the buyer on the arriving means of transport (such as a truck) ready for unloading at the named place of destination. The buyer has to bear all costs and risks of loss of or damage to the goods from that moment.

⑥ **DPU (Delivered at Place Unloaded (---- named place of destination))**

The seller delivers when the goods, once unloaded from the arriving means of transport (a vessel or aircraft, etc.), are placed at the disposal of the buyer at the named place of destination or at the agreed point within that place. The buyer has to bear all costs and risks of loss of or damage to the goods from that moment.

⑦ **DDP (Delivered Duty Paid (---- named place of destination))**

The seller delivers when the goods are placed at the disposal of the buyer, cleared for import on the arriving means of transport (such as a truck) ready for unloading at the named place of destination. The buyer has to bear all costs and risks of loss of or damage to the goods from that moment.

The seller is responsible for import customs clearance and pays the import tax.

< Rules for Sea and Inland Waterway Transport >

⑧ **FAS (Free Alongside Ship (---- named port of shipment))**

The seller delivers when the goods are placed alongside the vessel, on the quay or the barge, at the named port of shipment. The buyer has to bear all costs and risks of loss of or damage to the goods from that moment. This rule is commonly used for particular types of cargo such as lumber, etc.

⑨ **FOB (Free On Board (---- named port of shipment))**

The seller delivers when the goods are placed on board the vessel at the named port of shipment. The buyer has to bear all costs and risks of loss of or damage to the goods from that moment. This rule has been used for a long time and is applied for a conventional vessel or inland waterway transportation, but it is

来船または内陸水路（運河など）の場合に適用される。

⑩　CFR（運賃込み（指定仕向港））

　貨物の危険の移転時点はFOBと同様であるが、費用負担については輸入港までの運賃を含んだ（売主側が負担する）規則である。

⑪　CIF（運賃保険料込み（指定仕向港））

　貨物の危険の移転時点はFOBと同様であるが、費用負担については輸入港までの運賃および保険料を含んだ（売主側が負担する）規則である。

5．輸送方法とインコタームズ

(1) 輸送方法とインコタームズの不一致

　FOB、CFR、CIF規則は、本来は在来船用の規則であるにもかかわらず、コンテナ船輸送や航空機輸送、複合輸送にまで利用しているのが現状であるが、実際の輸送形態とインコタームズの示す義務と責任の移転時点とは一致していない。

　これらの規則における貨物の危険の移転時点はともに「本船の船上に物品が置かれたとき」であり、コンテナ貨物の受渡しの実態には合っていないのである。

　例えばコンテナ船の貨物であれば港湾地域のコンテナ・ターミナルで貨物が引き渡されたときに、実際には貨物は輸出者（またはその代理人）側の手を離れている。貨物が輸出者側の管理下でなくなってもなお、本船に積むまでは輸出者側の責任とするこれらの規則では、実態には合わないことがわかる。

　同様のことは、航空貨物や複合輸送の貨物の場合にもいえる。

　インコタームズは、もともと在来船による海上運送時代に誕生したものであるが、今日では通常の貨物はコンテナ船や複合輸送で運ばれるのが一般的になっており、在来船はコンテナ船の配船がない航路や、特別な貨物の場合などに利用されるにすぎなくなっている。

not applicable for a container ship.

⑩ **CFR (Cost and Freight (---- named port of destination))**

The seller delivers when the goods are placed on board the vessel in the port of shipment. The risks of loss of or damage to the goods are transferred from the seller to the buyer at the moment like FOB. The seller must pay the costs and the freight necessary to bring the goods to the named port of destination.

⑪ **CIF (Cost Insurance and Freight (---- named port of destination))**

The seller delivers when the goods are placed on board the vessel in the port of shipment. The risks of loss of or damage to the goods are transferred from the seller to the buyer at the moment like FOB. The seller must pay the costs and the freight necessary to bring the goods to the named port of destination.

The seller also has to obtain cargo insurance.

5. Incoterms and Modes of Transportation

(1) Inconsistency between the Modes of Transportation and Incoterms

Though the rules of FOB, CFR and CIF are originally established for conventional vessels, they are often used for transactions using container ships, air transportation and combined transportation in practice.

Under FOB, CFR and CIF, it is stated that all risks are transferred when the goods are placed on board the vessel in the port of shipment. Concerning conditions of risk transfer, FOB, CFR and CIF are not appropriate for the transportation using containers.

In the case of transportation by container ships, the exporter or their designated forwarder loses their control over the cargo at the point when they deliver the cargo to Container Yard (CY) or Container Freight Station (CFS). If the rule of FOB, CFR or CIF is applied, the risk of the cargo remains on the exporter until the shipment is completed and the exporter has to bear the risk of the cargo even after the exporter loses their control. It is not reasonable for the exporter to bear the risk without their control over the cargo.

The same applies to air transportation and combined transportation.

When Incoterms was first established, cargos were commonly transported by conventional vessels. Nowadays, however, cargos are transported mostly by container ships. The conventional vessels are used mainly for the routes without allocation of container ships and for transportation of particular cargos.

(2) 輸送方法に適したインコタームズ

　コンテナ船や複合輸送の場合、運送人の責任は貨物の受取り時点、つまりCY、CFSなどから開始する。貿易取引の中で重要な書類である船荷証券（B/L）や輸送証券も、運送人が貨物を受け取った時点で発行されており、運送責任の開始時点を示している。

　したがって、コンテナ貨物の場合の定型取引条件は、運送人への引渡し時点で輸出者から輸入者に危険が移転する規則である、FCA、CPT、CIP規則が適していることになる。

　このためインコタームズ2020では、輸送形態ごとに適した規則を明記し、グループ分けしている。

(2) Incoterms Appropriate for the Modes of Transportation

In the case of transportation by container ships or combined transportation, the carrier's responsibilities commence at the point of delivery, that is, CY or CFS. In addition, a Bill of Lading (B/L) or other transport document, which is important in international trade, is issued when the carrier receives the cargo and indicates the commencement of responsibilities assumed by the carrier.

Therefore, the rules of FCA, CPT and CIP are appropriate for the transportation using containers as the risk of the cargo is transferred from the exporter to the importer at the point of delivery of the cargo to the carrier.

Incoterms 2020 describes the rules appropriate for each mode of transport and is classified into groups.

6．見積価格の算出

　輸出商品の価格を決める場合には、つぎの諸経費を見積る必要がある。これを価格を建てるといい、建値（たてね）という。

① 　仕入価格（輸出梱包経費を含む）
② 　輸出諸掛り　…　事務諸経費

> ①＋②＝工場渡し価格（EXW価格）

③ 　国内輸送費

④ 　通関諸経費
　（a）通関諸掛り
　（b）積込費用

⑤ 　輸出業者諸経費
　（a）金利
　（b）通信費
　（c）管理諸経費
　（d）利益

> ①＋②＋③＋④＋⑤＝本船渡し価格（FOB価格）
> 　　　　　　　　　　またはCY渡し価格（FCA価格）

⑥ 　海上輸送費
　（a）海上運賃
　（b）海上保険料

> ①＋②＋③＋④＋⑤＝運賃保険料込み価格（CIF価格）
> 　　　　　　　　　　またはCY渡し価格（CIP価格）

6. Preparation for a Quotation

The following expenses are required to be estimated in order to set prices of export products.

This is called pricing.

① Purchasing Price (including export packing costs)

② Export Charges ··· Clerical Cost

> ① + ② = Ex Works (EXW Price)

③ Inland Transportation Charges

④ Customs Clearance Expenses
  (a) Customs Clearance Fee
  (b) Shipping Charges

⑤ Exporter's Expenses
  (a) Interest
  (b) Communication Expenses
  (c) Administrative Expenses
  (d) Profit

> ①+②+③+④+⑤= Free On Board (FOB Price)
> or Free Carrier (FCA Price)

⑥ Ocean Transportation Costs
  (a) Ocean Freight
  (b) Marine Insurance Premium

> ①+②+③+④+⑤=Cost Insurance and Freight (CIF Price)
> or Carriage and Insurance Paid To (CIP Price)

図表4－7　見積価格の算出表

輸出入取引の原価計算要素と勘定科目

製造業者		
原価要素	勘定科目	貿易条件
製造原価	製品	
営業費	営業費の各科目	
輸出梱包費用（製造者梱包）	営業費の各科目	
（小計）EXW販売価格	売上	

輸出者			
原価要素		勘定科目	貿易条件
商品仕入価格		仕入	
輸出梱包費用（自社梱包）		仕入	
輸出手続費用（各種輸出承認・許可等の取得費用、原産地証明書費用等）		仕入	
銀行関係諸費用	借入金利	支払利息割引料（営業外費用）	
	手形割引料（手形買取手数料）	支払利息割引料（営業外費用）	
輸出関係銀行手数料		仕入	
営業費		営業費の各科目	
利益			
（小計）EXW販売価格		売上	EXW
輸出倉庫保管費用		仕入	
輸出国内運送費用		仕入	
輸出通関諸費用（通関業者費用）		仕入	
船積諸費用		仕入	
（小計）FOB販売価格		売上	FOB、FCA
海上運賃		仕入	
（小計）CFR販売価格		売上	CFR、CPT
海上貨物保険料		仕入	
（小計）CIF販売価格		売上	CIF、CIP
【輸入地の費用】以下の費用はDAP、DDPの時だけ算入			
荷揚諸費用		仕入	
輸入倉庫保管料		仕入	
輸入国内運送費用		仕入	
（小計）DAP販売価格		売上	DAP
輸入通関費用		仕入	
関税		仕入	
消費税		仕入	
（小計）DDP販売価格		売上	DDP

Fig. 4-7 A List of Cost Elements for Preparation of a Quotation

Cost Elements and Account Titles in Export and Import Transaction

Manufacturer			
Cost Element		**Account Title**	**Trade Terms**
Manufacturing Cost		Finished Goods	
Operating Expenses		Each title of Operating Expenses	
Exporting Packing Costs (Packing by Manufacturer)		Each title of Operating Expenses	
(Subtotal) EXW Price		Sales	

Exporter			
Cost Element		**Account Title**	**Trade Terms**
Purchase Price of Finished Goods		Purchase	
Exporting Packing Costs (Packing by Exporter)		Purchase	
Exporting Procedural Costs (Costs Related to Obtaining Export Permits or Approvals, Certificates of Origin, etc.)		Purchase	
Bank-related Expenses	Interest on Loans	Interest Expense(Non-operating Expenses)	
	Bill Discounting (Negotiation Fee)	Interest Expense(Non-operating Expenses)	
Export-related Bank Charges		Purchase	
Operating Expenses		Each title of Operating Expenses	
Profit			
(Subtotal) EXW Price		Sales	**EXW**
Warehouse Fee in Exporting Country		Purchase	
Inland Transportation Charges in Exporting Country		Purchase	
Export Clearance Expenses (Freight Forwarder Fees)		Purchase	
Shipping Charges		Purchase	
(Subtotal) FOB Price		Sales	**FOB、FCA**
Ocean Freight		Purchase	
(Subtotal) CFR Price		Sales	**CFR、CPT**
Marine Insurance Premium		Purchase	
(Subtotal) CIF Price		Sales	**CIF、CIP**

Costs in Importing Country - The following costs are added only under DAP and DDP Rules.

Cargo Discharging Expenses		Purchase	
Warehouse Fee in Importing Country		Purchase	
Inland Transportation Charges in Importing Country		Purchase	
(Subtotal) DAP Price		Sales	**DAP**
Import Clearance Expenses		Purchase	
Customs Duty		Purchase	
Consumption Tax		Purchase	
(Subtotal) DDP Price		Sales	**DDP**

第5章
貿易取引の運送

Chapter 5
Transportation for International Trade

1. 主な貿易運送の種類

図表5-1　主な貿易運送の種類

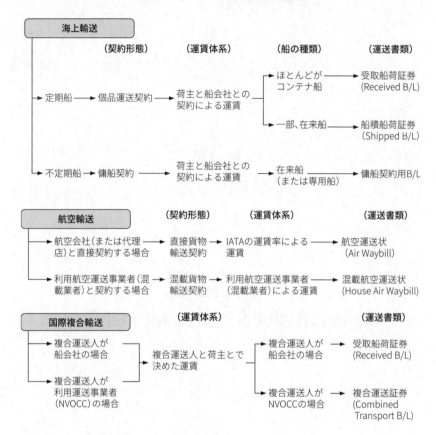

1. Major Modes of Transportation

Fig. 5-1 Major Modes of Transportation

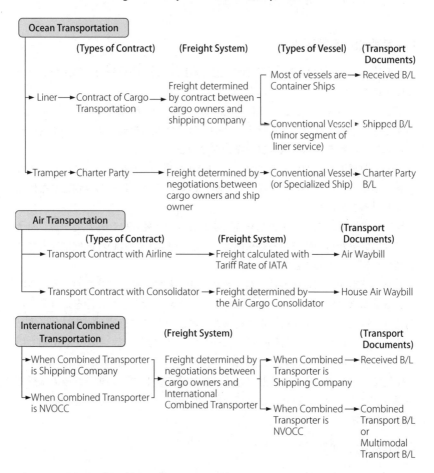

2. 海上輸送

　船舶による海上輸送には、定期船と不定期船とがあり、その輸送契約の形態も、運賃体系も、また運送書類も異なる。

(1) 定期船と不定期船

　定期船（Liner）とは、船会社が仕向地、出港予定日、運賃等を航海スケジュールにもとづき公表しているものをいう。

　荷主はこの航海スケジュールにもとづき、貨物の状態に合わせて仕向地行きの最も適した船を選び、船会社または船会社の代理店を通して口頭等で運送を申し込む。これを**スペース・ブッキング**という。

　一般の貿易取引における貨物は、一回の取引量が100トン以下というような少量貨物がほとんどのため、こうした貨物は通常定期船に他の貨物とともに船積みされることになる。

　現在の定期船はコンテナ貨物を輸送するコンテナ船がほとんどで、コンテナ船でない従来からの船である在来船は、コンテナ設備のない仕向地に輸送される場合など、ごくわずかである。

　一方、不定期船（Tramper）とは、大量の単一貨物の輸送にあたり、公表されている航海スケジュールとは別に、特にそのために傭船された船をいう。不定期船は、通常、コンテナ船でなく従来からの船である在来船が利用され、またそのうち特に特定の単一貨物の輸送に適したように造られたものを専用船といい、タンカーなどがその典型である。

　傭船契約を利用する貨物としては、一般に、包装せずそのままバラの状態で船積みされる、穀物、石炭、鉄鉱石などのバラ荷（バラ積み貨物　Bulk Cargo）が挙げられる。

(2) 定期船の運賃

　定期船の運賃率**タリフ・レート**（**Tariff Rate：表定運賃率**）では運送される貨物を品目別に細かく分類し、主要港間の基本運賃（Base Rate）が決められている。

　この基本運賃には、貨物の船への積み込み、および船からの荷卸しの費用が含まれており、このような運賃体系を**バース・ターム**（**Berth Term**）という。この定期船におけるバース・タームは、傭船契約のバース・ターム条件と区別して、特に**ライナー・ターム**（**Liner Term**）と呼ばれている。

2. Ocean Transportation

Ocean transportation can be divided into two categories: Liner and Tramper. They are different in terms of contract types, freight system, and transport documents, etc.

(1) Liner and Tramper

A "liner" refers to a ship whose sailing schedule is publicized showing ports of call, estimated dates of departure and freight rates.

After examining the sailing schedules of the liners, a shipper selects the best service in consideration of the freight and the port of destination, and applies to the shipping company or its designated agent for transport. This is called "Space Booking."

Consignments in international trade are generally less than 100 tons and are often loaded into the liner with other cargos.

In the liner services, container ships are usually used with some exceptions. For example, conventional vessels are used when the port of destination has no container facilities.

A "tramper" is a chartered vessel to transport a large amount of commodities of a single kind and it has no publicized sailing schedule. In a charter service, a conventional vessel or a specialized ship is usually used. A specialized ship, like a tanker, is designed to carry a particular kind of commodity.

A chartered vessel is generally used to carry bulk cargo such as cereal, coal and ironstone.

(2) Freight of Liners

The freight rates of liners are called "Tariff Rates".

In the list of tariff rates, cargos are carefully classified according to item, and "Base Rates" are set between major ports.

The base rates include cost of loading and discharge. These conditions of freight contract are called "Berth Terms". Berth term in liner transportation is called "Liner Term" to distinguish it from berth term in charter transportation.

　コンテナ船による輸送には、一荷主の貨物でコンテナが満載になる大口貨物の**FCL貨物**（**Full Container Load**）と、一荷主の貨物ではコンテナが満載にならないため、複数の荷主の貨物をコンテナに混載する、小口貨物の**LCL貨物**（**Less than Container Load**）とがあり、運賃率とその計算方法も異なっている。

　一荷主の貨物でコンテナ1本が仕立てられるFCL貨物の場合には、コンテナ内の貨物の重量には関係なく、標準サイズの20フィート・コンテナ、もしくは40フィート・コンテナ1本あたりいくらという、**ボックス・レート**が適用される。

　一方、複数の荷主の貨物を混載するLCL貨物の場合には、荷主ごとに貨物の品目や重量が異なるため、貨物の重量と容積から運賃を算出する**重量容積建て運賃**（タリフ上はW/Mと表記）となる。

　重量容積建て運賃の場合には、重量と容積の両方計ってそれぞれトンに直し、その数字の大きい方を**フレート・トン**（Freight Ton：運賃計算上のトン）として運賃を計算する。場所をとる貨物は容積で、重量が重い貨物は重量で運賃計算するためである。

　また、これらの基本運賃の他に、次のような調整運賃が発生することがある。

① 　BAF（Bunker Adjustment Factor）
　　　燃料費の急騰などの変動に対応するための調整運賃。アジア航路では**FAF**（Fuel Adjustment Factor）と表記される場合もある。

② 　CAF（Currency Adjustment Factor）
　　　運賃は米ドル建てのため、実際にその国通貨に換算するときの為替相場が変動した場合、その為替差損（益）に対応するための調整運賃。基本運賃の何％として計算される。アジア航路では**YAS**（Yen Appreciation Surcharge）として導入されている。

（3）傭船契約の運賃

　傭船契約の運賃は、傭船のつど荷主と船会社とで合意のうえ決定される。

In the case of transportation by container ships, the cargos are divided into two categories: Full Container Load Cargo (FCL cargo) and Less than Container Load Cargo (LCL cargo). An FCL cargo is a container filled with a single consignor's cargos, while an LCL cargo is loaded into a container with other consignor's cargos to make the whole container full. The freight rates and their calculation method depend on these categories.

In the case of FCL cargo, "Box Rate" is applied. This is the rate per 20 or 40 foot standard container. The weight of the cargo does not matter.

In contrast, in the case of LCL cargo, the freight rates are determined "by weight or measure, whichever is greater" (described as "W/M" on the tariff). In this case, both weight and measure are converted to tons. This ton is called "Freight Ton" (ton for freight calculation).

In addition to base rates, the following surcharges may be applied:

① BAF(Bunker Adjustment Factor):
Surcharges to cover the rising in fuel costs
In Asia, it can be described as "FAF" (Fuel Adjustment Factor).

② CAF(Currency Adjustment Factor):
Surcharges to cover currency fluctuations between US dollars and other currencies as the freight rates are in US dollars
CAF is calculated as a certain percentage of base rates. In Asia, "YAS" (Yen Appreciation Surcharge) is adopted.

(3) Freight of Charter Party

Freight of charter party is decided by negotiations between cargo owners and owners of chartered ships in each case.

（4）船荷証券（B/L）

　在来船による輸送の場合には、貨物が本船上に船積みされた時点で船荷証券（B/L：Bill of Lading）が発行されるが、コンテナ船による輸送の場合には、船会社が貨物を受け取った時点でB/Lが発行される。

　船荷証券は手形や小切手と同様の**有価証券**であり、輸入地で輸入者が貨物を引き取るためには、この船荷証券が必要となる。また、どのように発行されるかによって、幾つかの種類がある。

Ａ．船積船荷証券（Shipped B/L）と受取船荷証券（Received B/L）

　定期船で用いられる船荷証券の基本形式として、「**船積船荷証券（Shipped B/L）**」と「**受取船荷証券（Received B/L）**」の２種類がある。

（a）船積船荷証券（Shipped B/L）

　船積船荷証券（Shipped B/L）は、貨物が輸出者側立会いの下で特定の船舶に積み込まれたときに発行されるもので、On Board B/Lともいわれる。貨物の船積みに本船上に設置されているクレーンが使用される在来船では、船積船荷証券（Shipped B/L）が発行されるので、このB/Lは、貨物が特定の船舶に船積されたことの証拠となる。

(4) Bill of Lading

In the case of transportation of a cargo by a conventional vessel, a shipping company issues a Bill of Lading (B/L) when they load the cargo on board (a conventional vessel). On the other hand, in the case of transportation of a cargo by a container ship, the shipping company issues a B/L when they receive the cargo.

A B/L is negotiable securities like a bill or a check and is required when an importer receives the goods in the importer's country. There are several types of B/Ls and they can be categorized by the way of issuance.

A. Shipped B/L and Received B/l

The two most basic forms of B/L used for liners are a shipped B/L and a received B/L.

(a) Shipped B/L

A shipped B/L is issued by a shipping company when a cargo is loaded into an intended vessel in the presence of an exporting party. It is also called "On Board B/L". In the case of transportation by a conventional vessel whose on-board cranes are used to load cargos, a shipped B/L is issued. The B/L is a proof that the cargo has been loaded on board an intended vessel.

(b) 受取船荷証券（Received B/L）

　一方、受取船荷証券(Received B/L) は、貨物が船積みに先駆けて、コンテナ・ターミナル内にあるコンテナ・ヤード（Container yard：CY）またはコンテナ・フレート・ステーション（Container Freight Station：CFS) で引き渡される。

図表5－2　コンテナ・ターミナルの例

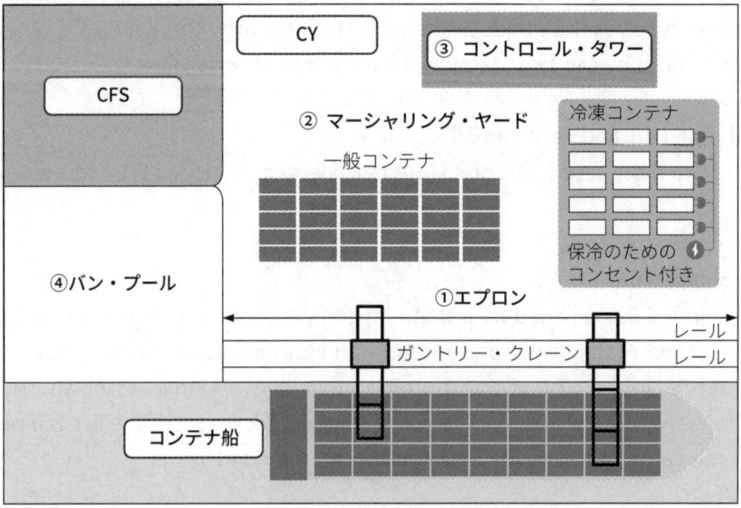

① エプロン　　　　　　　　　ガントリー・クレーンでコンテナの積卸しがされる場所
② マーシャリング・ヤード　　積卸しのためのコンテナを置いておくところ
③ コントロール・タワー　　　ヤードのオペレーションを管理する司令室
④ バン・プール　　　　　　　空きコンテナの置き場

　CYもCFSも船会社によって運営されており、船会社は貨物をコンテナ・ターミナルで受け取るとReceived B/Lを発行する。Received B/Lは船会社が貨物を受け取ったことの証拠となる。

(b) Received B/L

In the case of transportation of a cargo by a container ship, the cargo is delivered to Container Yard (CY) or Container Freight Station (CFS) located in the container terminal prior to the loading operation.

Fig. 5-2   Container Terminal

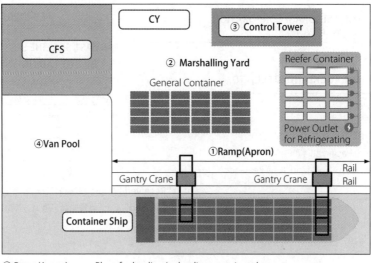

① Ramp(Apron)	Place for loading/unloading containers by gantry crane
② Marshalling Yard	Place to keep containers before loading or after unloading
③ Control Tower	Command office of container yard operation
④ Van Pool	Place to keep empty containers

Both CY and CFS are controlled by a shipping company and they issue a received B/L when they receive the cargo at the container terminal. The received B/L is a proof that the cargo has been received by the shipping company.

　その船荷証券が船積船荷証券（Shipped B/L）なのか、受取船荷証券（Received B/L）なのかは、B/L表面の約款の出だしを確認すると判断することができる。

図表5－3　受取船荷証券（Received B/L）

A shipped B/L and a received B/L can be distinguished by reading the very first word written in the B/L clause printed on the face side of a B/L.

Fig.5-3　Received B/L

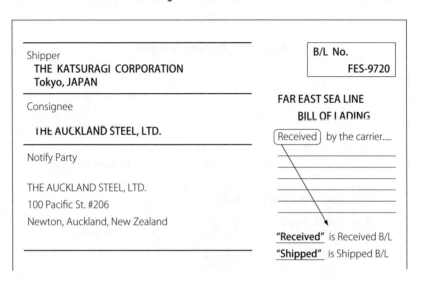

(c)受取船荷証券と On Board Notation

　受取船荷証券（Received B/L）であっても、最終的に、船積終了後に船への積み込みを完了した旨と積込み年月日を記載すれば、船積船荷証券（Shipped B/L）と同様に扱われる。この船積み証明のことを、「**On Board Notation**」といい、B/L下部に日付と署名がされることで行われる。

図表5－4　On Board Notation

Exchange rate	Prepaid at Tokyo, JAPAN	Payable at	Place and date of issue TOKYO, JAPAN OCT. 19, 20XX
	Total Prepaid in Yen	No. of original B/L THREE(3)	FAR EAST SEA LINE

LADEN ON BOARD THE VESSEL

Date **TOKYO, JAPAN**　　Signature

October 20, 20XX　　　- Signature -

- Signature -

On Board Notation

Ｂ．無故障船荷証券（Clean B/L）と故障付船荷証券（Foul B/L）

　船会社に貨物が持ち込まれたとき、その物品や包装に瑕疵（キズのこと）があった場合には、発行されるB/Lにその旨の付加条項または特記が記載される。これらの特記のことを「**リマーク**」という。

　例）１ case broken（１箱破損）
　　　Old barrels repaired, contents leaking（古樽、修理あり、中身もれ）

　リマークは、その瑕疵が船会社の運送によってできたものではなく、船会社に持ち込まれた時点から存在していたものであることを示している。したがって、このようなリマークつきのB/Lにもとづく貨物を受け取った輸入者は、船会社に運送責任を追及することはできず、直接輸出者にクレーム（賠償請求）していくことになる。

　リマークのついたB/Lを**故障付船荷証券**（**Foul B/L**）といい、リマークのついていないB/Lを**無故障船荷証券**（**Clean B/L**）という。

(c) Received B/L and On Board Notation

The received B/L with a notation of ① completion of loading into the vessel, and ② date of the loading, can be treated in the same way as a shipped B/L. Such notation is called "On Board Notation", which is evidenced by entering the date and signature at the bottom of the B/L.

Fig.5-4   On Board Notation

Exchange rate	Prepaid at Tokyo, JAPAN	Payable at	Place and date of issue TOKYO, JAPAN OCT. 19, 20XX
	Total Prepaid in Yen	No. of original B/L THREE(3)	**FAR EAST SEA LINE**

LADEN ON BOARD THE VESSEL

Date **TOKYO, JAPAN**   Signature

October 20, 20XX   - Signature -

- Signature -

On Board Notation

B. Clean B/L and Foul B/L

When a shipping company finds any damages on a received cargo or on outer packages, they write down the description of the circumstances of the damages or take notes on the B/L. Those notes are called "Remark".

e.g. -1 case broken

- Old barrels repaired, contents leaking

Such remarks raise presumption that there had been damages on the goods not during transportation but before the shipping company received them. In this case, an importer who received such cargo transported under the B/L with remarks can not make a claim against the shipping company. The importer has to claim compensation for the damage against the exporter directly.

A B/L with such remarks is called "Foul B/L", and a B/L with no remarks is called "Clean B/L".

C．B/L（船荷証券）の性質

B/Lの特徴として、次のようなものがある。

① 船会社が輸出港で貨物を受け取ったことを示す「受取証」
② 輸入港で貨物を受け取るための「引換証」
③ 貨物の引渡し請求権を証券化した「有価証券」
④ 貨物の所有権を移転させる流通性を持つ「流通証券」

3．航空輸送

（1）直接貨物輸送契約と混載貨物輸送契約

航空輸送契約には、「**直接貨物輸送契約**」と「**混載貨物輸送契約**」とがある。

A．直接貨物輸送契約

直接貨物輸送は、荷主が航空貨物代理店を通して、または航空運送事業者（つまり航空会社）と直接契約し、空港から空港までの輸送契約となる。実際には、ほとんどが代理店を通しての契約である。

航空貨物代理店は航空会社との代理店契約にもとづいて、集荷、運送の引受け、運送状の発行を行う。通常、代理店は、国際民間航空運送事業に従事する国際定期航空会社の国際団体である**国際航空運送協会（IATA）**の代理店資格を取得しており、IATA加入の航空会社であればすべて、代理店としての業務を行うことができる。

B．混載貨物輸送契約

混載貨物輸送（利用航空運送）とは、自らは航空機を持たない運送人である**利用航空運送事業者**（通称：**混載業者**）が、複数の荷主から小口の貨物を集荷して1つの大口貨物にまとめ、自らが荷主となって航空会社と輸送契約をする形態をいう。

C. Characteristics of B/L

Followings are characteristics of a B/L.

① "Receipt" issued by a shipping company who shipped the goods at port of loading.
② "Claim check" for an importer to take delivery of the cargo at port of discharge.
③ "Negotiable Securities " embodying the right to request delivery of the cargo.
④ "Negotiable instrument" with which the title to the goods transfers.

3. Air Transportation

(1) Transportation Contract with Airline and Transportation Contract with Consolidator

Air transportation contract can be divided into two types: transportation contract with an airline and transportation contract with a consolidator.

A. Transport Contract with Airline

One of the two types of contract is a transport contract with an airline. In this case, a shipper concludes a contract directly with an airline for airport-to-airport transportation. In most cases, the contract is made through an air cargo agent. Under an agency contract with an airline, the air cargo agent collects and transports cargos. The agent issues air waybills as well. Usually, the agent is certified by the International Air Transport Association (IATA) which is formed by international airlines engaged in the international scheduled air traffic. The agent can provide services for all IATA member airlines.

B. Transport Contract with Consolidator

The other type of contact is a contact with an air freight forwarder (commonly known as a consolidator). In consolidated cargo transportation (consolidation of air cargo), the consolidator concludes a transport contract as a shipper with an airline after collecting small lot cargos and putting them into one large lot. The consolidator does not have their own aircrafts and they make a contract for carriage of small lot cargos with each actual shipper.

　航空運賃は重量が大きくなるにしたがって運賃率が安くなる「重量逓減制」をとっているので、混載業者は小口貨物を大口貨物にまとめることでこの重量逓減制等を利用し、個々の小口貨物の荷主が直接航空会社に貨物を持ち込むよりも安い運賃を提供している。

　したがって、混載業者は、小口の貨物を持ち込む個々の荷主に対して、仕向地までの独自のタリフ（Tariff：運賃率）を持ち、そのタリフの運賃と航空会社のタリフの運賃との差額が、主として混載業者の収入となる。

図表5－5　混載貨物輸送の仕組み

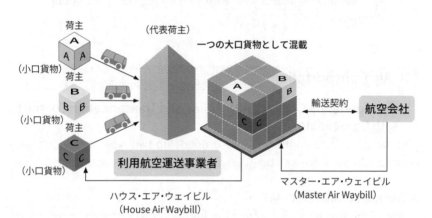

　これらの混載業者は、運送契約についても独自の運送約款を持っており、その約款と運賃率などにもとづいて、荷主との間で運送契約が締結されることになる。

　航空輸送契約の形態は、以上の直接貨物輸送契約と混載輸送契約のほか、チャーター（不定期）輸送契約もある。これは海上輸送における不定期船の傭船契約と同様、荷主と航空会社との間で、運送期間、日時を指定して、各航空会社が独自に設定した運賃で航空機の全スペースを借り切る契約をいう。

A freight rate for air cargo decreases as the weight of the cargo increases. The consolidator takes advantage of this system by putting small lot cargos into one large lot and receives lower freight rates from an airline company. This makes the consolidator possible to offer lower freight rates to small lot cargo shippers comparing the freight which they would be offered from the airline company if each of them contracted individually.

The consolidator receives payment for carriage from each small lot shipper under its own tariff. The consolidator's income is equal to the balance between their tariff and the tariff set by the airline company.

Fig.5-5　Structure of Consolidated Transportation

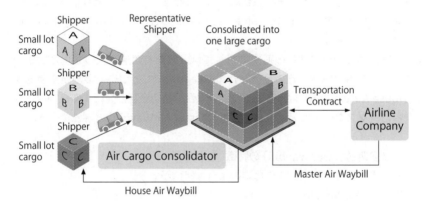

The consolidator has their own transport clause as well as their tariff. On the basis of their clause and tariff, they conclude a contract with a shipper.

In addition to the above transport contract with the airline and transport contract with the consolidator, there is also a contract for charter transportation in a very rare occasion. Same as in a charter party in ocean transport, a shipper charters the whole space of aircraft under the airline's own tariff.

（2）航空運送状（Air Waybill）

Ａ．直接貨物輸送契約の航空運送状

　直接貨物輸送契約では、運送契約が航空会社の運送約款、規則、運賃率など
にもとづいて締結されると、IATAの規則にもとづいた航空運送状（Air Waybill）
が発行される。

Ｂ．混載貨物輸送契約の航空運送状

　個々の小口貨物の荷主と混載業者との間で混載貨物輸送契約が締結される
と、個々の荷主からの小口貨物をまとめて大口貨物とした混載業者が、代表荷
主となって航空会社と運送契約を結ぶことになる。このとき混載業者には、航
空会社から通常の航空運送状（Air Waybill）が交付され、このAir Waybillは混載
業者によって保管される。

　一方、個々の小口貨物の荷主に対しては混載業者が運送人の立場となるの
で、混載業者が航空会社の発行したAir Waybillにもとづいて**混載航空運送状**
（**House Air Waybill**）を発行する。この場合の航空会社が発行する航空運送状
を特に、**マスター・エア・ウェイビル**（**Master Air Waybill**）と呼んでいる。

Ｃ．航空運送状（Air Waybill）の特徴

　航空運送状（Air Waybill）には次のような特徴がある。

（a）有価証券ではない

　海上輸送の場合、B/Lが貨物の引渡し請求権を証券化した書類だったので、貨
物の引取り時にはB/Lの呈示が必要であった。

　しかし、Air Waybillは海上輸送の場合のB/Lと同様、輸送契約の証拠書類では
あるが、貨物の引渡し請求権が証券化されてはいない。したがって、航空貨物
の受取りには航空運送状を必要としない。

（b）受取式（Received）かつ記名式である

　Air Waybillには、貨物の荷受人（Consignee）欄に、特定人名が記載されてお
り、貨物が到着した時、その特定人だけが貨物を引き取る権利を持つ。

(2) Air Waybill

A. Air Waybill of Transport Contract with Airline

In transport contract with an airline, the airline issues an air waybill based on IATA regulations.

B. Air Waybill of Transport Contract with Consolidator

Under a transport contract with each actual shipper, a consolidator collects small lot cargos and put them into one large lot. The consolidator, as a shipper of the one large lot cargo, concludes a transport contract with an airline. The airline issues an air waybill to the consolidator. The consolidator holds the air waybill issued by the airline.

The consolidator serves as a carrier for each actual shipper and issues the consolidator's air waybill based on the airline's air waybill. The consolidator's air waybill is called "House Air Waybill". The airline's air waybill is called "Master Air Waybill".

C. Characteristics of Air Waybill

Followings are characteristics of air waybill.

(a) Air waybills are not negotiable securities.

In the case of ocean transportation, a B/L is required to be presented to receive cargos because the B/L embodies the right to receive them.

Although an air waybill is a documentary evidence of transport contract like a B/L, the right to receive an air cargo is not embodied in the air waybill. Therefore, the air waybill is not required to be presented to receive the air cargo.

(b) Air waybills are issued as "received" and "straight".

In an air waybill, the name of a specific party is stated in the consignee field.

Only the specific party has the right to take delivery of the air cargo when it arrives at its destination.

4．国際複合輸送

(1) 国際複合輸送とは

2つ以上の異なった輸送手段（モード）を組み合わせて、輸送責任を一貫して1人の運送人が引受ける輸送形態を複合輸送という。

複合輸送は、コンテナの発展に伴い発達してきた。コンテナ輸送においては、コンテナに積み込んだ貨物をそのままの状態で他の輸送手段に積み替えることが容易であり、また、荷役も天候に左右されることなく行えることから、複数の輸送手段を用いて貨物受取人の指定地まで一貫して輸送することが可能になったのである。

図表5－6　複合輸送

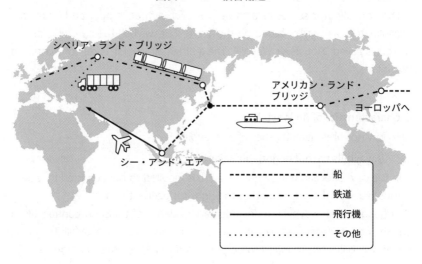

(2) 複合運送人

複合輸送を一貫して引受ける運送人を「**複合運送人**」と呼んでいる。複合運送人には、船会社がなる場合と、自らは国際輸送手段（船舶、航空機、列車など）を持たない**利用運送事業者**（**NVOCC**：Non-Vessel Operating Common Carrier）がなる場合とがある。

複合輸送は、当初船会社が引受ける形で発達してきた。コンテナの発展に伴い、単に港までではなく、列車に積替えたりしてもっと内陸地まで一貫した責

4. International Combined Transportation

(1) Combined Transportation

In international combined transportation, more than two modes of transport are combined and one carrier takes the responsibility throughout transportation.

The development of international combined transport has been accelerated by increasing demands for container transportation. In container transportation, containers can be easily transferred from one transport mode to another and their loading and unloading are not affected by weather. This easy handling of the containers makes it possible to deliver cargos using several modes of transport to the destination.

Fig.5-6　Combined Transportation

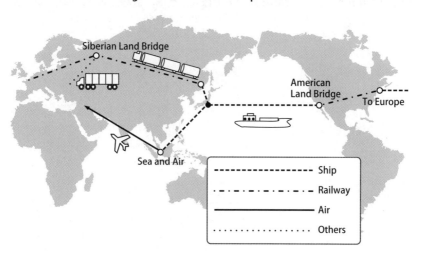

(2) Combined Transport Operators

A carrier who undertakes the combined transportation is called "Combined Transport Operator". A combined transport operator is either a shipping company or an NVOCC (Non-Vessel Operating Common Carrier) which does not have their own means of international transportation such as ships, aircrafts and trains.

Combined transportation was used to be undertaken by the shipping company. As needs for transportation by containers were increased, the shipping company started providing intermodal transport service in addition to its traditional port-

任体制で輸送を引受けるようになったのである。

　しかしこの場合には、複合運送人の船会社の航路が、その輸送方法の中に含まれていることが必要で、次第にそれ以外の輸送手段の組み合わせが要求されるようになったため、船会社以外にもNVOCCがいろいろな輸送手段の輸送業者を利用して、その貨物の全輸送区間に対して一貫した輸送責任を持つサービスを提供するようになった。

(3) 国際複合輸送の運送書類

　船会社による複合輸送では、通常の受取船荷証券（Received B/L）を使用している。

　NVOCCによる複合輸送では、日本のNVOCCが発行する運送証券は、**複合運送証券**（**Combined Transport Bill of Lading**、または**Multimodal Transport Bill of Lading**）を用いているが、その様式、目的、機能は通常のB/Lとほとんど同じである。

to-port transport. The shipping company takes the responsibility throughout the transportation in this type of combined transportation.

However, in this case, at least one of the shipping company's shipping routes must be included in the combined transportation. In response to various needs for the combination of other modes of transport, non-vessel operating common carriers (NVOCCs) began to provide services by combining suitable carriers of different modes taking full responsibility for the entire route of transportation.

（3）Transport Document of International Combined Transportation

In combined transportation undertaken by a shipping company, a received B/L is issued as a transport document. On the other hand, in combined transportation undertaken by an NVOCC, a "Combined Transport Bill of Lading" or a "Multimodal Transport Bill of Lading" is issued by its own form and handled almost the same way as an ordinary B/L.

第6章
貨物海上保険

Chapter 6
Marine Cargo Insurance

1．英文貨物海上保険証券

　異なる国の間で行われる貿易取引であるため、外航貨物海上保険はわが国だけでなく世界各国で流通する必要がある。世界各国にまたがる被保険者や損害発生時に査定を行うAgentに理解してもらう必要があることから、約款の内容や準拠法なども重要な問題となる。

　そこで日本の保険会社では、保険証券の流通性や信頼性を高めるために、世界の海上保険市場の中心的な役割を担ってきた英国で使用されている約款と同一のものを使用している。

　現在保険証券には2つの書式があり、それぞれ「S.G.Form（1963）」「MAR Form（1982）」と呼ばれている。

　S.G.Form（1963）は、200年以上前に作られたイギリスのロイズ S.G.保険証券（Lloyd's S.G. Policy）をもとに作られている。S.G.Form（1963）には、「保険金クレームについては英国の海上保険法および判例に準拠する」旨が規定されている。

　S.G.Form（1963）上の海上保険約款は、3,000以上の判例にのっとっており、それらの判例を通じてその1語1語の解釈が確立しているため、その解釈が難しい。

　このため、1979年UNCTAD（国連貿易開発会議）において、発展途上諸国より、S.G.Form（1963）の約款に対する改定の要請がなされ、その結果、新しいわかりやすい約款がMAR Form上に規定された。

2．協会貨物約款（ICC）

　海上保険証券は、ロンドン保険業者協会の制定したLloyd's S.G. Policyをもとに作られていた。しかし、この保険証券の本文だけでは多様化した貿易の実態をカバーしきれないため、今日では各種の特別約款を保険証券に添付、挿入することにより、その内容を補充している。

　こうした特別約款の1つが、ロンドン保険業者協会制定の「協会貨物約款（ICC：Institute Cargo Clauses）」（ICC）と呼ばれるものである。このICCは、ほとんどの貨物海上保険に使用されている。

3．旧ICCと新ICC

　S.G.Form（1963）およびMAR Form（1982）の2つの書式には、それぞれその

1. Marine Cargo Insurance Policy

As trade transactions are conducted between different countries, marine cargo insurance policies need to be negotiable not only in Japan but also around the world. In order that the assured in the world and agents who render damage assessment can understand, the clauses or the governing law are important subjects.

Japanese insurance companies use the clauses identical to the ones used in the UK that has been playing a key role in the world's marine cargo insurance market.

There are two types of insurance forms in marine insurance: "S.G. Form (1963)" and "MAR Form (1982)".

The S.G. Form (1963) is based on Lloyd's S.G. Policy made in the UK more than 200 years ago. The S.G. Form (1963) includes the phrase "This insurance is understood and agreed to be subject to English law and usage as to liability for and settlement of any and all claims".

The clauses in the S.G. Form (1963) are difficult to be interpreted because the words used in the clauses are defined in different ways based on more than 3,000 cases of judicial decisions.

Therefore, developing countries put forward a proposal to revise the clauses in the S.G. Form (1963) at UNCTAD (United Nations Conference on Trade and Development) in 1979. The proposal was passed and the comprehensive clauses were stipulated in the MAR Form (1982).

2. Institute Cargo Clauses (ICC)

Marine cargo insurance policies were based on Lloyd's S.G. Policy established by Institute of London Underwriters. Nowadays, however, various special clauses have been attached and inserted into them for supplementation as their policy body cannot cover all risks in diversified trade transactions.

One of the special clauses is "ICC: Institute Cargo Clauses" established by Institute of London Underwriters. ICC is adopted in most of the marine cargo insurance.

3. ICC (1963) / ICC (1982)

Each form of the S.G. Form (1963) and the MAR Form (1982) includes each

ベースとなる約款が規定されており、ICC（1963）（いわゆる旧ICC）、ICC（1982）（いわゆる新ICC）と呼ばれている。

　なお、MAR FormおよびICC（1982）は2009年に改定され、最近ではこのICC2009による保険の引受けが次第に増加している。

4．損害の種類

　海上保険の対象となる損害には、貨物自体の損害と費用損害とがある。

（1）全損（Total Loss）

　運送契約をした貨物の全部が、船の沈没、座礁、衝突、火災といった海上固有の危険によって受ける損害。

　全損には、現実全損と推定全損（現実全損が確実視されるが証明できないときや、貨物の回収や修理が可能であっても費用がかかり採算に合わない貨物）がある。推定全損の場合は、委付という手続きにより全損として保険金を支払う。

（2）分損（Partial Loss）

　貨物の一部が滅失したり、損傷を受ける損害で、これには、「単独海損」と「共同海損」とがある。

Ａ．単独海損（Particular Average）

　海上輸送中、個々の貨物に発生した損害で、被害を受けた被保険者（荷主）の単独の負担となる分損

Ｂ．共同海損（General Average）

　本船が暴風雨などのために座礁、沈没、大火災等の危険に直面した場合、船と貨物の安全を確保するために、船長の権限で一部の貨物を海中投棄したりすることがある。この措置で生じた貨物の損失や応急処置費用を共同海損として、船会社および全荷主が共同で定められた割合に応じて負担する場合の分損をいう。

（3）その他の費用損害

　貨物への損害の他、損害防止費用、特別費用、救助費用、およびサーベイ費

ICC as fundamental clause: ICC (1963) in the S.G. Form (1963) and ICC (1982) in the MAR Form (1982).

The MAR Form and ICC (1982) were revised in 2009 and underwriting of such insurance contract is increasing.

4. Covered Loss / Damage

Marine cargo insurance covers damages of the cargo itself and the cost incurred.

(1) Total Loss

It is called "Total Loss" when all cargos are totally destroyed by the perils of the sea, such as the carrying vessel being sunk, stranded, collided and burnt.

There are two types of total loss: actual total loss and constructive total loss. The constructive total loss is adopted, for example, when an actual total loss is undoubted but uncertified, or when it turns out to be too expensive to collect or fix the cargo. In this case, insurance money is paid through a procedure called abandonment.

(2) Partial Loss

It is called "Partial Loss" when cargos are partially lost or damaged. There are two types of partial loss: "Particular Average" and "General Average".

A. Particular Average

When the cargos are damaged individually during the transportation, the cargo owner (the assured) should solely bear the damage for such cargos.

B. General Average

Some cargos on board might be disposed into the sea under the authority of master of the vessel to save the whole in case of emergency such as vessel being stranded, sunk, burnt and so on. The losses or damages of the cargos and the cost of temporary treatment are considered as a general average, and the shipping company and the cargo owners should contribute a portion according to shares of contributions.

(3) Other Damage of Cost

In addition to the damages of the cargos, the extra costs such as sue and

用などの付帯費用の損害も、海上保険の対象となる。

5．保険金額

　保険金額（Amount Insured）は、保険会社が1回の事故について損害のてん補として支払う最高限度の金額として、保険契約者と取り決めた金額をいう。

　保険金額は、売買契約で特に定めのない限り、インコタームズで、CIFまたはCIP価額の110％と定められており、加算された10％とは、輸入者の希望利益である。

6．各種の約款（新ICCバージョン）

　日本の海上保険証券が、保険証券の流通性や信頼性を高めるために、世界の海上保険市場の中心的な役割を担ってきた英国で使用されている約款と同一のものとなっていることはすでに見てきたが、そのベースとなっているのがICC（ロンドン保険業者協会貨物約款）である。

　このICCに各種の特別約款を保険証券に添付、挿入することにより、その内容を補充している。

①2009年版ロンドン保険業者協会貨物約款（ICC：Institute Cargo Clauses）
　協会貨物約款（A）
　協会貨物約款（B）
　協会貨物約款（C）
②協会貨物約款（航空貨物）（Institute Cargo Clauses（Air）（excluding sending by post））
③協会戦争約款（Institute War Clauses (Cargo)）
④協会ストライキ約款（Institute Strikes Clauses (Cargo)）

7．新ICCにおける基本条件

　新ICCによる貨物海上保険は、次の3つの基本条件の中から1つを選んで付保される。

labour charges, particular charges, salvage and survey costs can be also covered by marine cargo insurance.

5. Amount Insured

Amount Insured is the maximum amount of indemnity guaranteed by the insurance company against losses of or damages to the goods in a single accident. The amount insured should be decided between the applicant and the insurance company under the insurance contract.

Unless otherwise stated in the sales contract, the latest Incoterms provides that the amount insured should be not less than the amount of 110% of the CIF/CIP value. This additional 10% represents the importer's expected profit.

6. Various Clauses (ICC (2009))

As mentioned above, Japanese insurance companies use the clauses identical to the ones used in the UK that has been playing a key role in the world's marine cargo insurance market. Those clauses are based on "ICC: Institute Cargo Clauses" established by Institute of London Underwriters.

Various special clauses have been attached and inserted into ICC for supplementation.

①ICC (2009)：Institute Cargo Clauses
　Institute Cargo Clauses (A)
　Institute Cargo Clauses (B)
　Institute Cargo Clauses (C)
②Institute Cargo Clauses (Air) (excluding sending by post)
③Institute War Clauses (Cargo)
④Institute Strikes Clauses (Cargo)

7. Basic Conditions in ICC (2009)

Marine cargos are usually covered by one of the following three basic conditions in ICC (2009).

(1) ICC (A)

　ICC (A) は、約款で特に免責とされている第４〜７条部分以外の外来的、偶発的な危険は、全て包括的に担保される条件である。

　また、各種費用損害については、下記の担保内容となっている（(A)、(B)、(C) 共通）。

・共同海損、救助料…第４条〜７条等の免責危険以外の危険を回避するために支出され、精算もしくは決定された共同海損および救助料

・継搬費用…担保危険のため、被保険輸送が仕向地以外の港、または地で終了した場合の荷卸し、保管、および当初の仕向地への保険の目的の輸送のために適切かつ合理的に支出された追加費用

・損害防止費用…保険でてん補される損害につき、その損害を防止、軽減するための、また第三者に対する権利の保全に要した適切かつ合理的な費用

---

(2) ICC (B)

　(B) 条件でてん補される内容は第１条に記載してあり、担保危険を列挙する形式での約款構成となっている。具体的には、下記の危険および損害を担保している。

＜原因を下記の事由に合理的に帰し得る保険の目的の滅失または損傷＞

・火災または爆発
・船舶または艀（はしけ）の座礁、乗揚、沈没または転覆
・陸上輸送用具の転覆または脱線
・船舶、艀（はしけ）、または輸送用具の水以外の一切の他物との衝突または接触
・避難港における貨物の荷卸し
・地震、噴火または雷

(1) ICC(A)

ICC(A) covers all risks of loss or damage attributable to external and incidental causes except as excluded by the provisions of Clause 4, 5, 6, and 7.

The coverage for expenses is as follows (common to (A), (B) and (C)).

> • General Average, Salvage Charges…General average and salvage charges, incurred, adjusted or determined to avoid loss from any cause except those excluded in Clauses 4, 5, 6 and 7
> • Forwarding Charges…Any extra charges properly and reasonably incurred in unloading, storing and forwarding the subject-matter insured to the initial destination in case the insured transit is terminated at a port or place other than the destination as a result of the risk covered
> • Minimising Losses…Any charges properly and reasonably incurred to avert or minimise loss recoverable under the insurance or required to ensure the rights against other third parties are preserved

(2) ICC(B)

ICC(B) covers loss or damage provided in Clause 1 as follows.

<Loss of or damage to the subject-matter insured reasonably attributable to >

> • fire or explosion
> • vessel or craft being stranded, grounded, sunk or capsized
> • overturning or derailment of land conveyance
> • collision or contact of vessel, craft or conveyance with any external object other than water
> • discharge of cargo at a port of distress
> • earthquake, volcanic eruption or lightning

<以下の事由に因る保険の目的の滅失または損傷>

> ・共同海損犠牲
> ・投荷または波ざらい
> ・海、湖、または河川の水の船舶、船艙、輸送用具、コンテナ、
> 　リフトバンまたは保管場所への侵入
> ・船舶または艀への積込み、またはそれらからの荷卸し中におけ
> 　る水没、または落下による梱包1個ごとの全損

　（B）は免責規定は（A）と同一だが、「1人または複数の人の悪意ある行為による保険の目的の全体または一部の意図的損傷または意図的破壊」は免責となっている（（B）（C）共通）。

(3) ICC (C)

　（C）条件でてん補される内容は第1条に記載してあり、担保危険を列挙する形式での約款構成となっている。具体的には、下記の危険および損害を担保している。
　免責規定は（B）条件と同一である。

<原因を下記の事由に合理的に帰し得る保険の目的の滅失または損傷>

> ・火災または爆発
> ・船舶または艀の座礁、乗揚、沈没または転覆
> ・陸上輸送用具の転覆または脱線
> ・船舶、艀、または輸送用具の水以外の一切の他物との衝突または
> 　は接触
> ・避難港における貨物の荷卸し

<以下の事由に因る保険の目的の滅失または損傷>

> ・共同海損犠牲
> ・投荷

　免責事由に該当しない場合にてん補される危険が、各約款の担保危険として（A）約款、航空約款を除き列記されている。All Risksタイプの両約款は包括的

\<Loss of or damage to the subject-matter insured caused by\>

- general average sacrifice
- jettison or washing overboard
- entry of sea, lake or river water into vessel, craft, hold, conveyance, container or place of storage
- total loss of any package lost overboard or dropped whilst loading on to, or unloading from, vessel or craft

Exclusion provisions of (B) are similar to those of (A). However, "deliberate damage to or deliberate destruction of the subject-matter insured or any part thereof by the wrongful act of any person or persons" is not covered under (B) (common to (B) and (C)).

(3) ICC (C)

ICC(C) covers loss or damage provided in Clause 1 as follows.
Exclusion provisions of (C) are the same as those of (B).

\<Loss of or damage to the subject-matter insured reasonably attributable to \>

- fire or explosion
- vessel or craft being stranded, grounded, sunk or capsized
- overturning or derailment of land conveyance
- collision or contact of vessel, craft or conveyance with any external object other than water
- discharge of cargo at a port of distress

\<Loss of or damage to the subject-matter insured caused by\>

- general average sacrifice
- jettison

The risks covered, except as excluded by the exclusion provisions, are listed in the clauses other than ICC(A) and Institute Cargo Clauses (Air) (excluding sending by post). Under ICC(A) and Institute Cargo Clauses (Air) (excluding sending by post) which cover all risks, Clause 1 provides to the effect that the insurance

に担保するため「免責事項として記載する場合を除き、保険の目的の滅失または損傷の一切の危険を担保する」との主旨が第1条に規定されている。

なお、(B)(C)条件で不担保とされている危険は、原則として、付加危険を選択することにより、担保危険として追加することが可能となる。

新ICCの各条件の担保範囲をまとめると、次のようになる。

図表6－1　新ICC各条件の担保危険

○印は担保、×印は免責（ただし特約を付ければ担保可）

担保危険、担保損害	A	B	C
火災・爆発	○	○	○
船舶・艀（はしけ）の沈没・座礁	○	○	○
陸上輸送用具の転覆・脱線	○	○	○
輸送用具の衝突	○	○	○
船舶、艀（はしけ）への積込み、それらからの荷卸中の海没、落下による梱包1個ごとの全損	○	○	×
海・湖・河川の水の輸送用具・保管場所への侵入	○	○	×
地震・噴火・雷	○	○	×
雨・雪などによる濡れ	○	×	×
破損・曲がり・へこみ、擦損・かぎ損	○	×	×
盗難、抜荷・不着	○	×	×
外的な要因を伴う漏出・不足	○	×	×
共同海損・救助料、投荷	○	○	○
波ざらい	○	○	×

（注）×印は保険会社により特約をつけることにより担保可となる場合あり

covers all risks of loss or damage to the subject-matter insured except as excluded by the exclusion provisions.

However, in principle, the risks not covered under (B) and (C) can be covered by paying extra premium.

The following list shows the coverage in ICC (2009).

Fig. 6-1   Coverage in ICC(2009)

○ : covered, ✕ :excluded (however, covered by special clauses)

Risk Covered	A	B	C
Fire or explosion	○	○	○
Vessel or craft being sunk or stranded	○	○	○
Overturning or derailment of land conveyance	○	○	○
Collision of conveyance	○	○	○
Total loss of any package lost overboard or dropped whilst loading on to, or unloading from, vessel or craft	○	○	✕
Entry of sea, lake or river water into conveyance or place of storage	○	○	✕
Earthquake, volcanic eruption or lightning	○	○	✕
Water damage due to rain or snow	○	✕	✕
Breakage, bending or denting, friction or hook damage	○	✕	✕
Theft, pilferage or non delivery	○	✕	✕
Leakage or shortage associated with external factors	○	✕	✕
General average and salvage charges, jettison	○	○	○
Washing overboard	○	○	✕

(Note)The risks shown as"x"can be covered by attachment of special clauses in some insurance companies.

８．戦争危険とストライキ危険

　2009年版ICCによるこれらの基本条件は、(A)(B)(C)の各約款において、戦争危険は第6条で、ストライキ危険は第7条でそれぞれ免責しているのでカバーしない。これらの危険についてもてん補したい場合には、特別約款として「**協会戦争約款（Institute War Clauses（Cargo））**」や「**協会ストライキ約款（Institute Strikes Clauses（Cargo））**」を追加契約することが必要となる。

　実際の実務では、各保険会社では協会戦争約款と協会ストライキ約款が追加されているのが標準となっている（不要な場合にのみ申告する）。

９．付加危険

　ICC（C）または（B）で付保されていない、次のような危険に対しては、追加保険料を支払うことによってそれらの危険を担保することができる。

　ただし、ICC（A）には、下記の追加危険は一括担保されている。

図表6－2　付加危険

追加危険	略語
雨淡水ぬれ損（Rain &/or Fresh Water Damage）	RFWD
盗難、抜荷、不着損害（Theft, Pilferage &/or Non delivery）	TPND
破損（Breakage）	B' kge
まがり、へこみ（Bending &/or Denting）	BD
漏損（Leakage）	L' kge
不足損害（Shortage）	S' tge
手かぎおよび油損（Hook & Oil Damage）	H & O
他貨物との接触による損害（Damage caused by Contact with Other Cargo）	COC
汗、むれ損（Sweat & Heating）	S&H
錆・酸化及び変色（Rust, oxidation and discoloration）	R.O.D.
かび損（Mould & Mildew）	MM
ねずみ食い、虫食い（Rats & Vermin）	RV
自然発火（Heating Spontaneous Combustion）	HSC
汚染（Contamination）	
投荷、波ざらい(Jettison &/or Washing Overboard)	JWOB

8. Coverage against the Risk of War & Strikes

The risks of War or Strikes are not covered by the basic terms of the ICC (2009) as they are excluded by the provisions of Clause 6 (war) and Clause 7 (strikes). They can be covered only by adding special clauses to the contract, such as "Institute War Clauses (Cargo)" and "Institute Strikes Clauses (Cargo)".

In practice, Institute War Clauses (Cargo) and Institute Strikes Clauses (Cargo) are added normally (notify an insurance company only if unnecessary).

9. Extraneous Risk

The special risks shown below are not covered by ICC(B) and ICC(C), while ICC(A) covers all of them. They can be covered by paying extra premium.

Fig.6-2 Extraneous Risk

Extraneous Risk	Abbreviation
Rain &/or Fresh Water Damage	RFWD
Theft, Pilferage &/or Non delivery	TPND
Breakage	B' kge
Bending &/or Denting	BD
Leakage	L' kge
Shortage	S' tge
Hook & Oil Damage	H & O
Damage caused by Contact with Other Cargo	COC
Sweat & Heating	S&H
Rust, oxidation and discoloration	R.O.D.
Mould & Mildew	MM
Rats & Vermin	RV
Heating Spontaneous Combustion	HSC
Contamination	
Jettison &/or Washing Overboard	JWOB

10．新旧ICCの担保条件の比較

　旧ICC（協会貨物約款）には、A/R（All Risks）、WA、およびFPAの3つの条件があるが、これらは新ICC（A）（B）および（C）にそれぞれに対応している。

　しかし完全に同じではなく、両約款には差異がある。

　新約款の大きな特色として、分損の概念を放棄したこと、基本3条件にそれぞれ担保危険、免責事項を明記してわかりやすくしたことにより、自己完結型の約款としたことがあげられる。

　新ICC（A）は、包括的に危険を担保する点では旧ICCのA/R（All Risks）条件と変わらないが、免責事項の違いにより担保責任の差異がある。

　旧ICCのWAおよびFPA条件は、全損については証券本文で規定された海上危険についてすべてを担保することを前提として、単独海損をどのように担保していくかを念頭に置いて作成された約款だった。

　それに対して新ICC（B）および（C）は、全損、分損に関わりなく、それぞれ列挙された危険を担保するという考え方をとっている。

　また、旧ICCでは分損担保のWA条件と分損不担保のFPA条件の違いは、結局潮濡れ損を担保するか否かといった程度といわれていたが、新ICCでは分損担保、不担保の概念がなくなったため、（B）（C）それぞれの担保危険に基づいて理解することになった。

　新旧両約款の物的損害についての主な相違点を、新約款を基に図表化すると、図6－3のようになる。

10. Comparisons of Conditions between ICC (1963) and ICC (2009)

There are three main sets of clauses in ICC (1963): A/R (All Risks), WA and FPA. They correspond approximately to ICC(A), ICC(B) and ICC(C) in ICC (2009) respectively.

They are not identical each other and there are differences.

As a prominent characteristic of ICC (2009), the concept of partial loss has been abolished and risks covered and exclusions have been specified in each of three basic conditions. Accordingly, the clauses in ICC (2009) are self-contained.

ICC(A) is similar to A/R (All Risks) in ICC (1963) in terms of coverage of comprehensive risks. However, there are differences in exclusions.

WA and FPA in ICC (1963) are the clauses established by considering how to cover particular average on the basis that all the risks provided in the policy body are covered as to total loss.

In contrast, concerning ICC(B) and ICC(C), risks listed in each condition are covered regardless of total loss or partial loss.

Moreover, in ICC (1963), the difference between WA and FPA is said to be simply whether or not sea water damage is covered. In contract, in ICC (2009), there is no concept of "free from particular average" and "with average". So, risks covered in each of ICC(B) and ICC(C) are taken into consideration.

Major differences relating to cargo damages between ICC (1963) and ICC (2009) are below.

図表6－3　新約款と旧約款の相違点

新ICC	旧ICC	旧約款との物的損害に関する主な相違点
(A)	A/R	① オールリスクの標題はなくなったが、包括担保のオールリスクである ② 免責危険が旧約款では英国海上保険法の規定等によっていたが、新約款では約款上に具体的に明示された [てん補されなくなった損害] ・船会社の経済的破綻による損害（ただし、2009年の新約款の改定で、被保険者がその事実を事前に知らなかった場合においては、てん補されることになった） ・核兵器の使用による損害（旧約款には規定がなく、協会放射能汚染免責約款を適用して免責としていた）
(B)	WA	担保危険と免責危険が具体的に列挙された 免責歩合（フランチャイズ）が廃止された [新たにてん補されるようになった危険] ・湖水、河川の水など淡水の船舶、輸送用具、保管場所への侵入 ・地震、噴火、落雷 [てん補されなくなった危険] ・荒天遭遇による荷崩れ ・悪意の行為による意図的な損傷、破壊、火災等
(C)	FPA	担保危険と免責危険が具体的に列挙された [新たにてん補されるようになった危険] ・担保危険に原因する分損 　（旧約款では列挙された特定事故（SSBC等）のみ分損担保） [てん補されなくなった危険] ・積込み、荷卸し中の貨物1個ごとの全損

Fig.6-3 Differences between ICC(1963) and ICC(2009)

ICC (2009)	ICC (1963)	Major Changes Relating to Cargo Damages from ICC (1963)
(A)	A/R	1) The name "All Risks" is not included, but it covers all risks. 2) Exclusions are specified in the clauses. In ICC (1963), exclusions are in accordance with provisions of Marine Insurance Act, 1906, etc. [Loss or damage no longer covered] - Loss or damage caused by insolvency or financial default of shipping companies (However, under the revision in 2009, if the assured is not aware of such insolvency or financial default in advance, loss or damage caused by such insolvency or financial default is covered.) - Loss or damage caused by use of nuclear weapons (There is no provision and Institute Radioactive Contamination Exclusion Clause is applied in ICC (1963).)
(B)	WA	Risks covered and exclusions are listed specifically. Franchise has been abolished. [Risks newly covered] - Entry of lake or river water into vessel, conveyance or place of storage - Earthquake, volcanic eruption or lightning [Risks no longer covered] - Collapsing of cargo due to bad weather - Deliberate damage, destruction, fire etc. by wrongful acts
(C)	FPA	Risks covered and exclusions are listed specifically. [Risks newly covered] - Partial loss arising from risks covered (In ICC (1963), only the certain types of partial loss (caused by stranding, sinking, burning or collision (SSBC) etc.) are covered.) [Risks no longer covered] - Total loss of each cargo during its loading and discharging

11. 旧ICCにおける基本条件

(1) ICC (1963) における基本条件

ICC (1963) による貨物海上保険は、次の3つの基本条件の中から1つを選んで付保される。

①FPA (Free from Particular Average)　分損不担保

FPAは次の危険をてん補する。
- ・共同海損
- ・全損
- ・本船、はしけの座礁、沈没、大火災があった場合の分損、および本船の衝突に起因する分損事故 (SSBC)
- ・損害防止費用等の費用損害

②WA (With Average)　分損担保

FPAがカバーする損害に加えて、海水濡れ損などの海固有の危険によって被った分損を、一定の損害割合以上の場合にてん補する。

③A/R (All Risks)　全危険担保

FPA、WAでカバーする危険以外に、保険期間中、貨物の運送に付随して外部的な原因によって生じるあらゆる偶発的な事故による損害をてん補する（ただし、A/Rでも戦争、ストライキ、暴動などはカバーしない）。

11. Basic Conditions in ICC

(1) Three Basic Conditions in ICC (1963)

Marine cargos are usually covered by one of the following three basic conditions in ICC (1963).

①FPA (Free from Particular Average)

FPA covers;
- general average
- total loss
- partial loss caused by vessel or barge in stranding, sinking or burning and vessel collision (SSBC),
- cost to prevent damages

②WA (With Average)

In addition to FPA coverage, WA covers other partial losses caused by perils of the sea like sea water damage when the damage exceeds more than certain rate.

③A/R (All Risks)

In addition to FPA or WA coverage, A/R covers any other damages from every incidental accident arising out of external causes during transportation of the cargo within the insurance period. (A/R, however, does not cover the risk of War, Strikes, Riots and Civil Commotions.)

図表6−4　旧保険証券（旧ICC）のてん補内容の概要

海損の種類	損害の種類	てん補範囲	保険条件		
共同海損	共同海損	・共同海損犠牲損害 ・共同海損費用 ・共同海損分担額	F P A（分損不担保）	W A（分損担保）	A／R（オールリスク担保）
単独海損	全損	・現実全損 ・推定全損			
	特定分損	・沈没・座礁・大火災による損害（S.S.B.） ・衝突（C.）、火災、爆発及び避難港における荷卸しに合理的に起因する損害 ・積込み、積替え、荷卸中の梱包1個ごとの全損			
	費用損害	・損害防止費用、その他の特別費用（避難港などでの荷卸し、保管、積替え、継搬などの費用） ・救助料、付帯費用（サーベイ費用等）			
	その他の分損	・特定分損以外の分損（潮濡れ、高潮・津波・洪水による濡れ損、流失損、その他荒天による分損）			
	各種の付加危険	個別追加可能（控除免責歩合〔EXCESS〕の取決） 盗難、破損、淡水濡れ、不着等 各種付加危険一括担保（免責歩合なし）			
不担保損害		遅延、保険の目的（貨物の梱包等）の固有の欠陥もしくは性質に起因した滅失・損傷、費用	全条件		

（注）
①FPA、WA条件に各種の付加危険を個別に追加付保することも可能。
②WA条件ではその他の分損については小損害の免責歩合（FRANCHISE）が適用されるが特約により不適用とするのが一般的である。
③特定分損の沈没、座礁は船舶以外の運送手段では、たとえば航空機の墜落、陸上輸送具の転覆、脱輪等に読み替える。

Fig.6-4   Coverage in ICC(1963)

Types of Average	Types of Damage or Loss	Covering Area	Conditions		
General Average	General Average	General Average Sacrifice General Average Expenditure Amount of Partial Loss for General Average	FPA (Free from Particular Average)	WA (With Average)	A/R (All Risks)
Particular Average	Total Loss	Actual Total Loss Constructive Total Loss			
	Certain type of Partial Loss	Damages by stranding, sinking, burning (S.S.B.) Damages caused by vessel collision, fire, explosion or to discharge of cargo at a port of distress Total loss of each package at loading, transshipment or discharging			
	Damage of cost	The cost to prevent further damages, other special charges(cost of unloading, warehousing, transshipment, or forwarding at a port of refuge) Salvage and survey cost			
	Other Partial Loss	Partial Loss other than certain type of partial loss above(sea water damage, other water damage or washed away loss caused by high water, tsunami or flood, partial loss caused by other heavy weather)			
	Other extraneous risks	Individual additional contract is available(subject to EXCESS (deductible percentage is provided in the insurance policy)). Theft, Breakage, Fresh Water Damage, Non Delivery, etc.			
		All risks of loss or damage are insured (memorandum percentage is not applicable).			
Uncovered Loss or Damage		Loss or damage caused by delay, inherent nature or vice of the cargo (for example, package, etc.)	Common to All Conditions		

(Note):①Additional contract to FPA or WA can be made to cover other extraneous risks.
②Under WA, "FRANCHISE" is applied to the other partial losses. Losses or damages which do not exceed the percentage specified in the policy are exempted from insurance coverage. Most of the cases, exporters or importers make a special contract to eliminate this exemption.
③"Stranding" or "Sinking" in the category of certain type of partial loss is for ocean transportations. For other means of transportations : e.g. airplane crash, rollover accident, derailment, etc.

（2）戦争危険およびストライキ、暴動危険のてん補

ICC（1963）によるこれらの基本条件は、戦争やストライキといった危険は、保険証券表面のイタリック約款で免責しているのでカバーしない。これらの危険についてもてん補したい場合には、特別約款として「協会戦争危険担保約款（Institute War Clauses（Cargo））」や「協会同盟ひ業暴動騒乱担保条項（S.R.C.C. Clauses）」を追加契約することが必要となる。

12．保険でてん補されないもの

次のものは通常の保険証券ではカバーされない。

図表6−5　保険でてん補されない危険

免責事項	A	B	C
故意・違法行為による損害	×	×	×
荷造り・梱包の不完全・コンテナ内への積付不良による損害	×	×	×
貨物固有の瑕疵または性質による損害（自然の消耗、通常の減少、発汗、蒸れ、腐敗、変質、錆など）	×	×	×
航海、運送の遅延に起因する損害	×	×	×
間接費用（慰謝料、違約金、廃棄費用など）	×	×	×
貨物が陸上にある間の戦争危険による損害	×	×	×
原子力・放射能汚染危険による損害	×	×	×
化学・生物・生物化学・電磁気等の兵器による損害	×	×	×
通常の輸送過程ではない保管中などのテロ危険による損害	×	×	×
船主、管理者、用船者、または運行者の支払不能、または金銭債務不履行による滅失、損傷または費用（注）	×	×	×
戦争危険（別途特約をつけることで担保可）	×	×	×
ストライキ危険（別途特約をつけることで担保可）	×	×	×

（注）ただし、保険の目的物を船舶に積込む時に、被保険者がそのような支払不能または金銭債務不履行が、その航海の通常の遂行を妨げることになり得ると知っているか、または通常の業務上当然知っているべきである場合に限る。

(2) Coverage against the Risk of War & S.R.C.C. (Strikes, Riots and Civil Commotions)

The risks of War or Strikes are not covered by the basic terms of the ICC (1963) as they are excluded by the Italic clause on the face of insurance policy. They can be covered only by adding special clauses to the contract, such as "Institute War Clauses (Cargo)" and "Institute Strikes Riots and Civil Commotions Clauses" (S.R.C.C. Clauses).

12. Uncovered Loss / Damage

Insurance does not cover the following losses or damages.

Fig. 6-5   Uncovered Loss or damage

Exclusions	A	B	C
Loss or damage attributable to wilful misconduct	×	×	×
Loss or damage caused by insufficiency of packing or stowage in a container	×	×	×
Loss or damage caused by inherent vice or nature of the subject-matter insured (ordinary wear and tear, ordinary loss, sweat, heating, decay, change in quality, rust, etc.)	×	×	×
Loss or damage caused by delay in voyage or transportation	×	×	×
Indirect expense (solatium, penalty, disposal costs, etc.)	×	×	×
Loss or damage caused by war while the subject-matter insured is placed on land	×	×	×
Loss or damage caused by radioactive contamination	×	×	×
Loss or damage caused by chemical, biological, biochemical, electromagnetic weapons, etc.	×	×	×
Loss or damage attributable to terrorism occurred outside the ordinary course of transit including the storage period	×	×	×
Loss, damage or expense caused by insolvency or financial default of the owners, managers, charterers or operators (Note)	×	×	×
War risk (which can be covered by special clauses)	×	×	×
Strikes risk (which can be covered by special clauses)	×	×	×

(Note) Provided that, at the time of loading the subject-matter insured on board the vessel, the Assured are aware, or in ordinary course of business should be aware, that such insolvency or financial default could prevent the normal prosecution of the voyage.

13. 確定保険と予定保険

　貨物海上保険契約では、貨物の危険が開始する前に、保険証券に記載が必要な事項について契約者が告知する義務があり、通常それは保険の申込書に記載することで行われる。

　この保険の申込み時に必要な項目がすべて確定している場合には、「確定保険契約」ができるが、その項目の一部、たとえば貨物の数量や金額、あるいは船名などが前もって確認できない場合もある。

　その場合には、不確定の項目をそのままに、概算保険金額で「予定保険契約」を締結し、項目が確定したら確定保険に切り替える方法をとる。

　売買契約上の貿易条件（インコタームズ）により貨物の危険を負担することになる契約当事者は、危険の開始時期からリスクをカバーしておかなければ万一の事故に備えることはできない。たとえば、インコタームズの貿易条件により、輸入者が海上保険を付保する場合、輸入者は輸出地での貨物の輸送状況を的確に把握することができないので、保険の申込みに必要な危険の開始時期がいつなのかを事前に知ることができない。事前に十分な情報の入手が難しい輸入者の場合には、無保険状態になってしまうことが出てくる。そこで、予定保険制度というものが存在するのである。

　予定保険の場合、後日船積み内容が確定し明細が判明したときに、改めて確定申込みを行う。予定保険の申込みに対しては、保険料、手数料は不要であり、確定保険申込み時に保険料が請求される。

　予定保険契約は、船積みごとに個別に行うこともできれば、長期にわたって保険会社と契約することも可能である。

（1）個別予定保険（Provisional Insurance）

　個別取引ごとの保険契約時に、船名が未定、保険金額が未定など、告知事項に不明または未定箇所のあるような場合に予定保険契約をすると、「個別予定保険証券（Provisional Policy）」が発行される。

　未定または不明事項が後日確定したときには、改めて確定申込みをして保険料を支払い、「確定保険証券（Definite Policy）」（通常の保険契約証書）の発行を

13. Definite Insurance Contract and Provisional Insurance Contract

When obtaining marine cargo insurance, an applicant must declare necessary information by filling in an application form before risks for their own cargos in a transaction start.

At the time of making the application, when all of the necessary entries are completed, a "Definite Insurance Contract" is concluded. However, if some information is unconfirmed, such as the quantity, the invoice value of the goods and the name of the carrying vessel, a "Provisional Insurance Contract" is concluded by an estimated amount insured. When all the unconfirmed information is provided, then the provisional insurance contract is converted to the definite contract.

It is necessary to insure the cargo before risks start for whoever is obliged to bear the risks under the trade terms in the contract. When the importer procures marine cargo insurance according to the trade terms, the cargos are usually loaded in the exporting country without the presence of the importer and the importer can not recognize when the risk starts. If it is difficult for the importer to obtain enough information to arrange insurance, they should be responsible for the losses of or damages to the uninsured cargos. This is why a provisional insurance contract exists.

The provisional insurance contract is converted to the definite contract when the shipping details are confirmed. Neither insurance premium nor handling charge is imposed at the time of making the application for the provisional insurance, however, the insurance premium is charged when the definite insurance contract is concluded.

The provisional insurance contract can be made both for an individual shipment and for several shipments during a fixed period of time agreed with the insurance company.

(1) Provisional Insurance Contract for Individual Shipment

When the importer makes an insurance contract according to the trade terms at the individual shipping, some necessary information to declare to the insurance company, such as the name of the carrying vessel and the invoice amount, is often still uncertain or unconfirmed. Under such situations, the importer obtains a provisional insurance contract for the individual shipment.

When the uncertain or unconfirmed information becomes definite after

受ける。

(2) 包括予定保険（Open Cover）

　個々の運送に対してではなく、一定期間中の全ての船積みについて確定保険を申し込むことを包括的に約束する契約で、大量に、しかも継続的に貨物を輸出入する場合に利用される。

　まず包括予定保険契約をするが、この時点では一部の告知事項について未確定あるいは不明なものがある。その後実際の個別の船積みごとに明細が確定したら、保険会社に確定通知として通知することになる。

　包括保険契約の場合は、輸出者が付保するケースと輸入者が付保するケースの両方があり得る。

　契約時に保険会社は、「包括予定保険証券（Open Policy）」、または「包括予定保険特約書（Open Contract）」を発行し、後日確定申込みを受けたときに確定保険証券または「保険承認状（Certificate of Insurance）」を発行する。

　輸入貨物の場合には、保険会社は、保険証券の代わりに保険承認状を発行するのが一般的である。保険承認状は保険証券の内容を簡略化したもので、保険証券と同様の効果がある。

receiving the shipping advice from the exporter, the importer declares this information to the insurance company. The provisional insurance is then converted to the definite insurance by this declaration. A "Definite Policy" is issued when the importer pays the insurance premium.

(2) Open Cover Contract

An open cover is an insurance contract which covers several shipments, not each shipment, during a fixed period of time. This contract is made when shipments take place repeatedly.

At first, an open cover contract is concluded. At this point, some necessary information to declare to the insurance company is still uncertain or unconfirmed. When the uncertain or unconfirmed information becomes definite in each actual shipment, this information is declared to the insurance company.

An open cover contract can be concluded by an exporter or by an importer.

The insurance company issues an "Open Policy" or an "Open Contract" at the time of concluding the open cover contract. Upon the receipt of the definite declaration, the insurance company issues the definite policy or a "Certificate of Insurance".

The insurance company usually issues a certificate of insurance, instead of an insurance policy, for the imported cargos. The certificate of insurance is a simplified form of an insurance policy and has the same effect as the policy.

第7章
代金決済方法

Chapter 7
Methods of Settlement

1．外国との決済手段の種類

　外国との代金決済手段は、荷為替手形による決済と送金による決済との2つの手段に大きく分けられる。

図表7-1　外国との決済手段の種類

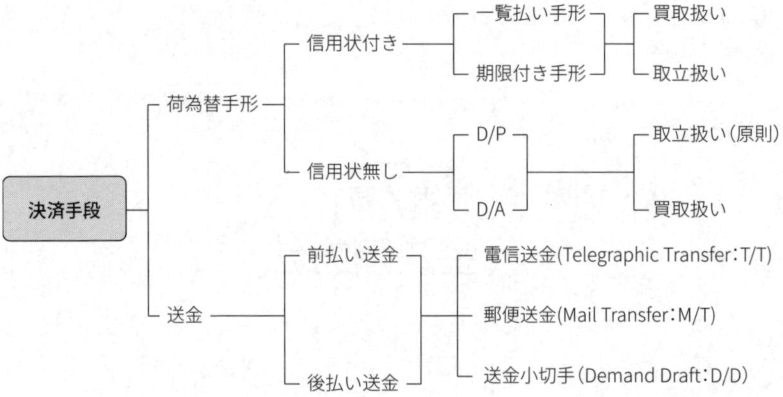

2．荷為替手形による代金決済

(1) 信用状取引

　信用状 (L/C：Letter of Credit) とは、

> ①　輸入者の取引銀行が輸出者に対して、
> ②　輸出者がL/Cどおりの船積書類を銀行に呈示することを条件に、
> ③　輸入者に代わって代金の支払を約束した保証状

のことである。

　したがって、輸出者がL/C条件どおりの手形と船積書類を銀行に呈示した場合には、輸出者の取引銀行が信用状発行銀行の代わりに、輸出者に対して手形代金を立て替え払いしてくれる。これを「手形の買取り」という（図表7-2参照）。

1. Methods of Settlement in International Trade

Methods of settlement are divided into two types: payment by documentary bill and payment by remittance.

Fig. 7-1   Methods of Settlement in International Trade

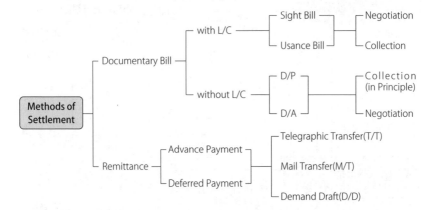

2. Settlement of Documentary Bill

(1) Transactions under Letter of Credit

An L/C, a Letter of Credit, is a letter

> ① issued by an importer's bank to an exporter and
> ② with which the importer's bank guarantees the payment
> ③ under the condition that the exporter presents shipping documents in accordance with terms and conditions of the L/C.

When the exporter presents a bill of exchange with the shipping documents in accordance with the terms and conditions of the L/C, an exporter's bank pays the bill on behalf of the issuing bank. This is called "Negotiation" (see Fig. 7-2).

図表7−2　貿易取引のしくみ(信用状取引の場合)

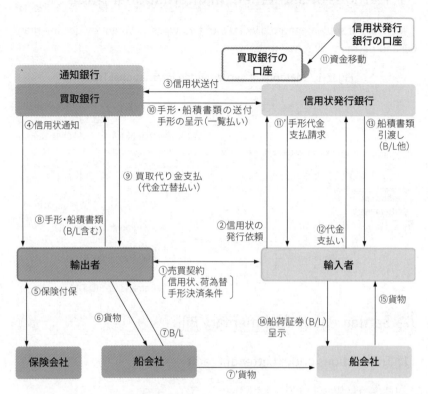

① 　輸出者と輸入者が売買契約のときに、**信用状**（L/C：Letter of Credit）（輸入者の取引銀行による代金支払いを確約した保証状）を使って取引をすることを条件として契約する。このとき代金支払の方法として、**為替手形**を使い、これを信用状と組み合わせることを取り決める。

② 　輸入者は契約条件にしたがって、自分の取引銀行に信用状の発行を依頼する。

③ 　輸入者の取引銀行は、輸入者の信用をチェックし、信用状を発行するかどうかを決める。問題がなければ、輸出地の銀行に向けて信用状が発行される。

④ 　輸出地の銀行経由で輸出者あてに信用状が通知される。輸出者に信用状を通知する銀行のことを**通知銀行**といい、信用状の真偽を確認している。

⑤ 　信用状を通知された輸出者は、信用状条件どおりの書類を銀行に呈示しないと代金の支払確約がされないため、条件にしたがって必要書類を入手、作

Fig.7-2 Flow of Foreign Trade (Transactions under L/C)

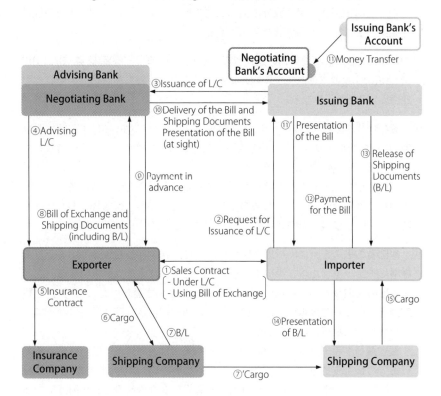

① When concluding a contract, the exporter and the importer agree about settlement by bill of exchange under L/C (Letter of Credit). An L/C is a letter with which the importer's bank guarantees the payment on behalf of the importer.

② The importer requests the importer's bank to issue an L/C in accordance with the contract. Issuing the L/C is often paraphrased as opening the L/C.

③ The importer's bank examines the importer's credit eligibility before issuing an L/C. After checking the credit eligibility, the importer's bank sends an L/C to its correspondent bank in the exporting country. The importer's bank is called "Issuing Bank".

④ The bank in the exporter's country advises the exporter of the L/C after verifying the authenticity of the L/C. This bank is called "Advising Bank".

⑤ The exporter prepares the documents complying with the terms and conditions of the L/C. The issuing bank can refuse the payment unless the

成する。

　たとえば信用状で保険証券の提示が要求されていた場合には、保険会社と保険契約を締結し、保険証券を入手する。

⑥⑦　また、信用状上で貨物の運送書類として、海上輸送の**船荷証券**（B/L: Bill of Lading）が要求されていた場合には、貨物を船会社に持ち込み、それと引き替えにB/Lを入手する。

⑧　その他、輸出者が自分で作成する商品の送り状（インボイス）や、梱包明細書（パッキング・リスト）などを信用状条件どおりに作成し、条件に合致した船積書類（各種書類の総称）を用意する。

　同時に船で出荷した貨物の代金請求書として為替手形を作成する。この為替手形は貨物代金の請求のためのものであることから、**荷為替手形**と呼ばれている。輸出者はこれらの手形、船積書類を自分の取引銀行に持ち込む。

⑨　輸出者の取引銀行は、手形、船積書類が信用状条件と合致していることを厳格にチェックした後、手形上に記載された商品代金を立替払いする。これを**手形の買取り**といい、手形を買い取った（代金の立替払いをした）銀行を**買取銀行**という。この事例では、買取銀行と通知銀行とは同じ銀行になっているが、異なる銀行の場合もある。

　買取銀行が手形代金を立替払いしてくれるのは、あくまで信用状による発行銀行の代金支払確約があるからである。立替払いしても、あとで（手形期日に）必ず信用状発行銀行からその代金の返却を受けられることが前提になっている。したがって買取銀行は、信用状による代金支払確約の条件である船積書類について、信用状条件と合致したものかどうかを厳格にチェックする。

　手形の買取りによって、輸出者は貨物の出荷とほぼ同時にその代金を回収できたことになる。これが信用状と荷為替手形を組み合わせることの大きな利点で、このことから、信用状上で輸出者は**受益者**（Beneficiary）と呼ばれる。

⑩　手形を買い取った買取銀行は、手形と船積書類を信用状発行銀行に送付（国際郵便またはクーリエサービス（書類宅配便）など）し、手形を発行銀行に呈示（支払いを求めるために見せること）してその代金の支払いを求める。

⑪　信用状発行銀行は、輸出地で代金立替払いをしてくれていた買取銀行に、双方で定められた方法で代金を返却する。この図の場合は、信用状発行銀行

exporter presents the shipping documents stipulated in the L/C.

If presentation of an insurance policy or a certificate is required by the L/C, the exporter needs to insure the cargo and obtain the insurance policy or the certificate.

⑥⑦   When a B/L (Bill of Lading) is required as a transport document by the L/C, the exporter receives a B/L from the shipping company in exchange for the cargo.

⑧   The exporter makes and obtains other documents, like a commercial invoice or a packing list, to meet the terms and conditions of the L/C.

The exporter draws a bill of exchange to request the payment for the shipped cargo to the issuing bank. The exporter presents the bill accompanied by the shipping documents to the exporter's bank. This bill with the shipping documents is called "Documentary Bill".

⑨   After checking if the bill and shipping documents comply with the terms and conditions of the L/C, the exporter's bank undertakes the payment for the bill in advance on behalf of the issuing bank. This is called "Negotiation". A bank which negotiates bills is called "Negotiating Bank". A negotiating bank can be an advising bank.

The negotiating bank can pay in advance because the payment is guaranteed by the issuing bank under the L/C. Since the issuing bank guarantees the payment under the condition that the shipping documents comply with the terms and conditions of the L/C, the negotiating bank examines the shipping documents.

This negotiation gives the exporter the benefit that they can collect the export proceeds right after completing the shipment. This is one of the biggest advantages of using a documentary bill with L/C. From this point, an exporter is called "Beneficiary" in an L/C.

⑩   After the negotiation, the negotiating bank sends the bill and the shipping documents to the issuing bank by mail or courier service, requesting the payment.

⑪   The issuing bank reimburses the negotiating bank for the amount of the bill in the way mutually agreed by the both parties. In this case, the issuing bank credits the amount of the bill to the account of the negotiating bank at the issuing bank. Ways of reimbursement vary according to the combination of banks involved in a transaction.

に預けられていた買取銀行の勘定に入金している。代金の返却方法は、銀行同士の組合せによって様々な方法がある。

⑪′　信用状発行銀行は輸入者に手形代金の支払いを求める。

⑫　輸入者は手形代金を発行銀行に支払う。

⑬　発行銀行は届いた貨物の引き取りに必要な船積書類を輸入者に引き渡す。ここで、代金の支払後船積書類が交付されていることに注意されたい。

　発行銀行は海外の輸出者に対して輸入者の代金の支払いを確約しているので、万一輸入者が代金を支払わなかったら代わってそれを輸出者に支払わなければならない。そこで、輸入者の代金支払を確実なものとするために、貨物の引き取りに必要な書類と引き替えに代金を支払うしくみとなっている。つまり、輸入者は貨物を引き取りたければ書類が必要で、書類を入手したければ代金を支払わねばならないことになっており、いわば銀行が書類を担保にとっているのと同じことになる。

⑭⑮　輸入者は銀行から交付された書類のうち、**船荷証券（B/L）**を船会社に提出し、それと引き替えに貨物を引き取る。

　銀行がなぜ手形を買い取るかというと、書類さえL/C条件に合致すれば、手形の期日に必ずL/C発行銀行が手形代金を支払ってくれることがわかっているからである。

　このように、L/Cと荷為替手形とを組み合わせることにより、輸出者は前払いでも後払いでもなく、商品の出荷とほぼ同時に代金を受領することができることになる。同時に、海外の取引相手である輸入者に対する信用不安も解消されるメリットがある（特に初めての取引の場合）。

　ただしこの手形の買取りは、輸出者の提出した船積書類がL/C条件と合致していることが前提条件なので、もし輸出者が呈示した書類がL/C条件と合致しない場合（**ディスクレパンシー：Discrepancy**）には、手形の買取りは受けられないことに注意が必要である。この場合には原則として代金取立手形として処理されるので、輸出者にとっては後払いに近い形となってしまう。

⑪′ The issuing bank requests the importer to settle the amount of the bill.

⑫ The importer settles the amount of the bill to the issuing bank.

⑬ The issuing bank releases the shipping documents, which are necessary for the importer to receive the cargo. It must be noted that shipping documents are delivered only after the payment.

If the importer fails to make the payment, the issuing bank must reimburse the amount of the bill instead according to the guarantee of the payment to the exporter. The importer needs the B/L to receive the cargo. The issuing bank delivers the shipping documents in exchange for the importer's payment. That is, the issuing bank holds the B/L as security.

⑭⑮ The importer receives the cargo from the shipping company in exchange for the B/L.

A negotiating bank negotiates bills of exchange because the negotiating bank understands that an issuing bank is obliged to pay the bills when the shipping documents comply with the terms and conditions of an L/C.

By using a documentary bill with L/C, an exporter can receive the payment right after completing shipment, not settled by advance payment or deferred payment. The exporter has the benefit that they can avoid the credit risk of the importer as a foreign trading partner especially in the first transaction.

It is essential that the shipping documents presented by the exporter comply with the terms and conditions of the L/C. When those documents do not meet the terms and conditions of the L/C, the bill can not be negotiated. The conflict between the documents and the terms and conditions of the L/C is called "Discrepancy". When any discrepancies are found, the bill can not be negotiated. The amount of the bill will be paid after the importer settles the payment. This settlement is, from the exporter's view, almost the same as deferred payment.

(2)一覧払手形と期限付手形

A．一覧払手形による代金決済

図表7－3　信用状取引における輸出為替手形(第一券)の例

BILL OF EXCHANGE

FOR U.S$94,054.00

NO　1234

October 22,20XX

ΛT XXXXXXXX SIGHT OF THIS FIRST BILL OF EXCHANGE (SECOND OF THE SAME TENOR AND DATE BEING UNPAID) PAY TO **TOKYO CITY BANK, LTD**. OR ORDER THE SUM OF SAY U.S. DOLLARS NINETY FOUR THOUSAND FIFTY FOUR ONLY.

VALUE RECEIVED AND CHARGE THE SAME TO ACCOUNT OF THE AUCKLAND STEEL, LTD. 100 Pacific St. #206, Newton, Auckland, New Zealand

DRAWN UNDER THE BANK OF AUSTRALIA, LTD.

L/C No. SG-36-25　DATED SEP. 25, 20XX

TO THE BANK OF AUSTRALIA, LTD.
　　（信用状発行銀行名）

THE KATSURAGI CORPORATION

- Signed -

F. Nakagawa

Shipping Manager

---

(2) Sight Bill and Usance Bill

A. Settlement by Sight Bill

Fig.7-3   An Example of Bill of Exchange (First Original) with L/C

BILL OF EXCHANGE

FOR U.S$94,054.00

NO 1234
October 22,20XX

AT XXXXXXXX SIGHT OF THIS FIRST BILL OF EXCHANGE (SECOND OF THE SAME TENOR AND DATE BEING UNPAID) PAY TO **TOKYO CITY BANK, LTD**. OR ORDER THE SUM OF SAY U.S. DOLLARS NINETY FOUR THOUSAND FIFTY FOUR ONLY.

VALUE RECEIVED AND CHARGE THE SAME TO ACCOUNT OF THE AUCKLAND STEEL, LTD. 100 Pacific St. #206, Newton, Auckland, New Zealand

DRAWN UNDER   THE BANK OF AUSTRALIA, LTD.

L/C No. SG-36-25   DATED   SEP. 25, 20XX

TO THE BANK OF AUSTRALIA, LTD.
    (Name of L/C Issuing Bank)   THE KATSURAGI CORPORATION
                                    - Signed -
                                    F. Nakagawa
                                    Shipping Manager

図表7－4 一覧払手形決済のしくみ

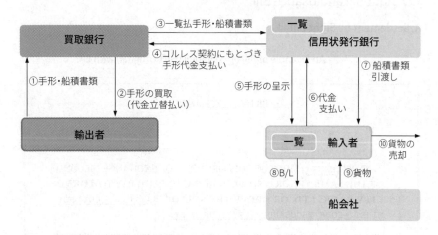

B．期限付手形（ユーザンス手形）による決済
（a）一覧後定期払い（At ○○days after sight）

手形の支払人が手形を一覧後、指定された期間後に支払う方法をいう。

手形の**At ××× × sight**の×××部分には、通常30、60など30日単位の期間が入る。支払人が手形を一覧した時点では、将来の手形期日に支払うことの約束だけを行い、代金の実際の支払いは期日まで支払猶予される。この支払い約束を**引受け**という。

Fig.7-4 Settlement by Sight Bill

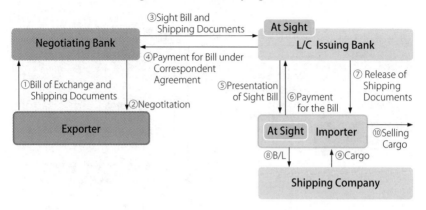

B. Settlement by Usance Bill

(a) Bill payable after a Fixed Period after Sight (At ○○days after sight)

A payer (hereinafter referred to as a drawee) of a bill pays the bill after a fixed period of days after sight.

In most cases, the period of days is often a multiple of 30 days such as 30 or 60, shown in the bill as at xxx days after sight. At the sight of the bill, the drawee only promises that they will pay the amount of the bill on the due date. This is called "Acceptance" and the actual payment will be extended until then.

図表7－5　一覧後定期払い手形の決済のしくみ

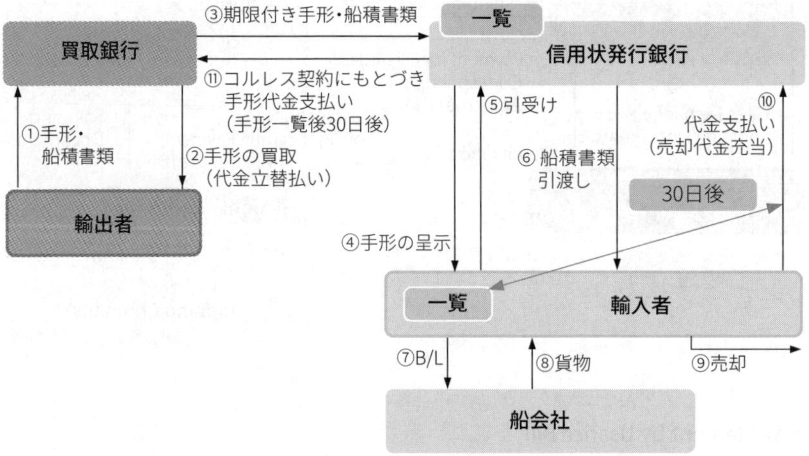

（b）確定日後定期払い（At ○○days after △△ date）

　手形の支払人はある確定日後、指定された期間後に支払う。ある確定日（たとえばB/L dateなど）が期間の起算日となる。しくみは一覧後定期払いと同様である。

（3）信用状にもとづかない荷為替手形の決済

A．D/P手形とD/A手形

　D/PとはDocuments against Payment の省略形であり、手形の支払人は一覧払手形を決済することで船積書類を受領できる。

　D/AとはDocuments against Acceptanceの省略形であり、手形の支払人は期限付手形を引受けることで船積書類を受領できる。しかし一部の期限付手形では、支払人が手形代金を支払うまで船積書類を受領できない。実務上では一般的に、L/Cなしの一覧払手形を**D/P手形**、L/Cなしの期限付手形を**D/A手形**と呼んでいる。

Fig.7-5 Settlement by Usance Bill

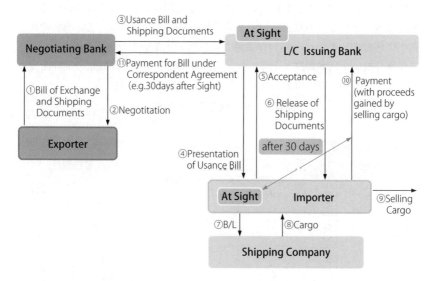

(b) Bill Payable after a Fixed Period after a Specified Date (At ○○days after △
△ date)

The drawee pays after a fixed period of days after a specified date. The specified
date like B/L date should be the initial date of reckoning. This works the same
as a bill payable after a fixed period of days after sight.

(3) Settlement of Bill of Exchange Without L/C

A. D/P Bill and D/A Bill

D/P is the abbreviation of Documents against Payment, which allows a payer
to receive shipping documents at the same time of paying a sight bill.

D/A is the abbreviation of Documents against Acceptance, which allows a
payer to receive shipping documents at the same time of accepting a usance
bill. However, some usance bills do not allow the payer to receive the shipping
documents until they pay the bill.

In practice, a sight bill without L/C is often called "D/P Bill", and the usance
bill without L/C is called "D/A Bill".

Ｂ．D/P、D/A手形の取立扱い

信用状のない場合の手形については、その代金回収が保証されないので、輸出者の取引銀行は代金立替払いである手形の買取を拒否する。この場合の輸出者への代金の支払いは、銀行が海外から代金の支払いを受けてから行われる。この取り扱いを**代金取立**という。代金取立は銀行にとっては取立の委任を受けただけで法的な拘束力は何もなく、手形上何ら責任を負わない。

図表７－６　代金取立のしくみ

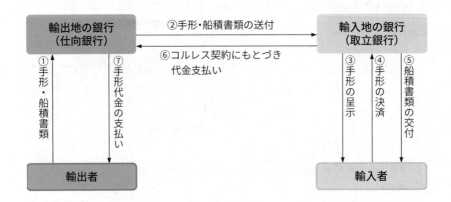

Ｃ．D/P、D/A手形の買取扱いと輸出手形保険

信用状なしの荷為替手形決済では、取立扱いが原則であるが、信用状なしであるにもかかわらず例外的に手形を買取る場合には、代金回収に対するリスクが大きいので、輸出地の銀行はそのリスクを保険でカバーした上でこれらの手形を買取る。

日本におけるこの保険の詳細については、株式会社日本貿易保険（NEXI）のウェブサイトを参照のこと。

https://www.nexi.go.jp/

B. Collection by D/P or D/A Bill

The exporter's bank refuses to negotiate the bill without L/C because the importer's bank does not guarantee the payment. The exporter's bank pays the exporter only after the importer settles the payment. This is called "Bill for Collection". The banks are only entrusted with collecting bills and they have no legal obligation to complete the collection.

Fig.7-6　Collection of Bill

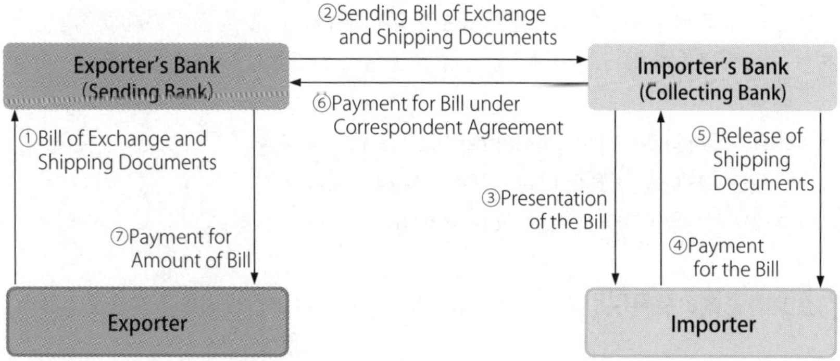

C. Negotiation of D/P or D/A Bill and Export Bill Insurance

The bill without L/C is settled by collection in principle. When the exporter's bank exceptionally negotiates the bill without L/C, the bank insures against the risk of the dishonor of the bill. This is because the importer's bank does not guarantee the payment.

Please refer to the web site of Nippon Export and Investment Insurance ("NEXI") for the details of the insurance.

https://www.nexi.go.jp/

3．送金による代金決済

(1) 前払い送金と後払い送金

　送金による代金決済は、いつ送金するかによって、前払い送金と後払い送金とに分けられる。

(2) 送金方法

　送金による代金決済には、銀行経由の銀行為替と郵便局経由の郵便為替とがあり、銀行経由の銀行為替は、さらに次の3つの種類に分かれている。

> ①　電信送金（T/T：Telegraphic Transfer）
> ②　普通送金（郵便付替）（M/T：Mail Transfer）
> ③　送金小切手（D/D：Demand Draft）

　企業対企業の貿易取引においては、そのほとんどが銀行経由の電信送金である。

A．電信送金（T/T）

図表7−7　電信送金（T/T）のしくみ

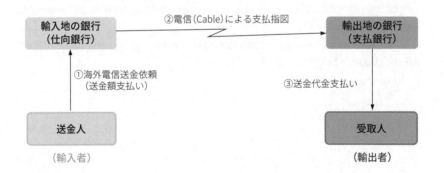

3. Settlement by Remittance

(1) Advance Payment and Deferred Payment

Payment by remittance is divided into two: advance payment and deferred payment in terms of when to make a remittance.

(2) Methods of Remittance

There are two methods of payment by remittance: bank transfer through bank and postal transfer through postal office. Also, there are three methods of remittance in bank transfer.

> ① T/T: Telegraphic Transfer
> ② M/T: Mail Transfer
> ③ D/D: Demand Draft

Telegraphic transfer through bank is used in most B to B transactions.

A. Telegraphic Transfer (T/T)

Fig.7-7   Telegraphic Transfer (T/T)

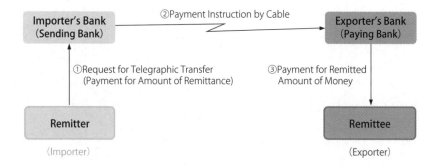

B．普通送金（郵便付替）（M/T）

電信送金としくみは同じだが、仕向銀行から支払銀行への支払指図が郵便により行われる方法をいう。

C．送金小切手（D/D）

Demand Draftとは、小切手を郵送する方法による送金のことである。かつて送金に為替手形が用いられていたためこの名称で呼ばれる。

図表7－8　送金小切手による送金(D/D)のしくみ

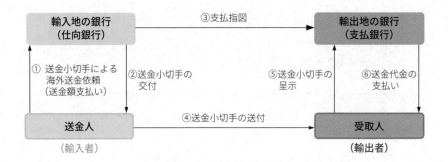

B. Mail Transfer (M/T)

M/T differs from T/T only in that a sending bank sends a payment instruction to a paying bank by post.

C. Demand Draft (D/D)

D/D is a remittance by sending check. The name D/D comes from the fact that bill (draft) was used for remittance in the past.

Fig.7-8   Demand Draft (D/D)

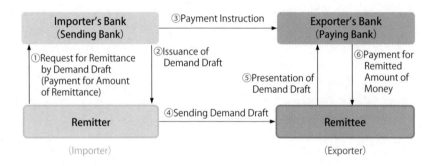

第**8**章
輸出の通関・船積み

Chapter **8**
Export Clearance and Shipment

1. 輸出実務の流れ

図表8－1 輸出実務の流れ（コンテナ船、CIP建て送金取引の場合）

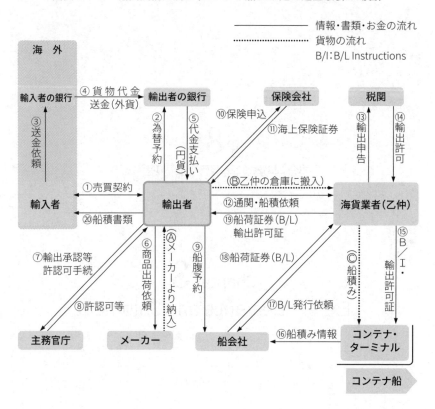

① 海外の輸入者と売買契約を締結する。

② 契約上の取引通貨が外貨の場合には、海外からの送金（④）は契約通貨どおりとなるので外貨となる。このとき、外貨ではなく、外貨を円に換えて受け取りたい（⑤）場合には、④⑤の時点で外国為替相場を使用する必要がある。

　もし外国為替相場が④⑤の時点で円高に動いていたら、輸出者にとっては不利になってしまうので、為替変動リスクを回避するために、輸出者は売買契約を締結した時点で将来④⑤の時点で使用する相場を銀行に予約しておく。

1. Flow of Export Practice

Fig.8-1　Flow of Export Practice
(by Container Ship, on CIP Basis, by T.T. Remittance)

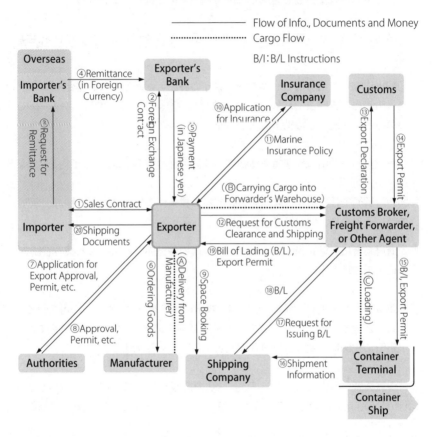

① An exporter concludes a sales contract with an overseas importer.

② When foreign currency is agreed as transaction currency under the contract, the remittance from overseas (④) is made in such foreign currency as agreed. However, if the exporter prefers to receive Japanese yen (⑤), currency exchange rate is required to be applied at the time of ④ and ⑤.

If Japanese yen appreciates at the time of ④ and ⑤, the exporter would be disadvantaged. To avert currency exchange risks, at the time of conclusion of the sales contract, the exporter and its bank agree to exchange currencies at a specified foreign exchange rate applied to the time of ④ and ⑤.

③　契約上の支払期限までに輸入者が輸入地の銀行へ送金依頼を行う。

④　輸入地の仕向銀行から、輸出地の被仕向銀行へ外貨で送金されてくる。

⑤　②で予約された相場を適用し、円で輸出者に送金が支払われる。

⑥　国内メーカーから商品や、原材料、部品等の調達が必要な場合には発注する。

⑦⑧輸出に際して法令にもとづき関係省庁の許認可が必要となる場合には、税関への輸出申告時までに許認可の申請をし、取得しておく（許認可が取れていないと、税関からの輸出許可がおりない）。

⑨　売買契約で輸出者が運賃を負担する貿易条件の場合には、船の予約を行う。

⑩⑪売買契約で輸出者が保険料を負担する貿易条件の場合には、貨物海上保険の申し込みをし、保険証券を入手する。

⑫　海貨業者に、Shipping Instruction（S/I）で輸出通関と貨物の船積み手続きの代行を依頼する。

⑬⑭海貨業者が輸出者に代わり、税関へ輸出の申告を行い、輸出の許可を得る。　　貨物が輸出に際して法令にもとづく許認可の必要な貨物だった場合には、申告時に税関に必要な許認可が取れていることを証明する。

⑮　海貨業者が輸出者に代わって、⑫のS/Iの情報にもとづいてB/L Instructions（B/I）を作成し、貨物をコンテナ・ターミナルへ持ち込んで船積みの依頼を行う。

⑯　貨物が船積みされたら、コンテナ・ターミナルから船会社へ船積み情報が通知される。

⑰⑱貨物の船積み確認後、海貨業者が船会社にB/Lの発行依頼をし、B/Lの発行を受ける。

⑲　海貨業者が税関から受領した輸出の許可証（Export Permit：E/P）と、船会社から受領したB/Lを輸出者に渡す。

③　The importer applies for remittance with its bank by the due date agreed under the contract.

④　The foreign currency remittance is made from the sending bank in the importing country to the paying bank in the exporting country.

⑤　The exporter receives the remittance in Japanese yen at the foreign exchange rate agreed in ②.

⑥　If necessary, the exporter places an order for goods, materials or parts with a domestic manufacturer.

⑦⑧　In case that the goods for export are subject to permits and/or approvals from relevant authorities under the laws and regulations of the exporting country, the exporter is required to apply for and obtain such permits and/or approvals. (Unless such permits and/or approvals are obtained, the customs will not issue an export permit.)

⑨　In accordance with the trade terms agreed, if the exporter must pay the costs of carriage, the exporter books shipping space with a shipping company.

⑩⑪　In accordance with the trade terms agreed, if the exporter must pay the insurance premium, the exporter concludes an insurance contract with an insurance company and obtains the insurance policy.

⑫　The exporter issues a shipping instruction requesting its customs broker, freight forwarder or other agent to clear export customs and arrange a shipment of the goods on behalf of the exporter.

⑬⑭　The customs broker, freight forwarder or other agent files an Export Declaration with the customs on behalf of the exporter and an Export Permit (E/P) is issued. If the goods are subject to permits and/or approvals under the laws and regulations of the exporting country, the exporter proves at the time of filing that it has already obtained such permits and/or approvals required in accordance with the laws and regulations of the exporting country.

⑮　The customs broker, freight forwarder or other agent prepares B/L Instructions (B/I) based on the information provided by the exporter's shipping instruction and brings the goods into the container terminal for loading.

⑯　After the shipment has been completed, the shipping company is advised of the shipment information from the container terminal.

⑰⑱　When the shipment has been confirmed, the customs broker, freight forwarder or other agent requests the shipping company to issue the B/L and the B/L is issued.

⑲　The customs broker, freight forwarder or other agent delivers the E/P and the B/L to the exporter.

⑳　輸出者は、契約時に輸入者が必要書類として指定したものを、直接輸入者へ送付する。このとき、保険証券裏面に、輸出者が白地裏書を行う。

2．輸出通関の流れ

(1) 輸出通関の流れ

図表8−2　輸出通関の流れ

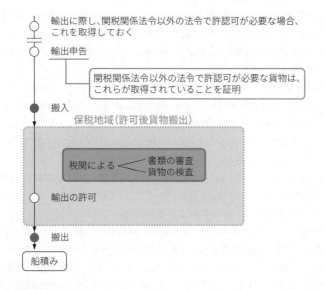

(2) 保税地域

輸出貨物を通関するためには、税関へ輸出申告後、まず貨物を「保税地域」へ搬入しなければならない。

保税地域は輸出入貨物の検査や審査を行うために、税関が指定し監視している地域である。輸出貨物を保税地域に搬入し、輸出許可がおりると通関は完了する。

3．法令による輸出規制

輸出しようとする貨物は必ず税関で輸出の許可を受けなければならないが、

⑳ The exporter sends the required documents designated by the importer at the time of conclusion of the contract directly to the importer. At this time, the exporter blank endorses on the back of the insurance policy.

2. Export Clearance

(1) Flow of Export Clearance

Fig.8-2 Flow of Export Clearance (in Japan)

(2) Bonded Area

In Japan, in order to clear export goods through customs, the goods must be carried into one of bonded areas after an export declaration.

The bonded areas are designated and controlled by the customs. The goods for export and import are stored and inspected in the bonded areas. When an export permit is obtained from the customs after the export goods are carried into the bonded area, the export clearance procedure is completed.

3. Laws and Regulations of Export

An exporter of goods must obtain an export permit at the customs. At the

そのときに、もし法令で輸出する貨物に関し許可や承認等の許認可が必要な場合には、事前にこれらの許認可を取得し、税関に輸出申告をする際にそれらが取得されていることを証明しなければならないことになっている。

4．輸出通関・船積み

　貨物の船積みについては、実際には専門業者である海貨業者（乙仲）に通関手続とともに業務を委託することになるが、どのような手順で貨物が船積みされ、最終的に船荷証券（B/L）が発行されることになるのかを知っておくことは、輸出者にとっても輸出業務全体を把握するうえでとても重要である。

　コンテナ船へ貨物を積み込む場合には、海貨業者は貨物をコンテナ・ターミナル内のCY（コンテナ・ヤード）またはCFS（コンテナ・フレート・ステーション）に持ち込む。

(1) コンテナ・ターミナル

　コンテナ船専用の巨大な施設を「コンテナ・ターミナル」といい、「コンテナ・ヤード（CY：Container Yard）」と「コンテナ・フレート・ステーション（CFS：Container Freight Station）から構成されている。

図表8－3　コンテナ・ターミナルの例

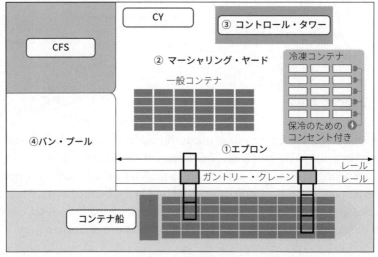

①エプロン　　　　　　　　　　ガントリー・クレーンでコンテナの積卸しがされる場所
②マーシャリング・ヤード　　　積卸しのためのコンテナを置いておくところ
③コントロール・タワー　　　　ヤードのオペレーションを管理する司令室
④バン・プール　　　　　　　　空きコンテナの置き場

time of export clearance, if the goods are subject to permits and/or approvals under the laws and regulations of the exporting country, the exporter is required to obtain such permits and/or approvals prior to customs clearance and prove that it has already had such permits and/or approvals.

4. Export Clearance and Shipment

In order to understand the whole export operation, it is important for an exporter to know how goods are actually shipped and how a Bill of Lading (B/L) is issued, although the exporter's designated customs broker, freight forwarder or other agent carries out the operation in practice.

For containerized cargos, the customs broker, freight forwarder or other agent carries cargos into a Container Yard (CY) or a Container Freight Station (CFS) located in a container terminal.

(1) Container Terminal

Container Terminal is gigantic facilities used exclusively for container ships, and it is consisted of areas called CY and CFS.

Fig. 8-3 An Example of a Container Terminal

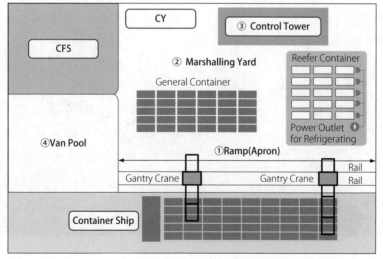

① Ramp(Apron)	Place for loading/unloading containers by gantry crane
② Marshalling Yard	Place to keep containers before loading or after unloading
③ Control Tower	Command office of container yard operation
④ Van Pool	Place to keep empty containers

A．コンテナ・ヤード（CY：Container Yard）

CYとは、コンテナを本船に積み込んだり、取り卸したりする場所、つまり海上輸送と陸上輸送との接点の役割をする地域のことをいう。

一荷主の貨物でコンテナ一単位が満載された大口貨物（FCL貨物　後述）は、海貨業者によって直接このCYへ運び込まれる。

B．コンテナ・フレート・ステーション（CFS：Container Freight Station）

CFSとは、貨物の量がコンテナ1個に満たない小口貨物（LCL貨物　後述）を取り集めてコンテナに詰め合わせしたり、船から卸したコンテナから詰め合わせていた小口貨物を取り出して仕分けしたりする場所のことで、通常はCYの一部あるいはそれに隣接した地域に設置されている。

図表8－4　コンテナ・ターミナルの様子

A. Container Yard

CY is an area where land transportation and ocean transportation are connected. Cargos are loaded onto or unloaded from container ships in a CY.

A container filled with a single consignor's cargos (Full Container Load Cargo: FCL cargo) is carried directly into the CY by a customs broker, freight forwarder or other agent.

B. Container Freight Station

CFS is usually located in or next to a CY. A unit of cargos that is not large enough to fill the whole container (Less than Container Load Cargo: LCL cargo) is collected in a CFS and loaded into a container with other consignors' LCL cargos. The LCL cargos are unloaded from containers and are sorted in a CFS.

Fig. 8-4　Container Terminal

(2) FCL貨物とLCL貨物

　コンテナを利用した貨物には、輸出者（荷主）の貨物だけで１つのコンテナを満載にできる大口貨物「**FCL貨物（Full Container Load）**」と、一荷主の貨物では量が少なく１つのコンテナを満載にできないため、他の荷主の貨物と混載することになる小口貨物「**LCL貨物（Less than Container Load）**」の２種類がある。FCL貨物は**CY（コンテナ・ヤード）**に直接持ち込まれて船積みされ、LCL貨物は**CFS（コンテナ・フレート・ステーション）**に持ち込んで他の貨物と混載したうえでCY経由で船積みされる。

　FCL貨物の場合には荷主である輸出者（またはその委託者）がコンテナ詰めを行い、コンテナに施封（シール）してCYに持ち込む。

　LCL貨物は、主として複合一貫輸送を行うNVOCCにより取り扱われるので、NVOCCの施設またはCFSで他の荷主の貨物と混載され、混載後、コンテナに施封（シール）されて、CYに持ちこまれ、CYから船積みされる。

　このときの書類の流れをみてみると、図８−５のようになる。

(2) FCL Cargo and LCL Cargo

Containerized Cargos are divided into two categories: FCL cargo and LCL cargo. An FCL cargo is a container filled with a single consignor's cargos, while an LCL cargo is loaded into a container with other consignor's small amounts of cargo to make the whole container full. The FCL cargo can be directly brought into a CY and loaded onto a container ship. In the case of LCL cargo, exporters or their designated customs brokers, freight forwarders or other agents bring their cargo into a CFS and the cargo is co-loaded into a container. After being containerized, the cargo is shifted to the CY and loaded onto the container ship.

In the case of FCL cargo, exporters or their agents pack and seal their containers by themselves, and carry them into the CY.

On the other hand, LCL cargos are mostly handled by an NVOCC who undertakes the combined transportation. The LCL cargos are co-loaded into a container with other consignors' cargos in facilities of the NVOCC or in the CFS.

After co-loading, the containers are sealed, shifted to the CY and loaded onto the container ship.

Fig. 8-5 shows the flow of the documents involved in a shipment.

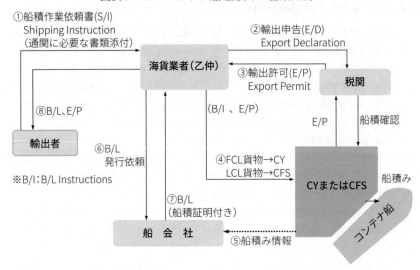

図表8－5 コンテナ船 船積みの書類の流れ

(3) コンテナ船への船積み

① 輸出者が海貨業者（乙仲）にShipping Instructionで通関・船積みの手続を依頼する。

② 海貨業者が税関に輸出申告（E/D：Export Declaration）をする。

③ 海貨業者が税関から輸出の許可を受け、輸出許可証（E/P：Export Permit）を受領する。

④ 海貨業者がShipping InstructionにもとづきB/L Instructions（B/I）を作成し、E/Pとともに、貨物を船積み前にCYまたはCFSに持ち込む。

⑤ FCL貨物は直接CYより、LCL貨物はCFSで混載されてからCY経由で船に積み込まれ、税関はE/P等で船積みを確認する。
船積み後、船積み情報がコンテナ・ターミナルから船会社へ連絡される。

⑥ 海貨業者は船積日が記載されたB/Lを受領するために、貨物の船積後、船会社にB/L発行を依頼する。

⑦ 船会社が、船積日が記載されたB/L（船荷証券）を交付する（CIF、CFR、CPT、CIP契約の場合には運賃を支払ってから交付を受ける）。

Fig.8-5 Flow of Shipping Documents of Container Ship

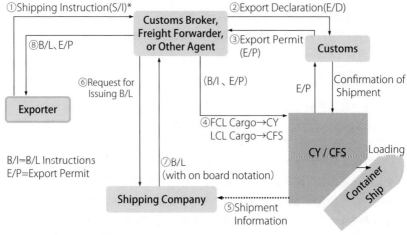

*Documents required for Cusoms Clearance must be attached to Shipping Instruction.

(3) Making Shipment by Container Ship

①　An exporter issues a shipping instruction requesting its customs broker, freight forwarder or other agent to clear customs and arrange a shipment of the goods.

②　The customs broker, freight forwarder or other agent files an Export Declaration (E/D) to the customs.

③　An Export Permit (E/P) is issued by the customs.

④　The customs broker, freight forwarder or other agent prepares B/L Instructions (B/I) and brings the goods into a CY or a CFS along with the E/P.

⑤　Containerized cargos are loaded onto a container ship from the CY. LCL cargos are co-loaded into a container in the CFS, shifted to the CY and loaded onto a container ship. The customs confirms the shipment by the E/P, etc.

　　After the shipment has been completed, the shipping company is advised of the shipment information from the container terminal.

⑥　The customs broker, freight forwarder or other agent requests the shipping company to issue the B/L with the date of loading.

⑦　The shipping company delivers the B/L with the date of loading. Under CIF, CFR, CPT or CIP rules, the customs broker, freight forwarder or other agent pays the freight on behalf of the exporter.

⑧　海貨業者が荷主である輸出者に、B/L、E/Pを返却する。

　前記⑦で船会社から交付されるB/Lは、貨物をCYまたはCFSの運送人に引渡したとき発行されるため、**受取船荷証券（Received B/L）**となる。

(4) 船積通知

　船積みが終了すると、輸出者は輸入者に、E-mailやFaxなどで速やかに船積通知（Shipping Advice）を行う。船積通知には通常、貨物の明細、金額、船名、出航日などが記載されている。

　契約で輸入者が保険を付保する貿易条件の場合には、輸入者は最初予定保険付保しているので、輸入者はこの通知にもとづいて確定保険に切り替えることになる。また輸入者は船積通知にもとづいて貨物の受け入れ準備も始める。

　信用状決済や、D/P、D/A決済では、輸入者が貨物を引き取るのに必要な船積書類は銀行を経由して輸入者に交付されるので、通常輸入者がその書類を入手するまでには日数がかかることがある。このため輸出者は、船積書類のコピーを船積案内状に添付して、航空便やクーリエサービス（書類宅配便）を利用して送付することもある。

　また航空貨物の場合には、輸入地において通関や貨物の引取りに必要な航空運送状（エアー・ウェイビル：Air Waybill）やインボイスは、貨物と一緒に送られるので、輸入者の荷受けの準備のためにも一刻も早く船積通知を行うことが必要である。

⑧　The customs broker, freight forwarder or other agent hands over the B/L and the E/P to the exporter.

The above-mentioned B/L is a Received B/L as it is issued when the cargo is received by the shipping company at the CY or the CFS.

(4) Shipping Advice

The exporter should send a shipping advice to the importer by E-mail or FAX as soon as the shipment is completed. The shipping advice, in general, includes details of the cargo, invoice amount, name of the vessel, and sailing schedule, etc.

If the transaction is based on the trade terms under which marine insurance shall be obtained by the importer, the importer usually effects the provisional insurance first. After receiving the shipping advice, the importer, then, switches the provisional insurance to the definite insurance and also starts to prepare for receiving the goods.

Under the transaction based on a letter of credit (L/C), D/P without L/C or D/A without L/C, it may take a while for the importer to receive the original shipping documents since the documents are delivered through the banks. In such cases, the importer sometimes requests the exporter to send a full copy of the shipping documents by airmail or courier along with the shipping advice to receive the goods as soon as possible.

In the case of air cargo, a prompt shipping advice is appreciated. As an Air Waybill and invoices are attached to the air cargo, the shipping advice makes it possible for the importer to prepare for customs clearance and receiving the cargo.

第9章
輸入の通関・荷受け

Chapter 9
Import Clearance and Receiving Cargo

1. 輸入実務の流れ

図表9−1　輸入実務の流れ
（コンテナ船、CPT建て送金取引の場合）

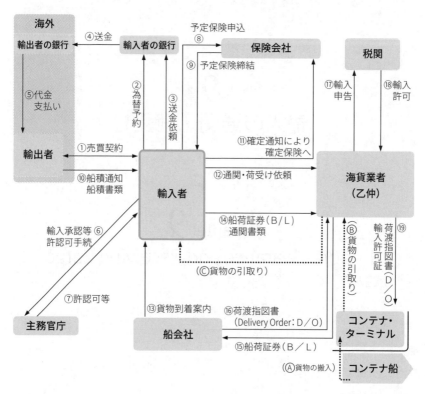

①　海外の輸出者と売買契約を締結する。

②　売買契約が外貨建ての場合には、輸出地への送金（④）は契約通貨どおりとなるので外貨となる。このとき、外貨に代わって円で代金を支払いたい場合（③）には、この時点で外国為替相場を使うことになる。

　③の時点で相場が円安に移行していた場合には輸入者が予定よりも多く支払わなければならないことになるので、その時使用する相場を銀行にあら

1. Flow of Import Practice

Fig.9-1 Flow of Import Practice
(by Container Ship, on CPT Basis, by T.T. Remittance)

———————— Flow of Info., Documents and Money

························· Cargo Flow

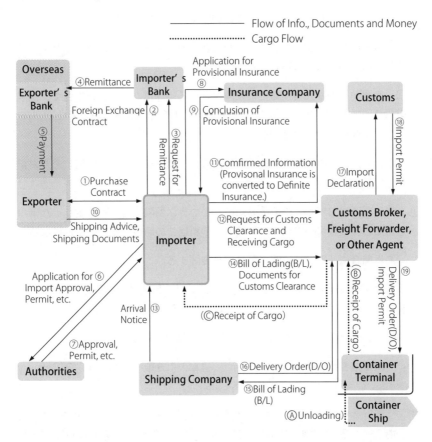

① An importer concludes a purchase contract with an overseas exporter.

② When foreign currency is agreed as transaction currency under the contract, the remittance to overseas (④) is made in such foreign currency as agreed. However, if the importer prefers to make payment in Japanese yen, currency exchange rate is required to be applied at the time of ③.

If Japanese yen depreciates at the time of ③, the importer must pay more than the expected amount. To avert currency exchange risks, the importer and its bank agree in advance to exchange currencies at a specified foreign

かじめ予約しておく。

③　契約上の支払期限までに輸入者が輸入地の銀行へ送金依頼を行う。

④　輸入地の仕向銀行から輸出地の被仕向銀行へ外貨で送金される。

⑤　海外から送金が到着し、輸出者の口座に入金される。

⑥⑦　輸入に際して国内の法令で許認可が必要な貨物の場合には、主務官庁に許認可の申請をして取得しておく。

⑧⑨　売買契約で輸入者が貨物に保険付保する条件になっていた場合で、保険申し込み時に確定できない告知事項がある場合には予定保険の申し込みをし、予定保険契約を締結する。

⑩　輸出者が貨物の船積みを終え、輸入者に船積通知をする。同時に必要書類を送付してくる。

⑪　輸入者は輸出者からの船積通知にもとづき、保険会社に不確定だった事項を告知し、確定保険に切り替える。保険料はこの時点で支払うことになる。

⑫　海貨業者に荷受けと通関の手続きを委託する。

⑬　貨物が輸入地に到着し、船荷証券（B/L）のNotify Party（着荷通知先）欄に記載されている輸入者へ、船会社から貨物の到着案内が行われる。

⑭　輸入者は海貨業者へB/Lと通関に必要な書類を渡す。

⑮⑯　海貨業者が船会社へB/Lを呈示し、貨物の引き取りに必要なD/O（Delivery Order：荷渡指図書）の交付を受ける。

⑰⑱　海貨業者が輸入者に代わり、税関へ輸入申告をして輸入の許可を受ける。もしその貨物が輸入に際して法令にもとづく許認可の必要な貨物だった場合には、この輸入申告時にそれらの許認可が取得されている（⑦）ことを証明する。

⑲　海貨業者がコンテナ・ターミナルでD/Oを呈示して貨物を引き取り、輸入者に引き渡す。

exchange rate applied to the time of ③.

③　The importer applies for remittance with its bank by the due date agreed under the contract.

④　The remittance is made in the agreed foreign currency from the sending bank in the importing country to the paying bank in the exporting country.

⑤　The exporter receives the remittance paid into its bank account.

⑥⑦　In case that the goods for import are subject to permits and/or approvals from relevant authorities under the laws and regulations of the importing country, the importer is required to apply for and obtain such permits and/or approvals.

⑧⑨　If the importer makes an insurance contract in accordance with the trade terms agreed, when some necessary information provided on an application form is unconfirmed, a provisional insurance contract is concluded.

⑩　After the shipment has been completed, the exporter sends a shipping advice to the importer. At the same time, the exporter sends the required documents to the importer.

⑪　Based on the above shipping advice, the importer switches the provisional insurance contract to the definite insurance contract by declaring the confirmed information to the insurance company. At this point, the importer pays the insurance premium.

⑫　The importer requests a customs broker, freight forwarder or other agent to carry out procedures associated with receiving the cargo and import clearance.

⑬　When the cargo arrives in the importing country, an arrival notice is sent by the shipping company to the importer indicated as the notify party on the Bill of Lading (B/L).

⑭　The importer delivers the B/L as well as the documents required for import clearance to the customs broker, freight forwarder or other agent.

⑮⑯　The customs broker, freight forwarder or other agent presents the B/L to the shipping company and receives a Delivery Order (D/O) which is required for receipt of the cargo.

⑰⑱　The customs broker, freight forwarder or other agent files an Import Declaration with the customs on behalf of the importer and an Import Permit is issued. If the goods are subject to permits and/or approvals under the laws and regulations of the importing country, the importer proves at the time of filing that it has already obtained such permits and/or approvals required in accordance with the laws and regulations of the importing country (⑦).

⑲　The customs broker, freight forwarder or other agent receives the cargo at the container terminal by presenting the D/O and delivers it to the importer.

2．輸入通関の流れ

通常の輸入通関手続は次のような流れで行われる。

図表9－2　輸入通関の流れ

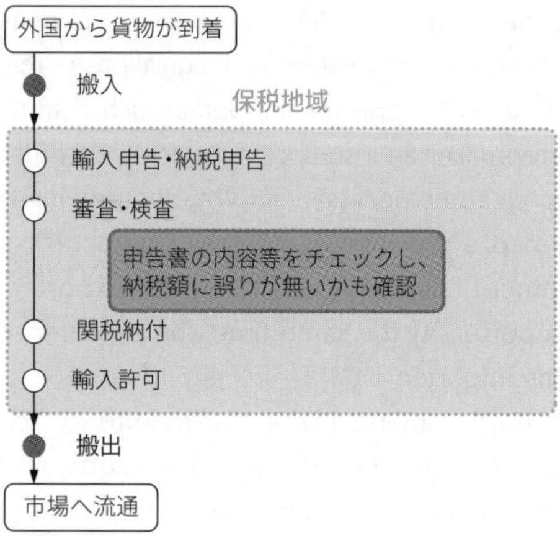

外国から貨物が到着

● 搬入　　　　　　保税地域

○ 輸入申告・納税申告

○ 審査・検査

　　申告書の内容等をチェックし、
　　納税額に誤りが無いかも確認

○ 関税納付

○ 輸入許可

● 搬出

市場へ流通

3．輸入の法規制

　輸入しようとする貨物は必ず税関で輸入の許可を受けなければならないが、そのときに、法令で輸入する貨物に関し許可や承認等の許認可が必要な場合には、事前にこれらの許認可を取得し、税関へ輸入申告をする際にそれらが取得されていることを証明しなければならないことになっている。

4．関税制度

(1) 関税の算出方法

　関税額　＝　課税標準　×　税率

関税は、輸入貨物の価格を課税標準として課税される場合と、数量を課税標

2. Flow of Import Clearance

Fig.9-2 shows a flow of import clearance.

Fig.9-2   Flow of Iport Clearance (in Japan)

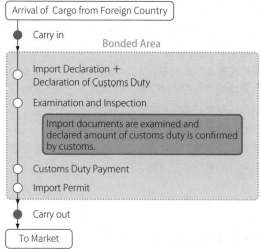

3. Laws and Regulations of Import

An importer of goods must obtain an import permit at the customs. At the time of import clearance, if the goods are subject to permits and/or approvals under the laws and regulations of the importing country, the importer is required to obtain such permits and/or approvals prior to customs clearance and prove that it has already had such permits and/or approvals.

4. Tariff System

(1) Calculation Method of Customs Duties

Amount of Customs Duties = Tax Base × Duty Rate

Customs duties are imposed based on the price or quantity of goods at the

準として課税される場合とがある。輸入貨物の課税価格が課税標準として利用される場合には、従価税率が適用され、他方で貨物の数量、重量、容積等が課税標準として利用される場合には、従量税率が適用される。一部の貨物には、これらが組み合わさった従価従量税率が適用される。

(2) 特恵関税制度

　一般特恵関税は、その国の法律で定められた一定の開発途上国（特恵受益国）からの輸入を促進することが目的で、それらの国の原産品を輸入する場合に課す関税を、一般の税率より低税率、または無税にしたりする制度である。

　これらの特恵受益国のうち、中でも後発開発途上国である一定の国に対しては、特別特恵受益国制度があり、特恵関税の適用対象となっている産品に対してはすべて無税となる。

　これらの特恵関税の適用を受けようとする場合には、原則として、輸出国側で発給した原産地証明書が必要である。

(3) 経済連携協定（EPA）等にもとづく税率

　経済連携協定（EPA：Economic Partnership Agreement）とは、二国間あるいは多国間での協定で、互いに関税等を免除または減額することにより、両国間の貿易や投資を自由化したり、人の往来や資本の移動を容易にし、当該協定締結各国間の経済的な連携を強化することを目指したものである。協定には貿易以外の分野についての内容も含まれているが、ここでいう「経済連携協定（EPA）等にもとづく税率」とは、そのうち、関税についての協定内容にもとづく税率を指している。

(4) 減免税、戻し税制度

　有税品である輸入貨物が一定の条件に適合する場合、関税の一部または全部が免除されることがある。

　納税義務の一部を免除するのを減税、すべてを免除するのを免税という。また、いったん納税済みの輸入貨物が、一定の条件に適合した場合に、納付した関税の一部または全部を納税者に払い戻すのが戻し税、納税者以外に払い戻すのが還付である。

time of import declaration. When the dutiable value of the imported goods is to be used as a tax base, an "Ad Valorem Rate" is applied to the item. On the other hand, when the quantity, weight or volume of the imported goods is to be used as a tax base, a "Specific Rate" is applied to the item. For some items, a combination of both the ad valorem and the specific rate is applied.

(2) Outline of Generalized System of Preferences (GSP)

Generalized System of Preferences (GSP) is aimed to promote import from certain developing countries or regions (GSP beneficiary countries), which are provided by applicable laws and regulations. For certain products originating from those beneficiary countries, lower duty rates are applied or duties are exempted.

Among the beneficiary countries, the least developed countries (LDCs) provided by applicable laws and regulations are eligible for special preferential treatment, and duty free treatment is applied to the designated products from those countries.

In order to receive the special preferential treatment, in principle, a Certificate of Origin issued in an exporting country is usually required.

(3) Duty Rates under Economic Partnership Agreements (EPAs)

The Economic Partnership Agreement (EPA) is a bilateral or multilateral agreement which objective is to reinforce economic partnership between or among the signatory countries by liberalizing trade and investment, and facilitating the movement of people and capital through exemption from or reduction of customs duties. The agreement includes provisions other than those of trade. However, the "duty rates under EPAs" means the duty rates under the provisions with respect to customs duties.

(4) Reduction and Exemption of Customs Duties

Customs duties may be reduced or exempted in case that dutiable imported goods satisfy certain conditions. Full amount or some part of customs duties which are already paid may be refunded to the taxpayer or repaid to a third party if the goods satisfy certain conditions.

5．貨物の荷受け

（1）コンテナ船の貨物の荷受け

　輸入者から通関・荷受け業務を委託された海貨業者は、B/LまたはL/G（後述
（2）参照）を船会社に呈示して「**荷渡指図書（D/O：Delivery Order）**」の交付を
受ける。

　このD/Oは、FCL貨物の場合にはコンテナ・ヤード（CY）オペレーターあてに、
LCL貨物の場合にはコンテナ・フレート・ステーション（CFS）オペレーターあ
てに発行してもらう。

　次に海貨業者は税関に輸入申告（I/D：Import Declaration）を行い、輸入の許
可（I/P：Import Permit）を受ける。コンテナ貨物はこの間にCYに荷卸しされ、
大口貨物であるFCL貨物はそのままそこに置かれ、混載された小口貨物である
LCL貨物は、コンテナごとCFSに運びこまれて仕分けされる。

　輸入の許可を受けた海貨業者は、D/OをCYまたはCFSのオペレーターにI/Pと
ともに提出し、貨物の引渡しを受ける。このとき貨物の状態を点検し記録して、
デバンニング・レポート（D/R：Devanning Report）等の貨物受け渡し書類を作
成し、船会社と荷受人が相互に署名する。

　荷主（通常はその委託を受けた海貨業者）は、貨物が損傷を負った状態で引
渡しを受けた場合には、後日運送人に損害賠償する可能性があるので、必ずリ
マーク（損傷状態の表記）のある書類を証拠として取り付けるようにしなければ
ならない。

　コンテナ貨物のうち、貨物引取り時に貨物の外観上の状態が確認できるLCL
貨物の場合、貨物に損傷があれば、デバンニング・レポート等の貨物受け渡し
書類にリマークをつけてもらい、船会社や運送業者の責任を明確にすることが
重要となる。必ず貨物の受領時点で外装の梱包に異状がないかを確認し、もし
異状があればその状態を受け渡し書類に記入してから、受け渡し書類に捺印し
て手渡すことが大切である（詳細は後述参照）。

5. Receiving a Cargo

(1) Receiving a Cargo from a Container Ship

In most cases, an importer's designated customs broker, freight forwarder or other agent carries out the following entire import operation on behalf of the importer. The customs broker, freight forwarder or other agent receives a Bill of Lading (B/L) from the importer and submits it to a shipping company. In exchange for the B/L, the shipping company issues a Delivery Order (D/O).

The D/O for a Full Container Load Cargo (FCL cargo) is made out to a Container Yard (CY) operator, whereas the D/O for a Less than Container Load Cargo (LCL cargo) is made out to a Container Freight Station (CFS) operator.

Then, the customs broker, freight forwarder or other agent makes an Import Declaration (I/D) to the customs and receives an Import Permit (I/P). In the meantime, the containerized cargos are unloaded from the container ship. The FCL cargo is stored in the CY. The container with LCL cargos is shifted to the CFS and devanned.

The customs broker, freight forwarder or other agent submits the D/O along with the I/P to the CY or the CFS operator to receive the cargo. Both the shipping company and the consignee or its customs broker, freight forwarder or other agent check the condition of the cargo then mutually sign the documents such as Devanning Report (D/R) before the cargo is taken from the CY or the CFS.

If the consignee or its designated customs broker, freight forwarder or other agent finds any damage on the cargo before receiving it, such party should obtain a remark, a description of the damage on documents from the shipping company, so that a claim for the damage can be filed at a later date.

Damages on LCL cargos can be visible as they are taken out of containers at the CFS before being handed over to the consignee or its customs broker, freight forwarder or other agent. For such visible damages, it is important to have the shipping company or the carrier make remarks on a devanning report or the like. External conditions of packages should be carefully checked before receiving the cargo.

図表9－3　コンテナ貨物引取りの書類の流れ

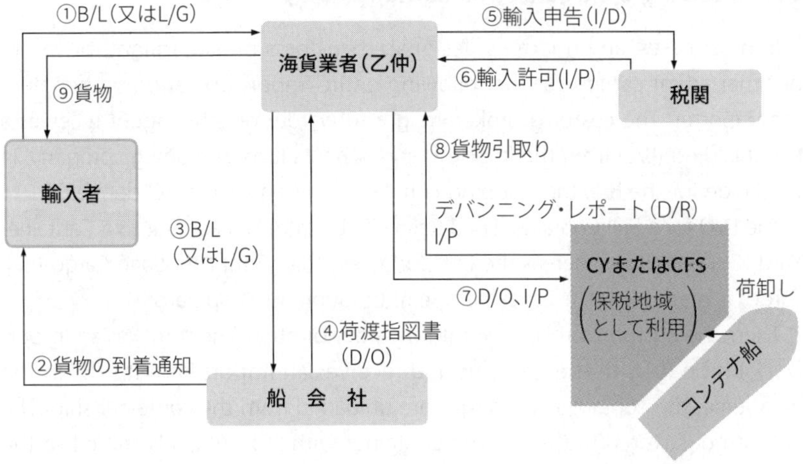

(2) B/Lなしでの貨物の引取り

　海上貨物は通常、有価証券である船荷証券（B/L）と引き替えに引き取るが、最近は船の高速化などで、近距離からの輸入の場合には、船積書類が着く前に貨物が先に到着してしまうことが頻発するようになった。貨物は届いたが、貨物の引取りに必要なB/Lはまだ届いていないというこのような事態を、B/Lの危機という。B/Lの危機への対応策としては、次のような方法がある。

A．L/G（保証状荷渡し）

　従来から最もよく利用されてきた方法が、L/G（Letter of Guarantee：保証状荷渡し）である。

　L/Gとは、B/Lなしで貨物を引き取ることについて、万一船会社に損害を与えた場合には、その損害を補償する旨を約束した保証状で、輸入者の信用を補てんするために銀行が連帯保証しているものである。

　L/Gで貨物を引き取るには、まず船会社からL/Gの用紙を交付してもらい、輸出者からの船積案内などによって船名や貨物の明細などがわかった時点で内容を記入し、輸入者自身が署名する。

　銀行に発行してもらったL/GをB/Lの代りにして、輸入者は貨物を船会社か

Fig.9-3 Flow of Documents for Receiving a Container Cargo

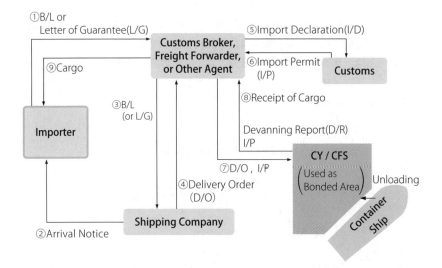

(2) Receiving a Cargo without a B/L

An ocean cargo is generally released in exchange for a B/L, which is a form of negotiable securities. Due to the adoption of high-speed vessels, a cargo often arrives before shipping documents are delivered especially in the case of shipments coming from countries nearby. Followings are countermeasures to receive a cargo without a B/L.

A. Letter of Guarantee (L/G)

A Letter of Guarantee (L/G) is one of the countermeasures to receive a cargo without a B/L and has been often used in practice.

In the L/G, an importer gives an assurance to a shipping company that the importer compensates the shipping company for the damage caused by receiving the cargo without a B/L. The L/G is usually co-signed by an importer's bank to add the credibility to the importer.

The importer usually uses the shipping company's L/G form. As soon as details of the shipments such as the name of vessel, description of the goods, etc. are informed by a shipping advice or the like from the shipper (the exporter), the importer fills out and signs the form.

The importer receives the cargo from the shipping company in exchange

ら引き取る。その後B/Lが到着したら、これを船会社に提出して預けてあったL/Gと交換する。

　船会社から回収したL/Gは銀行に返却され、銀行はL/Gを発行してから回収までの連帯保証期間に応じて、輸入者に保証料を請求する。

　この方法は、銀行の保証料が必要なため、B/Lの危機が頻発するとコスト面で負担になることから、これに代わる方法として次のような方法が採られるようになってきている。

図表9－4　L/Gのしくみ

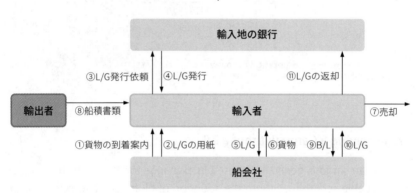

B．Sea Waybill

　B/Lが有価証券であるため、貨物の引き取り時にB/Lの呈示が必要となることから、これに代えて、初めから有価証券でない海上運送状を発行することが行われている。このような海上運送状を「Sea Waybill」という。有価証券でないSea Waybillの場合、貨物の引き取り時に運送状を船会社に呈示する必要がなく、自社が運送状上の荷受人であることを証明すれば足りる。

　ただし、信用状取引などの銀行にとっての与信取引においては、Sea Waybillは担保としての価値を持たないため敬遠される傾向があり、また、商慣習に裏打ちされた一定のルールや法的解釈などが確立されておらず、関係当事者全員に受け入れられている方法とは言い難い面がある。したがって現状としては、船積書類が輸出者から輸入者に直送される送金の場合に利用されている。

for the L/G instead of the B/L. When the original B/L arrives later, the importer submits the B/L to the shipping company in exchange for the L/G.

The importer returns the L/G to the bank which co-signed and pays a guarantee commission to the bank for the term of guarantee, which starts from the date of issuance of the L/G and ends at the date of its return to the bank.

The importer must pay the guarantee commission to the bank when using the L/G. If the importer tries to receive a cargo without a B/L by using the L/G every time the cargo arrives before arrival of the B/L, the commission piles up accordingly and the importer suffers from the increased cost as a result. To avoid this extra payment, many importers are adopting following measures replacing the L/G.

Fig.9-4   L/G

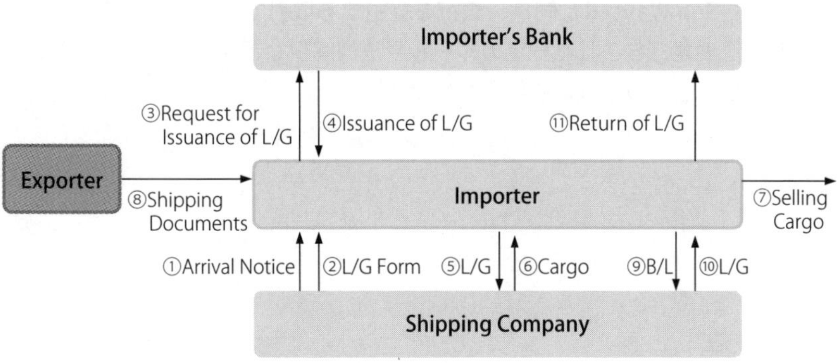

B. Sea Waybill

Due to the nature of B/L being negotiable securities, it is required to submit the original B/L in order to take delivery of the cargo. A non-negotiable transport document called "Sea Waybill (SWB)" has been adopted to replace a function of B/L. When a SWB is issued, a consignee can take delivery of the cargo by identifying themselves as the consignee stated on the SWB and the original SWB is not required to take the delivery.

However, it should be noted that banks usually do not accept the SWB as security in the case of transactions under L/C, as the SWB is not negotiable. Also, the SWB is not widely accepted by every party concerned as its definite rules and legal interpretations based on trade practices have not been established yet.

Therefore, the SWB is often used when contracts are on telegraphic transfer basis and shipping documents are directly sent from the exporter to the importer.

Ｃ．Surrendered B/L（元地回収B/L）

　原則としてB/Lは、輸入地で貨物の引渡しが完了したときに有価証券として
の価値を失う。輸出者が指示することにより、B/Lは例外的に輸出地で回収済
みとすることができるが、そのようなB/Lを**Surrendered B/L**という。B/Lが回
収された後は、荷受人は自社がB/L上の荷受人（Consignee）であることを船会
社に対して証明すれば、Surrendered B/L現物を船会社に提示することなく貨
物を引き取ることができる。

　船会社がSurrendered B/Lを求められた場合、船会社は有価証券としてのB/L
を発行し、B/L上に"Surrendered"と表記して、輸出地側でそのB/Lを回収する。
輸入者は自社がSurrendered B/Lの荷受人であることを、そのSurrendered B/L
のPDF等の電磁的記録やFAXを船会社に提示して証明すれば貨物を引き取るこ
とができる。Surrendered B/Lは**Express B/L**などとも呼ばれることもある。

　しかし、Sea Waybillと同様、銀行を経由する取引では敬遠されることが多
く、商慣習に裏打ちされた一定のルールや法的解釈などが確立されていないた
め、主として送金の場合に利用されている。

C. Surrendered B/L (B/L voided in exporting country)

In general, a B/L loses its value as negotiable securities when a delivery of the cargo is completed in an importing country. At the request of an exporter, the B/L can be exceptionally voided in the exporting country and such B/L is called "Surrendered B/L". When a B/L is surrendered, a consignee can take delivery of the cargo by identifying themselves as the consignee stated on the surrendered B/L to a shipping company and the original surrendered B/L is not required to take the delivery.

When the shipping company is requested for a surrendered B/L, they issue the B/L as negotiable securities, mark "Surrendered" on the B/L and void the B/L in the exporting country. The surrendered B/L is faxed or scanned into PDF etc. and sent to the importer from the exporter. When the importer presents the faxed or scanned surrendered B/L to identify themselves as the consignee stated on the surrendered B/L to the shipping company, the importer can receive the cargo.

The surrendered B/L is also called "Express B/L".

Equally to the Sea Waybill, banks usually do not accept the surrendered B/L as security in the case of transactions under L/C, as the surrendered B/L is not negotiable securities. Also, the surrendered B/L is not widely accepted by every party concerned as its definite rules and legal interpretations based on trade practices have not been established yet.

Therefore, the surrendered B/L is often used when contracts are on telegraphic transfer basis and shipping documents are directly sent from the exporter to the importer.

第10章
クレーム

Chapter 10
Claims

1．貨物の点検

　輸入者として最も大切なことは、引渡しを受けた貨物を直ちに点検することである。そうすることによって損傷や事故を早期に発見し、すぐにクレーム手続に入れることになるからである。

　運送人への運送クレームの場合には、運送人への損害賠償請求に時効がある上、その損害賠償請求権を確保するためには、決められた手続を行っていることが前提条件となる。

　また、輸出者に直接クレームする貿易クレームの場合にも、通常売買契約締結時に、クレーム方法やその対処などを決めており、決められた期間内に輸出者に通知することが義務づけられているのが普通である。

　このため、輸入者の持つ損害賠償請求の権利を実効あるものにするためには、これらの手続をもれなく済ませていることが非常に大切になってくる。

2．発生の確認

　輸入者は、貨物が損傷を負った状態で本船から荷卸しされたり、倉庫から搬出されてきた場合、必ずリマーク（損傷状態の表記）のある書類を証拠としてとりつけるようにする必要がある。

　コンテナ船のLCL貨物であればデバンニング・レポート（Devanning Report）等の貨物受渡書類にリマークを記載してもらい、船会社や運送業者の責任を明確にしておくことが重要である。

　必ず貨物の受領時点で、外装の梱包に異状がないかを確認することが大切である。

3．事故通知（予備クレーム）

　B/Lが無故障船荷証券（貨物に瑕疵のある旨のリマークがつけられていないB/Lのこと）であるのに、貨物の荷渡し時に発行されるデバンニング・レポート等の貨物受け渡し書類に損傷についてのリマークがある場合には、その貨物は船積された時点では何の損傷もなかったのに、輸送途上で損傷が起こったことになる。

　このように輸送中に発生した貨物の事故について、わが国における運送人への損害賠償請求権は、船荷証券統一条約、国際海上物品運送法（国内法）にもとづくB/L約款によって、いかなる場合も、貨物受取りの後、1年以内に訴訟を提起しない場合は消滅すると規定されている。

1. Examination of Cargo

It is very important for an importer to examine external conditions of packages right after taking delivery. If they find any damage on their packages, they should start to prepare for filing a claim for the damage immediately.

In the event of a claim against a carrier, the importer should file a claim for damage within the given time frame. In addition, they should follow the procedure set by an insurance company to secure the right to claim compensation for damages.

In the event of a claim against an exporter, the importer is usually obliged to notify the exporter of damage within the given time frame according to the claim procedure agreed in the sales contract.

It is vital for the importer to complete the procedure properly to execute the right to claim compensation for damages.

2. Finding Damages

An importer should obtain a remark, a description of the damage, on a document if their cargo is unloaded from a ship with damage or carried out from a warehouse with damage.

It is important to have the shipping company or the carrier make remarks on a delivery receipt such as a devanning report or the like. External conditions of packages should be checked before receiving the cargo.

3. Notice of Loss or Damage (Preliminary Claims)

When a clean B/L is issued and a remark is noted on a delivery receipt, it is possible that the cargo has been damaged during the transportation.

In Japan, a right to claim compensation against a carrier for any loss or damage occurred during transportation expires if an importer does not file a lawsuit within one year after receiving cargo. This statute of limitation is stipulated in B/L clauses based on International Convention for the Unification of Certain Rules relating to Bills of Lading as well as the relevant domestic law.

In order to claim compensation for loss or damage, it is necessary to give a carrier a notice in writing before or at the time of taking the goods from the carrier's premises.

　そして、この損害賠償請求権を主張するためには、貨物引渡しのときまでに、書面で事故の通知をすることが必要とされている。貨物受取り時の書類にリマークがある場合には、この通知が行われたとみなされるが、この場合も別途書面で通知を出しておくことが望ましい。

　問題は、その滅失、損傷が、貨物の受取り時には外部から認められず、リマークなしで貨物が引取られた場合である。

　B/L約款はこのような場合、貨物の受取り後（運送人による引渡し後）、3日以内に運送人に対して書面で、滅失、損傷があった旨およびその概要を通知しなければ、B/L記載どおり無事故で貨物が引渡されたものとみなす―と規定している。

　したがって輸入者は、貨物受取りの際に貨物の損傷が発見できず、後で発見した場合、貨物の受取りの日から3日以内に船会社に対して**事故通知（Claim Notice）**を行うことが必要である。

　この事故通知（Claim Notice）は、損害賠償請求権を留保するとの意思を申し出て、求償権を確保することが目的なので、**予備クレーム**ともいわれている。

　求償権を予備クレームで確保したうえで、原則として運送人の立会いを求めて損害を評価し、後日損害鑑定人にサーベイを依頼した結果船会社の責任であることが確定すると、損害数量、損害額が確定するので、正式に損害賠償請求をすることになる。このクレームのことを**本クレーム**という。

　事故通知に対して船会社は、数量不足などの明らかな落ち度以外のクレームについては、B/L上の免責約款を根拠に賠償責任を拒否してくるのが通例で、特に荒天遭遇の場合は「海難報告書」を根拠にしたりする。

　そのため、本クレームに際しては、専門の鑑定機関で調査してもらい、その鑑定報告書にもとづいて損害賠償請求をしていくことが必要である。

4．保険会社への通知とサーベイ

（1）保険会社への通知

　船会社への事故通知と同時に荷主は、保険会社または保険証券に記載されている揚げ地側のクレーム・エージェントに事故通知をする。

Although a remark noted on a delivery receipt is regarded as a notice of loss or damage, it is advisable to give the carrier a notice of loss or damage in writing.

The time frame is different when loss or damage is not apparent and the goods are removed from the carrier's premises without any remark.

B/L clauses stipulate that unless notice of the latent loss of or damage to the goods and the condition of the loss or damage is given to the carrier in writing within three days after delivery of the goods, it is assumed that the goods are delivered in good order as described in the B/L.

An importer, therefore, should send a claim notice to the carrier within three days after taking their cargo from the carrier's premises if they found latent loss or damage to their goods at later date.

The importer secures their right to claim compensation by sending this claim notice to the carrier in which they express their intention to reserve their right. This claim notice is also called "Preliminary Claim".

While the importer reserves their right, they conduct a damage survey, which usually takes place in the presence of the carrier. The survey is an investigation conducted by a special institution called surveyor in order to analyze/determine when and how goods were lost or damaged and who is responsible for the loss or damage. The surveyor also assesses the damage. If the surveyor comes to the conclusion that the carrier is responsible for the loss or damage, the importer officially files a claim for compensation against the carrier based on the assessment reported by the surveyor. This is called "Final Claim".

Upon receiving such claim notice, the carrier usually tries to deny their responsibility based on an exemption clause of the B/L except for apparent fault such as shortage of the goods.

The importer should have the surveyor examine the loss or damage and file the final claim for compensation based on the survey report received from the institution.

4. Notice to Insurance Company and Survey

(1) Notice to Insurance Company

In addition to a notice of loss or damage to the carrier, an importer should contact their insurance company or the insurance company's claim agent, which is usually printed on an insurance policy, at the place of receipt of the goods to notify the loss or damage.

(2) サーベイ（損害検査）による責任所在の究明

（1）の通知にもとづき、荷主は保険会社とサーベイが必要かどうかについて打合せをする。サーベイ（Survey）とは、貨物の損傷がいつ、だれの責任によって発生したのかを客観的に評価することで、サーベイヤー（Surveyor　損害鑑定人）と呼ばれる専門機関により行われる。

サーベイヤーは通常、保険会社から指定されるので、その指示にもとづき荷主がサーベイヤーを起用することになる。サーベイを利用した場合、その費用であるサーベイ料は、当初依頼者である輸入者が負担することになるが、実際にはその費用も後で保険金請求のときにあわせて保険会社へ請求することになる。

サーベイの結果は**サーベイ・レポート（Survey Report）**といわれる報告書で提示される。

また、損害の種類や規模によっては、サーベイヤーの起用が省略されることもある。

このときは保険会社と被保険者（輸入者）間で損害額を協定することになる。

5．保険金の請求

被保険者（輸入者）はサーベイ・レポートにもとづき、損害額、費用損害、サーベイ料などを、保険会社に任意の書式に必要書類を添えて請求する。

この保険会社への求償の際、船会社などの運送人にあてた事故通知と、それに対する返答があれば、必ずそれを添えて提出する必要があり、そのためにも船会社への事故通知は非常に重要といえる。

6．保険金の支払いと保険会社の代位請求

保険会社が輸入者からの損害のクレームにもとづいて保険金の支払いを行った場合、その支払いにより輸入者が持っていた運送人（船会社）に対する損害賠償請求権は、保険会社が代位（他人に代わってその地位につくこと）することになる。

つまり保険会社は、輸入者に保険金を支払うのと引き換えに、船会社に対する代位請求権を取得することになるので、輸入者に代わってその請求権にもとづいて船会社に求償していくことになる。

船会社などの運送人は、もし貨物の滅失や損傷に責任があった場合には、保険会社からの代位請求に対して、国際海上物品運送法などの法律に基づいて、一定の限度までの支払いを行わなければならないことになっている。

(2) Survey

The importer and their insurance company discuss and decide whether a survey is necessary or not.

The insurance company usually nominates a surveyor for the importer. Although the importer initially bears the cost of the survey, they charge the cost to the insurance company when filing claims for insurance.

The result of the survey is provided as a report called "Survey Report".

For certain damages, sometimes surveys are not required and the amount of insurance money is decided through negotiation between the insurance company and the importer.

5. Insurance Claims

The assured (an importer) makes an insurance claim for the damage, the survey cost, etc. with documents required for the claim. A copy of the claim notice to the carrier and the reply from them, if any, should be provided. This is why the claim notice to the carrier is important.

6. Insurance Money Payment and Subrogation

When an insurance company pays insurance money based on a claim by an importer, the right to claim compensation against a carrier transfers to the insurance company. This is called subrogation.

The insurance company claims compensation against the carrier based on the subrogated right as the insurance company acquires the right to claim compensation against the carrier in exchange for paying insurance money to the importer.

When the carrier is responsible for any loss or damage to goods, they have to compensate insurance company for the amount which the insurance company paid to the importer for the loss or damage. The amount, however, does not exceed the limit provided in International Convention for the Unification of Certain Rules relating to Bills of Lading and applicable domestic laws.

第11章
製造物責任（P/L）

Chapter 11
Product Liability (P/L)

1．製造物責任

(1) 製造物責任（P/L）とは

製造物責任（PL：Product Liability）とは、企業が製造、販売したもの（生産物）あるいは仕事の結果に起因して事故が発生した場合の賠償責任のことをいう。

(2) 無過失責任

米国、EU加盟国等では、早くから製造物責任は**無過失責任**を導入していた。

無過失責任とは、製品に欠陥があり、その欠陥が原因で第三者が損害を受けた場合、製造業者や流通業者などは過失がなくても、被害者に対して損害賠償責任を負うことをいう。

2．製造物責任への対応策

(1) PL対応策の重要性

米国では、1960年代に各種のPL訴訟が提起され、高額の判決が次々に出て社会問題となった。

このため、製品を輸出したり、海外で事業を行う法人は、PLに対する正確な知識を持ち、十分な対策を講じなければならなくなってきている。そのような備えがなければ、思わぬ損失を被るばかりでなく、場合によっては事業そのものの命取りにもなりかねない。

PLへの主な対応策としては、次の3つを挙げることができる。

① 製品安全対策（Product Safety：PS）
② PL予防策（Product Liability Prevention：PLP）
③ PL訴訟対策（Product Liability Defense：PLD）

(2) 製品安全対策

PL対策の第一は、何といっても安全なよい製品を製造することである。そのためには、例えば次のような対策が考えられる。

1. Product Liability

(1) Product Liability (P/L)

Product Liability is the liability to compensate for injury or damage to life, body or property caused by a defect in the product manufactured, sold or provided, and the service provided by business entities.

(2) Strict Liability

In the United States and EU countries, product liability claims have been based on strict liability since the early stages.

Under strict liability, manufacturers and distributors are liable for loss or damage caused by a defect in the product even if they are not negligent.

2. Protection against Product Liability Claim

(1) Importance of Protection against PL

In the United States, various kinds of PL lawsuits were filed in 1960's and became a social problem due to the series of court decisions ordering defendants to pay high compensation.

Therefore, companies exporting their products or doing business overseas must have accurate knowledge of the product liability and take sufficient countermeasures for it. Lack of such preparation will cause not only unexpected damage, but also fatal risk to their business.

The followings are the major points of protection against PL.

① Product Safety : PS
② Product Liability Prevention : PLP
③ Product Liability Defense : PLD

(2) Product Safety

The most effective protection against the product liability is to manufacture good and safety products with the following concepts.

Ａ．安全な設計

- ・ 予想されるユーザーのタイプの確認
- ・ 可能性のあるすべての危険の洗い出し
- ・ 政府や業界の安全基準・規則の確認
- ・ 安全性に関する立証可能な技術水準の確認
- ・ 過去の事故例、判例の分析
- ・ 代替設計の可能性と検討の評価
- ・ 専門コンサルタントや試験機関の利用

Ｂ．確実な製造

- ・ ミスの出ない製造設備および工程
- ・ 製造工程における適正な品質管理の実施
- ・ 製品安全管理者の設置
- ・ 確実な検査体制
- ・ 外部の効果的な査察体制
- ・ フィード・バック・システム

(3) PL予防対策

　安全な製品を作るとともに大切なのが、PL問題に巻き込まれないように常日頃から十分に気をつけ、準備を行うことである。

　また、万一PL訴訟が始まった場合に、米国特有の訴訟手続であるディスカバリー（証拠開示手続）に効果的に対応できるよう、あらかじめ準備をしておくことも必要である。

Ａ．仕様書

　仕様書について、次のような点を整理しておく必要がある。

① どういうテストを何回したか
② 開発当初からの設計変更を全部挙げ明確にしておく
③ 問題点や改良すべき点などをどう解決したか
④ 最終的に改善され、解決されたことを証明するレポートはあるか
⑤ 開発の経緯、製造、品質、検査などのデータをよく整理しておく

A. Safety Design
- Confirm expected user types
- Investigate possible risks
- Confirm safety standards and regulations of government and industry
- Confirm verifiable engineering levels related to safety
- Analyze past accidents and precedents
- Explore a possibility of alternative designs
- Make use of consultants and inspection agencies

B. Complete and Secure Manufacturing
- Establish a manufacturing process with zero defect
- Establish appropriate quality control in a manufacturing process
- Assign a product safety manager
- Establish a secure inspection scheme and system
- Make use of an external audit system
- Collect and analyze feedback

(3) Product Liability Prevention

Sufficient attention and preparation to prevent PL issues are necessary in addition to manufacturing the safety products.

It is also important to prepare for the "Discovery", which is a unique legal procedure (proof disclosure process) in the United States.

A. Specifications
The following points need to be checked in making specifications.

① Record types and numbers of tests which are performed
② Record every design change from the first
③ Record solution to problems and improvements
④ Prepare reports verifying the results of improvement, and solutions to the defects
⑤ Prepare complete and thorough data regarding quality, inspection, manufacturing and progress of development

B．カタログ

過大広告になっていないかチェックする。

C．適正な警告ラベルや取扱説明書の作成

D．製品販売後の監視と警告の実施

E．リコール体制の確立

F．適切な保険付保

（4）PL訴訟対策

訴訟をいつ起こされても迅速にかつ効果的に対応できるよう、常日頃から社内外の体制を整えておくことが望ましいといえる。

例えば米国に商品を輸出しているのであれば、PL専門の米国の法律事務所をあらかじめ選定し、情報を収集して、それを国内の社内関係者にフィード・バックすることなどが必要である。

3．PL保険

PL保険は、PL責任のリスクを回避するための有効な手段である。

（1）輸出PL保険

米国やEU諸国は、製造物責任（PL）についてすでに多くの経験と実績とがあり、PLについての社会意識も他国に比べて相対的に高い。米国やEU諸国等へ製品を輸出したり、現地で事業を行う法人は、PLに対する正確な知識を持ち、十分な対策を講じなければならない。そのような備えがなければ、思わぬ損失を被るばかりでなく、場合によっては事業の命取りにもなりかねない。

B. Catalogue

It is important to make sure an advertisement in a catalogue is not exaggerated.

C. Preparation of Appropriate Warning Labels and Handling Manuals

D. Monitoring the Products after Sale

E. Establishment of a Recall System

F. Appropriate PL Insurance Coverage

(4) Product Liability Defense

It is desirable to organize internal and external structures for an immediate and effective response in case of a lawsuit.

For example, for export to the United States, it is necessary to appoint a U.S. law firm specialized in the PL to collect information and share it with departments concerned.

3. Product Liability Insurance

Product liability insurance is an effective measure to cover risk of compensation for PL damages.

(1) Export PL Insurance

The United States and EU countries have more experiences and achievements in product liability cases and the degree of social consciousness of product liability is relatively high comparing to other countries. Companies exporting their products to the United States or EU countries, or doing business in these countries must have accurate knowledge of product liability and take sufficient countermeasures for it. Lack of such preparation will cause not only unexpected damage, but also fatal risk to their business.

A．輸出PL保険のてん補範囲

輸出PL保険では、通常次の損害が保険金支払いの対象となる。

> ①　法律上の賠償責任を負うことによって輸出者が被害者に支払うべき損害賠償金
> ②　訴訟解決のための諸費用。この保険では、保険会社が被保険者を守るための裁判または損害賠償請求の解決のために要した防御費用（たとえば裁判費用、弁護士報酬、示談解決のための費用など）

製品の欠陥により被保険者が被害者によって訴訟を起こされた時、輸出PL保険では保険会社は、被保険者（輸出者など）に対する訴訟が根拠のないもの、誤ったもの、あるいは不正のものであっても、被保険者を防御する権利と義務を有している。このことは、輸出者にとっては保険契約の最も大きなメリットであり、輸出PL保険を必要とする理由でもある。

ただし、米国での不法行為訴訟において裁決された懲罰的損害賠償金の場合は、保険会社は免責となる。懲罰的損害賠償金（Punitive Damages）とは、主に不法行為訴訟において、加害行為の悪性が高い場合に、加害者に対する懲罰および一般的抑止効果を目的として、通常の損害賠償の他に認められる損害賠償金のことである。

B．追加被保険者

輸出PL保険の被保険者は、通常、保険契約をした輸出者であるが、この他に海外の輸入者や販売者を追加被保険者として輸出PL保険を付保する場合がある。

この場合、輸出者は記名被保険者となり、追加被保険者とは記名被保険者が製造、販売を行った製品の流通過程に関わる者となる。ただし、追加被保険者が保険の適用を受けられるのは、記名被保険者の生産物に限られる。

輸出PL保険で輸出者が追加被保険者の設定が必要となるのは、次のような場合である。

A. Export PL Insurance Coverage

Generally, export PL insurance covers the following loss or damage.

> ① Compensation for victims when an exporter is legally liable for loss or damage
> ② Expenses required for the settlement of the claim. Those are defense costs which the insurance company pays for the trial to protect the insured, or costs to settle the claim. (e.g. judicial costs, attorney's fees, costs for out-of-court settlement)

When the insured is sued by victims due to a defect in a product, an insurance company has a right and obligation to protect the insured (such as exporters) even if the lawsuit itself is unfounded, incorrect or abusive. This is the greatest advantage of export PL insurance, and also the reason why exporters usually require the export PL insurance.

However, in the event punitive damages are awarded in the tort lawsuit in the U.S., the insurance company is exempted from such damages. Punitive damages are damages awarded in order to punish defendants and prevent the same from happening. Defendants are ordered to pay substantial compensation to plaintiffs in addition to actual damages if the defendants are found to be malicious and intentional.

B. Additional Insured

The insured of export PL insurance is usually the exporter who concludes the insurance contract. The exporter sometimes can obtain an insurance which also covers an importer and a distributor in the importing country as an additional insured.

In this case, the exporter is regarded as a named insured and the additional insured is a person or a company that deals in products which the named insured manufactures and sells. The additional insured is protected only when handling the products of the named insured.

Followings are the cases that the exporter needs to set the additional insured in their export PL insurance.

> ①　売買契約において、海外の輸入者や販売者等もカバーするPL
> 　保険を輸出者側が付保する条件がつけられている場合
> ②　輸出者が売買契約で契約責任を負わされる条件となっている
> 　場合

　②のケースで、もし製品の欠陥により海外の輸入者や販売者が被害者によって訴訟を起こされた場合、輸入者は売買契約条件にもとづいて、輸出者にその損害賠償責任を転嫁してくる。輸出者が付保した輸出PL保険で海外の輸入者や販売者が追加被保険者になっていた場合には、輸入者はその保険によって守られるため、輸出者に対して損害賠償責任を転嫁しない。

　発展途上国を中心とする国によっては、自国の保険市場の活性化、および外貨流出の回避を目的として、政府により外国の保険会社への付保が制限される場合がある（自国保険主義）。これに違反した場合罰金が課せられるので、輸出PL保険を手配する際には、相手国の制限を事前確認することが望ましい。

　なお、このような外国の保険会社での付保制限をとっている国であっても、輸出品の販売を海外子会社に委託している場合などはその対象にならないので、被保険者として追加することができる。

　これらの制限はしばしば変更されるので、それぞれのケースにおける最新情報を入手する必要がある。

（2）輸入PL保険

　商品を輸入したり、それを販売する企業においても、PLに対する正確な知識を持ち、十分な対策を講じなければならないのは同様である。輸入PL保険は、PL責任に対する効果的な方法である。

　輸入PL保険の手続きやてん補範囲は各国政府の制限や各国の保険会社の付保ルールや規則によって異なる。

> ① The exporter is required to obtain an insurance which also covers the importer and the distributor in the importing country in the sales contract.
> ② The exporter has contractual liability based on the sales contract.

In the case of ②, if the importer and the distributor in the importing country are sued by victims due to a defect in the product, the importer requests for indemnity to the exporter based on the sales contract. When the exporter maintains the export PL insurance which covers the importer and the distributor in the importing country as an additional insured, the importer is protected by the insurance. Therefore, the importer does not request for indemnity to the exporter.

In some countries, especially in some developing countries, governments may have restrictions on making contract with foreign insurance companies in order to develop their own insurance markets and prevent foreign currencies from outflowing (domestic insurance regulations). As violations of such restrictions are subject to a fine, it is advisable to check restrictions of trading partner's countries prior to arranging insurance.

However, even in the countries which have such restrictions, the exporter can add their subsidiaries as an additional insured in the case that the exporter consigns their export goods to their subsidiaries for distribution.

As these restrictions are frequently revised, it is required to obtain the latest information in each case.

(2) Import PL Insurance

Companies importing products or distributing them also should have accurate knowledge of the product liability and take sufficient countermeasures to prevent unexpected damage. Import PL insurance is an effective countermeasure against such damage.

The procedures and coverage of import PL insurance vary depending on governmental restrictions, or rules and regulations of insurance companies in each country.

第12章
紛争の解決方法

Chatper 12
Settlement of Disputes

1. 売手へのクレーム

売手である輸出者に責任のある損害や契約違反については、輸出者にクレームの申し立てをすることになる。

特に品質・数量に関して輸出者が契約違反をした場合には、買手である輸入者を救済するために、商品を受け取ってから一定期間内にクレーム通知（違反があった場合の損害賠償請求）を出すことを、輸出入者が売買契約を締結するときに契約書上に条件として明記している。

売手へのクレームの主なものとして、次のようなものが考えられる。

①　品質・数量に関するクレーム
- 品質不良 → 契約で打ち合せしたものより劣っている
- 品質相違 → 契約で規定されたものと違っている
- 着荷不足 → 数量についての違反
②　貨物受け渡しに関するクレーム
- 船積違反 → 契約品以外の船積
- 船積遅延 → 出荷および船舶・航空機のスケジュール変更

損害の原因がどこにあるかわからないために保険会社でも船会社でもクレームに応じない。したがって、明らかに売手である輸出者の契約違反による貨物の事故の他、損害については、とりあえず輸出者に対して予備的にクレームを申し立てておくことが望ましいといえる。

これは、契約書の中にクレームを申し立てる有効期限が取り決められており、その期限までにクレームを申し立てないと、そのクレームが無効となってしまうからである。

2. 紛争の解決手段

輸出者と輸入者との間でクレームが発生した場合には話し合いで解決することが最も望ましいが、もし解決が困難な場合にはどのように解決するかについて、売買契約を締結する時点で、契約書の中に明確に規定しておく必要がある。

1. Claim against Seller

In the event of loss or damage, or a breach of contract for which a seller (an exporter) shall be responsible and liable, a buyer (an importer) claims compensation against the seller.

The exporter and the importer should clearly state the procedure in case of breach of contract in a sales contract. In the case of a breach of contract, especially in quality and quantity of the goods, the buyer should send a written notice of claim to the seller within a specified period agreed in the sales contract after receipt of the goods.

Major examples of the claim against the seller are as follows:

① Claim concerning the quality and the quantity
  - Inferior quality
  - Quality Difference
  - Quantity shortage
② Claim concerning the delivery of the goods
  - Wrong item
  - Delayed shipment

When the cause of loss of or damage to the goods is uncertain, an insurance company and a shipping company may refuse to compensate for the damage.

Therefore, the importer should make a notice of claim to the exporter immediately not only when the damage is clearly caused by the exporter's breach of contract, but also when it is not clear who is responsible for the damage.

As a period in which the importer can make a claim against the exporter is usually stated in the sales contract, the importer loses the right to claim unless the importer makes a claim to the exporter during this period.

2. Dispute Resolution Method

It is desirable for the exporter and the importer to settle the claim by negotiation.

However, in case an amicable settlement between the exporter and the importer is not feasible, a settlement of dispute clause should be stipulated in the contract at the time of concluding the sales contract.

（1）解決方法

解決方法としては、斡旋、調停、仲裁、裁判（訴訟）などの方法がある。裁判以外の紛争解決方法は一般に**ADR（Alternative Dispute Resolution）**と呼ばれている。

斡旋は、第三者が解決のための助言を行い、その判断を当事者に任せるものである。調停は、解決案を両当事者に示すものだが、両当事者が合意しない限り成立しないので、結局最終的には仲裁または裁判となることが多いといえる。

（2）裁判と仲裁

裁判と仲裁は次のような点が異なる。

図表１２−１　裁判と仲裁との相違点

	裁判	仲裁
裁定地	自国または相手国	仲裁地を選択可（第三国でも）相手国でいきなり訴訟をおこされることを回避できる
裁定人	裁判官（専門的な分野については得意でないこともある）	仲裁人を自由に決められる（専門知識を持った者を指定できるので、現実的な解決が図れる。既存の仲裁機関を選ぶこともできる）
争点の公開の有無	公開	非公開（企業秘密が漏れない）
上訴の可否	上訴可	上訴不可
法的執行力	裁判管轄権があり、判決を外国で執行するのは容易ではない	仲裁に関する国際条約の加盟国間では、仲裁判断が法的執行力を持つ

このように、裁判は特定国の裁判所での裁定となるため、国をまたがる貿易取引の場合には現実的には裁判によって紛争を解決することは難しく、実際には契約書中に仲裁による解決を規定するのが一般的である。

(1) Settlement of Dispute

There are some methods for settlement of dispute such as Conciliation, Mediation, Arbitration and Lawsuit. The methods to settle the trade dispute other than lawsuit are called "Alternative Dispute Resolution (ADR)".

Conciliation is a method that a neutral third party only advises the parties to find a mutually satisfactory solution. Mediation is a method that a mediator indicates resolutions to the parties. As both the advice of conciliation and the resolution of mediation do not bind the exporter and the importer, mutual agreement is necessary for settlement. If the exporter and the importer cannot reach an agreement, they may need to proceed to arbitration or lawsuit.

(2) Lawsuit and Arbitration

Fig.12-1   Differences between Lawsuit and Arbitration

	Lawsuit	Arbitration
Place of Settlement	Country of Defendant or Country of Plaintiff	Decided by the Contract (Sudden lawsuit in counterparty's country can be avoided.)
Decision-maker	Judge (The judge may not have enough knowledge for a specific area.)	Arbitrator Decided by the Contract (An expert or an arbitral institution can be selected.)
Transparency	Open	Private (Business secret can be kept.)
Appeal	Appealable	Non-appealable
Legal Enforcement	Due to the jurisdiction, it is difficult to enforce the judgment in other countries.	Between the members of the International Convention on Arbitration, the award is enforceable by law.

As legal enforcement of the judgment is limited to the jurisdiction of the court, it is not easy to settle a dispute of trade business across the countries by lawsuit.

The exporter and the importer usually stipulate an arbitration clause in the sales contract.

（3）仲裁

Ａ．仲裁人と仲裁方法

　契約上の両当事者が仲裁によって紛争を解決することを望む場合、仲裁方法、仲裁場所、仲裁規則などを売買契約上の仲裁条項として取り決める必要がある。

　仲裁には常設仲裁機関による機関仲裁と、そのつど両当事者が仲裁人（Arbitrator）を定めるad hoc（アドホック）仲裁の2つがある。

①　機関仲裁（Institutional Arbitration）

　機関仲裁を選択した場合、両当事者は、世界中に設置されている仲裁規則（Arbitration Rules）を備えた常設仲裁機関のうち、どこの機関を利用するかを選択しなければならない。この場合の仲裁人は、その仲裁機関の仲裁規則によって選出される。

②　Ad hoc（アドホック）仲裁

　仲裁人によるAd hoc（アドホック）仲裁を選択した場合、両当事者は、売買契約書にもとづいて第三者を仲裁人として指名する。契約書上には、仲裁人の決め方が定められていなければならず、その仲裁人の示した判断に従って解決を図る。

Ｂ．仲裁に関する国際条約と仲裁判断

　貿易取引における紛争は、異なる法律が適用される、異なる国の間で起こるので、仲裁人によって示された判断（仲裁判断、裁定）が各々の国において有効かどうかが問題となってくる。

　仲裁人によって示された判断（仲裁判断、裁定）を各々の国において有効とするために、**仲裁に関する国際条約**というものがあり、その条約を締結している国同士の間では、仲裁判断がその国の中で法的に有効であることが、各々の国の法律によって認められている。

　たとえば日本で下された仲裁判断については、裁判所の確定判決と同等の効果が認められており、一定の条件のもとでは強制執行できることが承認されている。

(3) Arbitration

A. Arbitrator and Method of Arbitration

If both parties wish to solve disputes by arbitration, both parties should provide an arbitration clause in which they stipulate concerning type of arbitration, place of arbitration, applicable arbitration rules and so on in the sales contract.

There are two types of arbitration. One is an institutional arbitration, which is conducted by professional bodies providing arbitration services. The other is an ad hoc arbitration, which is conducted by arbitrators appointed by the seller and the buyer.

① Institutional Arbitration

When an institutional arbitration is chosen, both parties should select which arbitral institution they wish to use from many arbitral institutions in the world which have their own arbitration rules. The arbitrator is selected by the rules of such arbitral instituition.

② Ad Hoc Arbitration

When an ad hoc arbitration is chosen, both parties should appoint a neutral third party as arbitrator based on the sales contract. It should be stated how to choose the arbitrator in the sales contract. The dispute is resolved according to the judgment (award) of the arbitrator.

B. International Convention on Arbitration and Arbitral Award

International trade disputes arise between parties in different countries, where different laws and regulations govern. Therefore, it is a very important factor whether the arbitral award brought by the arbitrator is enforceable in each party's country.

In order to make the arbitral award enforceable, an international convention called "Convention on the Recognition and Enforcement of Foreign Arbitral Awards" is applied. In the contracting countries, the award of arbitration is legally enforceable based on each country's domestic laws.

For example, arbitral awards made in Japan have the same judicial effect as the final and conclusive judgments by Japanese courts. The party concerned can expect a compulsory execution under certain conditions.

付録

各種帳票集

Appendix

Trade Documents

印刷条項（裏面約款）の例

Example of Printed Clause (Terms and Conditions on Reverse Side)

GENERAL TERMS AND CONDITIONS

1. **TRADE TERMS** -- Seller and Buyer shall be governed by the provisions of INCOTERMS 20 , as amended, with regard to the trade terms, such as FCA, CPT, CIP, used herein, unless otherwise provided for herein.

2. **SHIPMENT** -- Partial shipment or delivery and/or transshipment shall be permitted. Each lot of partial shipment or delivery shall be regarded as a separate and independent contract.

   Date of bill of lading or air waybill shall be accepted as conclusive evidence of the date of shipment or delivery.

   If the vessel is not provided or nominated by Buyer in time for the shipment or delivery of the Goods under the terms of FCA, FAS or FOB or within any extension of time for such shipment or delivery granted by Seller, Seller may, at its option, extend the time of shipment or delivery of the Goods, or cancel this Contract or any part of thereof, without prejudice to any other rights and remedies Seller may have.

   In case of the mode of transportation for which the trade terms of FCA, CPT or CIP under which the Goods shall be handed over to the carrier should be used, for example, air transportation, transportation by container ships, or combined transportation, when trade terms such as FOB, CFR or CIF shall be applied, risk of loss of the Goods shall pass from Seller to Buyer upon delivery of the Goods to the carrier or its agent for transportation.

   In the event Seller shall charter a vessel for ocean transportation of the Goods, all charges and expenses for discharge of the Goods, including demurrage and other damages, which are to be for the account of the charterer against the shipowner or the chartered owner under the relevant charter party, shall be borne and paid by Buyer.

3. **PAYMENT** -- In case payment for the Goods shall be made by a letter of credit under this Contract, Buyer shall, unless otherwise provided for herein, establish in favor of Seller an irrevocable and confirmed letter of credit negotiable on sight draft through a prime bank of good international repute and satisfactory to Seller immediately after the conclusion of this Contract with validity of at least 20 days after the last day of the period of relative shipment or delivery. Such letter of credit shall be in a form and upon terms satisfactory to Seller and shall authorize reimbursement to Seller for such sums, if any, as may be advanced by Seller for consular invoices, inspection fees and other expenditures for the account of Buyer. Should payment under such letter of credit not be duly effected, Buyer shall, upon notice thereof from Seller, immediately make payment in cash to Seller directly and unconditionally.

   If payment for the Goods is not effected fully by Buyer when due under terms of payment, or, in case of payment to be made by a letter of credit, such letter of credit is not established in accordance with the terms of this Contract, Seller may cancel all or any part of this Contract at any time without prejudice to the rights of Seller to recover any damages incurred thereby and/or to enforce any other rights or remedies under applicable laws, and all accounts payable by Buyer to Seller for the Goods delivered under this Contract shall, upon Seller's declaration, become immediately due and payable in cash in full.

   If Buyer's failure to make payment or otherwise perform its obligations hereunder is reasonably anticipated, Seller may demand adequate assurance, satisfactory to Seller, of the due performance of this Contract by Buyer and withhold shipment or delivery of the undelivered Goods. Unless Buyer gives Seller such assurance within a reasonable time, Seller may, without prejudice to any other remedies it may have, cancel the portion of this Contract which relates to the undelivered Goods, and all accounts payable by Buyer to Seller for the Goods delivered under this Contract shall, upon Seller's declaration, become immediately due and payable in cash in full.

   All bank charges outside Japan, including collection charges and stamp duties, if any, shall be for the account of Buyer, provided that confirming commissions shall be for the account of Buyer, regardless of being charged within or outside Japan.

4. **INSURANCE** -- If this Contract is on a CIP or CIF basis, 110% of the invoice amount shall be insured by Seller, unless otherwise agreed herein.

5. **INCREASED COSTS** -- Any new, additional or increased freight rates, surcharges (bunker, currency, congestion or other surcharges), taxes, customs duties, export or import surcharges or other governmental charges, or insurance premiums, including those for war and strikes risks, which may be incurred by Seller with respect to the Goods after conclusion of this Contract, shall be for the account of Buyer and shall be reimbursed to Seller by Buyer.

6. **WARRANTY** -- UNLESS OTHERWISE EXPRESSLY STIPULATED ON THE FACE OF THIS CONTRACT, SELLER MAKES NO WARRANTY OF FITNESS OR SUITABLITY OF THE GOODS FOR ANY PARTICULAR PURPOSE OR SPECIAL CIRCUMSTANCE.

7. **CLAIM** -- No claim may be raised by Buyer against Seller with regard to the Goods unless Buyer notifies Seller of its claim by registered airmail, containing full particulars of the claim and accompanied by evidence thereof certified by an authorized surveyor within thirty (30) days after the arrival of the Goods at the port of destination, or within six (6) months after the arrival of the Goods at the port of destination in the event of a latent defect.

   Seller shall not be responsible to Buyer for any incidental, consequential or special damages. Seller's total liability on any or all claims from Buyer shall in no event exceed the price of the Goods with respect to which such claim or claims are made.

8. **PATENT, TRADEMARK, ETC.** -- Seller shall not be responsible to Buyer, and Buyer waives any claim against Seller, for any alleged infringement of patent, utility model, design, trademark or other industrial property right or copyright, in connection with the Goods except that infringement of any Japanese patent, utility model, design, trademark, or copyright.

   Buyer shall hold Seller harmless from any such alleged infringement on said Japanese rights arising from or in connection with any instruction given by Buyer to Seller regarding patent, utility model, design, trademark, copyright, pattern and specification.

9. **FORCE MAJEURE** -- In the event the performance by Seller of its obligations hereunder is prevented by force majeure, directly or indirectly affecting the activities of Seller or any other person, firm or corporation connected with the sale, manufacture, supply, shipment or delivery of the Goods, including but not limited to, act of God, flood, typhoon, earthquake, tidal wave, landslide, fire, plague, epidemic, quarantine restriction, perils of sea; war or serious threat of the same, civil commotion, blockade, arrest or restraint of government, rulers or people, requisition of vessel or aircraft; strike, lockout, sabotage, other labor dispute; explosion, accident or breakdown in whole or in part of machinery, plant, transportation or loading facility; governmental request, guidance, order or regulation; unavailability of transportation or loading facility; curtailment, shortage or failure in the supply of fuel, water, electric current, other public utility, or raw material including crude oil, petroleum or petroleum products; bankruptcy or insolvency of the manufacturer or supplier of the Goods; boycotting of Japanese goods; substantial change of the present international monetary system; or any other causes or circumstances whatsoever beyond the reasonable control of Seller, then, Seller shall not be liable for loss or damage, or failure or delay in performing its obligations under this Contract and may, at its option, extend the time of shipment or delivery of the Goods or cancel unconditionally and without liability the unfulfilled portion of this Contract to the extent so affected.

10. **SETTLEMENT OF DISPUTE** -- Any legal action taken by Buyer against Seller shall be brought in a Japanese court having competent jurisdiction over Seller, provided, however, that Buyer may submit any dispute between itself and Seller to arbitration in Japan in accordance with the rules of the Japan Commercial Arbitration Association in which case the award shall be final and binding on both parties.

    Any legal action by Seller against Buyer shall be brought in a court having competent jurisdiction over Buyer.

    Subsequent to the bringing of such legal action by either party or submission of dispute to arbitration by Buyer, the other party shall submit any claim it may have in connection with said action or arbitration to the court in which jurisdiction has first been established or in the case of such arbitration to the arbitrator or arbitrators appointed in accordance with such rules.

11. **LAW APPLICABLE** -- This contract shall be governed by and construed in all respects in accordance with the laws of Japan.

12. **WAIVER** -- No claim or right of Seller under this Contract shall be deemed to be waived or renounced in whole or in part unless the waiver or renunciation of such claim or right is acknowledged and confirmed in writing by Seller.

13. **ENTIRE AGREEMENT** -- This Contract is based on the terms and conditions expressly set forth herein and no other terms and conditions are binding on Seller without its agreement in writing to such other terms and conditions.

14. **HEADINGS** -- The headings are for convenience only and shall not affect the construction of this Contract.

Commercial Invoice（商業送り状）（送金用）
Commercial Invoice (for T.T. Remittance)

INVOICE

THE KATSURAGI CORPORATION

Date	October 18, 20××
Invoice No.	ASW-102-00
Ref. No.	

2-8-6 Shiba-Koen, Minato-ku
Tokyo 123-4567, Japan
Phone: 81(3)3456-7890   Fax:81(3)3456-7893

Buyer

THE AUCKLAND STEEL, LTD.
100 Pacific St, #206
Newton, Auckland, New Zealand

Payment Terms

T.T. Remittance 30 days after B/L date

L/C No.   Date

Vessel or	On or about	Issuing Bank
"FES-GO" 43/750	October 20, 20××	
From	Via	
TOKYO, JAPAN		
To		Remarks
AUCKLAND		

Marks & Nos.	Description of Goods	Quantity	Unit Price CIP AUCKLAND	Amount
	STAINLESS STEEL SHEETS AND COILS		IN US$	
	T6695 STAINLESS STEEL SHEETS 120cm × 150cm	80 SHEETS	US$550.00/SHEET	US$44,000.00
	T6696 STAINLESS STEEL SHEETS 200cm × 200cm	120 SHEETS	US$250.00/SHEET	US$30,000.00
	T6697 STAINLESS COILS	100 PIECES	US$200.00/PIECE	US$20,000.00
	ELEMENTS			US$54.00

AUCKLAND STEEL
AUCKLAND
CTN NO. 1-300
MADE IN JAPAN

TOTAL	200 SHEETS & 100 Pcs.	CIP US$94,054.00

THE KATSURAGI CORPORATION

− Signed −

authorized signature

Packing List（梱包明細書）（送金用）

Packing List (for T.T. Remittance)

PACKING LIST

THE KATSURAGI CORPORATION

2-8-6 Shiba-Koen, Minato-ku
Tokyo 123-4567, Japan
Phone: 81 (3) 3456-7890 Fax: 81 (3) 3456-7893

Date	October 18, 20××
Invoice No.	ASW-102-00
Ref. No.	

Buyer

THE AUCKLAND STEEL, LTD.
100 Pacific St, #206
Newton, Auckland, New Zealand

Payment Terms	
	T.T. Remittance 30 days after B/L date
L/C No.	Date

Vessel or FES-GO 43/750	On or about October 20, 20××	Issuing Bank
From TOKYO, JAPAN	Via	
To AUCKLAND		Remarks

Case No.	Description of Goods	Quantity	Net Weight	Gross Weight	Measurement
	STAINLESS STEEL SHEETS AND COILS				
1-80	T6695 STAINLESS STEEL SHEETS 120cm × 150cm	80 Cartons	800kg	850kg	18M3
81-200	T6696 STAINLESS STEEL SHEETS 200cm × 200cm	120 Cartons	1,200kg	1,300kg	30M3
201-300	T6697 STAINLESS COILS ELEMENT	100 Cartons	800kg	850kg	12M3
	AUCKLAND STEEL AUCKLAND CTN NO. 1-300 MADE IN JAPAN				
TOTAL		300 Cartons	2,800kg	3,000kg	60M3

THE KATSURAGI CORPORATION

－Signed－

authorized signature

第3章 Chap.3

Bill of Lading (B/L) (船荷証券) (送金用)
Bill of Lading (B/L) (for T.T. Remittance)

(Forwarding Agents)

Shipper	B/L No. FES-9720

THE KATSURAGI CORPORATION

FES LINE

FAR EAST SEA

BILL OF LADING

Consignee

THE AUCKLAND STEEL, LTD.

RECEIVED by the Carrier from the Shipper in apparent good order and condition unless otherwise indicated herein, the Goods, or the container(s) or package(s) said to contain the cargo herein mentioned, to be carried subject to all the terms and conditions provided for on the face and back of this Bill of Lading by the vessel named herein or any substitute at the Carrier's opinion and / or other means of transport, from the place of receipt or the port of loading to the port of discharge or the place of delivery shown herein and there to be delivered unto order or assigns.

Notify Party

THE AUCKLAND STEEL, LTD.
100 Pacific St. #206
Newton, Auckland, New Zealand

If required by the Carrier, this Bill of Lading duly endorsed must be surrendered in exchange for the Goods or delivery order.

In accepting this Bill of Lading, the Merchant agrees to be bound by all the stipulations, exceptions, terms and conditions on the face and back hereof, whether written, typed, stamped or printed, as fully as if signed by the Merchant, any local custom or privilege to the contrary notwithstanding, and agrees that all agreements or freight engagements for and in connection with the carriage of the Goods are superseded by this Bill of Lading.

In witness whereof, the undersigned, on behalf of Far East Sea Line, the Master and the owner of the Vessel, has signed the number of Bill(s) of Lading stated under, all of this tenor and date, one of which being accomplished, the others to stand void.

Pre-carriage by	Place of Receipt TOKYO CY	
Ocean Vessel "FES-GO"	Voy. No. 43/750	Port of Loading TOKYO
Port of Discharge AUCKLAND	Place of Delivery AUCKLAND CY	Final Destination(for the Merchant's reference only)

Container No.	Seal No. :Marks & Nos.	No. of Containers or P'kgs.	Kind of Packages:	Description of Goods	Gross Weight	Measurement
			"SHIPPER'S LOAD AND COUNT" "SAID TO CONTAIN"		3,000KGS	60.000M3
FES-081946-1	FES-MLB WA 123		200 SHEETS STAINLESS STEEL SHEETS			
			100 PIECES OF STAINLESS COILS			
	300 CARTONS		and ELEMENTS			
			Order No.T6695, 6696, 6697			
AUCKLAND STEEL						
AUCKLAND			" FREIGHT PREPAID "			
CTN NO. 1-300						
MADE IN JAPAN						
			SAY: ONE(1) CONTAINER ONLY.-			
			OR THREE HUNDRED(300) CARTONS ONLY			

Particulars furnished by the Merchant

TOTAL NUMBER OF CONTAINERS
OR PACKAGES (IN WORDS)

FREIGHT & CHARGES	Revenue Tons	Rate	Per	Prepaid	Collect
Ocean Freight	FREIGHT AS ARRANGED			FREIGHT AS ARRANGED	

ICS	Ex. Rate	Prepaid at TOKYO, JAPAN	Payable at	Place of B(s)/L Issue TOKYO, JAPAN OCTOBER 19, 20XX	Dated
B/L	@	Total Prepaid in Local Currency	Number of Original B(s)/L THREE(3)	**FAR EAST SEA LINE**	
		Laden on Board the Vessel		By **Signed**	

Date TOKYO, JAPAN, OCT. 20, 20XX By **Signed**

(JSA STANDARD FORM A)
SECOND ORIGINAL   (TERMS CONTINUED ON BACK HEREOF)

第3章　Chap.3

貨物海上保険証券（ICC2009）

Marine Insurance Policy (ICC2009)

MARINE CARGO POLICY
Nippon Kanzei Marine & Fire Insurance Co., Ltd.
Head office:1-1, Chiyoda 1 Chome, Chiyoda-ku, Tokyo 100-0000 Japan Phone: Tokyo (03)-1234-5678

Assured(s),etc	Invoice No.
THE KATSURAGI CORPORATION	ASW-102-00
(Code: 1234-2345-AB345-456)	Amount insured
Prov. No.　O/P No.	US$103,459.40

POLICY No.12-345-67890

Claim, if any, payable at/in	Conditions
New Zealand	**INSTITUTE CARGO CLAUSES (A)**

IMMEDIATE CLAIM NOTICE MUST BE GIVEN TO
THE EITHER OFFICE AS BELOW
KZ CLAIMS SERVICE INC., AUCKLAND OFFICE,
MARINE INSURANCE DIVISION. 200 PACIFIC ST. 500
NEWTON AUCKLAND NEW ZEALAND
(TEL:123-456-7777)(FAX:123-456-8888)
OR
KI CLAIMS SERVICE INC., WELLINGTON OFFICE,
MARINE INSURANCE DIVISION. 100 QUEEN ST. 25
OLDTON WELLINGTON NEWZEALAND
(TEL:012-345-9999)(FAX:012-345-0000)

Local Vessel or Conveyance	From(interior port or place of loading)		
Ship or Vessel	From	Sailing on or about	
"FES - GO"	TOKYO	OCT. 20, 20XX	
To/Transhipped at	Thence to		
AUCKLAND	INT. PLACE(S) IN NEW ZEALAND		

Subject-matter Insured

STAINLESS STEEL SHEETS AND COILS

SPECIMEN

Marks and Numbers as per Invoice No. specified above.　Valued at the same as Amount insured.

Signed in	Dated	No. of Policies issued
TOKYO	OCT. 18, 20XX	ONE

IMPORTANT
PROCEDURE IN THE EVENT OF LOSS OR DAMAGE FOR WHICH UNDERWRITERS MAY BE LIABLE
LIABILITY OF CARRIER, BAILEES OR OTHER THIRD PARTIES
It is the duty of the Assured and their Agents, in all cases, to take such measures as may be reasonable for the purpose of averting or minimising a loss and to ensure that all rights against Carriers, Bailees or other third parties are properly preserved and exercised. In particular, the Assured or their Agents are required:-
1. To claim immediately on the Carriers, Port Authorities or other Bailees for any missing packages.
2. In no circumstances, except under written protest, to give clean receipts where goods are in doubtful condition.
3. When delivery is made by Container, to ensure that the Container and its seals are examined immediately by their responsible official.
If the Container is delivered damaged or with seals broken or missing or with seals other than as stated in the shipping documents, to claim on the delivery receipt accordingly and retain all defective or irregular seals for subsequent identification.
4. To apply immediately for survey by Carriers' or other Bailees' Representatives if any loss or damage be apparent and claim on the Carriers or other Bailees for any actual loss or damage found at such survey.
5. To give notice in writing to the Carriers or other Bailees within 3 days of delivery if the loss or damage was not apparent at the time of taking delivery.
NOTE:- The Consignees or their Agents are recommended to make themselves familiar with the Regulations of the Port Authorities at the port of delivery.

INSTRUCTIONS FOR SURVEY
In the event of loss or damage which may involve a claim under this insurance, immediate notice of such loss or damage should be given to and a Survey Report obtained from the Claims Office or Agents specified in this Policy or Certificate.

DOCUMENTATION OF CLAIMS
To enable claims to be dealt with promptly, the Assured or their Agents are advised to submit all available supporting documents without delay, including when applicable:-
1. Original policy or certificate of insurance.
2. Original or certified copy of shipping invoices, together with shipping specification and/or weight notes.
3. Original or certified copy of Bill of Lading and/or other contract of carriage.
4. Survey report or other documentary evidence to show the extent of the loss or damage.
5. Landing account and weight notes at port of discharge and final destination.
6. Correspondence exchanged with the Carriers and other Parties regarding their liability for the loss or damage.

This insurance is subject to the following clauses printed or attached on the front or the back of this Policy:

Institute Cargo Clauses or other clauses specified above.
Institute War Clauses (Cargo)
Institute Strikes Clauses (Cargo)
Institute Radioactive Contamination, Chemical, Biological, Bio-Chemical and Electromagnetic Weapons Exclusion Clause
Institute Replacement Clause
Under Deck or On Deck Clause
Label Clause (applying to labelled goods)
Duty Clause (applicable only when import duty is separately insured under this Policy)

Wild Fauna and Flora Clause
Co-Insurance Clause (applicable in case of Co-Insurance)
Cargo ISM Endorsement
Termination of Transit Clause (Terrorism) 2009
Extension Clause for MAR Form
For sendings by Post, Institute War Clauses (Cargo) shall be replaced by Institute War Clauses (Sendings by Post), and Mail and Parcel Post Clause shall be additionally applied.
Sanction Limitation and Exclusion Clause
Other clauses, if any, specified above.

Notwithstanding anything contained herein or attached hereto to the contrary, this insurance is understood and agreed to be subject to English law and practice only as to liability for and settlement of any and all claims.

This insurance does not cover any loss or damage to the property which at the time of the happening of such loss or damage is insured by or would but for the existence of this Policy be insured by any fire or other insurance policy or policies except in respect of any excess beyond the amount which would have been payable under the fire or other insurance policy or policies had this insurance not been effected.

We, Nippon Kanzei Marine & Fire Insurance Co., Ltd. hereby agree, in consideration of the payment to us by or on behalf of the Assured of the premium as arranged, to insure against loss damage liability or expense to the extent and in the manner herein provided.

Where the Insurer pays for loss of or damage to the subject-matter insured, rights of ownership and/or any other proprietary rights of the Assured in remains of the subject-matter insured shall not transfer to the Insurer, unless the Insurer agrees in writing to take over such rights at the time of paying for the loss of or damage to the subject-matter insured.

In witness whereof, I the Undersigned of Nippon Kanzei Marine & Fire Insurance Co., Ltd. on behalf of the said Company have subscribed My Name in the place specified as above to the policies, the issued numbers thereof being specified as above of, the same tenor and date, one of which being accomplished, the others to be void, as of the date specified as above.

For Nippon Kanzei Marine & Fire Insurance Co.,Ltd.

- *Signed* -

AUTHORIZED SIGNATORY

貨物海上保険証券（ICC2009）裏面

Reverse Side of Marine Insurance Policy (ICC2009)

★An enlarged copy of the clauses printed hereon is available from this Company upon request.
★Only those clauses specified on the front shall apply to this insurance.

第3章 Chap.3

貨物海上保険証券（S.G.フォーム）

Marine Insurance Policy (S.G. Form)

MARINE CARGO POLICY

Nippon Kanzei Marine & Fire Insurance Co., Ltd.

Head office:1-1, Chiyoda 1 Chome, Chiyoda-ku, Tokyo 100-0000 Japan Phone: Tokyo (03)-1234-5678

Assured(s),etc.
THE KATSURAGI CORPORATION
(Code: 1234-2345-AB345-456)

Invoice No.
ASW-102-00

Amount insured US$103,459.40

POLICY
No.12-345-67890

Claim, if any, payable at/in **New Zealand**

IMMEDIATE CLAIM NOTICE MUST BE GIVEN TO
KZ CLAIMS SERVICE INC., AUCKLAND OFFICE,
MARINE INSURANCE DIVISION.
200 PACIFIC ST. 500, NEWTON AUCKLAND,
NEW ZEALAND
TELEPHONE:123-456777
FAX:123-456888 AND CLAIMS WILL BE
PAID BY THE SAID AGENT,

Conditions
ALL RISKS.

Local Vessel or Conveyance	From(interior port or place of loading)	
	INT. PLACE(S) IN JAPAN	
Ship or Vessel called the	**at and from**	**Sailing on or about**
"FES - GO"	TOKYO	OCT. 20, 20XX
arrived at /transhipped at	**thence to**	
AUCKLAND	INT. PLACE(S) IN NEW ZEALAND	

Goods and Merchandises

300 CARTONS OF STAINLESS STEEL SHEETS
AND COILS

SPECIMEN

Marks and Numbers as per Invoice No. specified above.　Valued at the same as Amount insured.

Signed in	Dated	No. of Policies issued
TOKYO	OCT. 18, 20XX	TWO

This insurance is subject to the following clauses printed or attached on the front or the back of this Policy.

Institute Cargo Clauses, or other clauses if specified above.
Institute War Clauses (Cargo)
Institute Strikes Riots and Civil Commotions Clauses
Institute Extended Radioactive Contamination Exclusion Clause
Institute Replacement Clause (applying to machinery)
Under Deck or On Deck Clause
Label Clause (applying to labelled goods)

Duty Clause (applicable only when import duty is separately insured under this Policy)
Wild Fauna and Flora Clause
Co-Insurance Clause (applicable in case of Co-Insurance)
Cargo ISM Endorsement
Termination of Transit Clause (Terrorism)

For sendings by Post, Institute War Clauses (Cargo) shall be replaced by Institute War Clauses (For the insurance of sendings by Post), and Mail and Parcel Post Clauses shall be additionally applied.
Other clauses, if any, specified above.

1. Warranted free of capture, seizure, arrest, restraint, or detainment, and the consequences thereof or of any attempt thereat; also from the consequences of hostilities or warlike operations, whether there be a declaration of war or not; but this warranty shall not exclude collision, contact with any fixed or floating object (other than a mine or torpedo), stranding, heavy weather or fire unless caused directly (and independently of the nature of the voyage or service which the vessel concerned or, in the case of a collision, any other vessel involved therein, is performing) by a hostile act by or against a belligerent power; and for the purpose of this warranty 'power' includes any authority maintaining naval, military or air forces in association with a power.

Further warranted free from the consequences of civil war, revolution, rebellion, insurrection, or civil strife arising therefrom or piracy.

2. Warranted free of loss or damage
(a) caused by strikers, locked-out workmen, or persons taking part in labour disturbances, riots or civil commotions;
(b) resulting from strikes, lock-outs, labour disturbances, riots or civil commotions.

Grounding or stranding in the Suez, Panama or other canals, harbours or tidal rivers not to be deemed a stranding under the terms of the policy, but to pay any damage or loss which may be proved to have directly resulted therefrom.

This Insurance does not cover any loss or damage to the property which at the time of the happening of such loss or damage is insured by or would but for the existence of this Policy be insured by any fire or other insurance policy or policies except in respect of any excess beyond the amount which would have been payable under the fire or other insurance policy or policies had this insurance not been effected.

⇒ In the event of loss or damage which may involve a claim under this insurance, no claim shall be paid unless immediate notice of such loss or damage has been given to and a Survey Report obtained from this Company's Office or Agents specified in this policy.

In case of loss or damage, please follow the "IMPORTANT" clause printed on the back hereof.

The descriptions to be inserted in the following clauses are as shown above.　**Be it known, That**
as well in his or their own Name, as for and in the Name and Names of all and every other Person or Persons to whom the same doth, may, or shall appertain, in part or in all, do make *Insurance*, and hereby cause himself or themselves and them and every of them, to be Insured, lost or not lost, at and from the port of　upon Goods and Merchandises, or Treasure, of and in the good Ship or Vessel called the　whereof is Master, for this present Voyage or whosoever else shall go for Master in the said Vessel, or by whatsoever other Name or Names the said Vessel, or the Master thereof, is or shall be named or called: - BEGINNING the Adventure upon the said Goods and Merchandises from the loading thereof on board the said Ship, and so to continue and endure, until the said Goods and Merchandises shall have arrived at　and until the same be there discharged and safely landed. And it shall be lawful for the said Vessel, in this Voyage, to proceed and sail to, and touch and stay at any Ports or Places whatsoever, (within the limits of the above Voyage) for necessary Provisions, Assistance or Repairs, without prejudice to this Insurance: the said Goods and Merchandises laden thereon for so much as concerns the *Assured*, are and shall be
Touching the Adventures and Perils which the said Nippon Kanzei Marine & Fire Insurance Co., Ltd. themselves are content to bear, and to take upon them in this Voyage; they are of the Seas, Men-of-War, Fire, Enemies, Pirates, Rovers, Thieves, Jettisons, Letters of Mart and Counter-Mart, Surprisals, Takings at Sea, Arrests, Restraints and Detainments of all Kings, Princes, and People, of what Nation, Condition, or Quality soever, Barratry of the Master and Mariners, and of all other Perils, Losses, and Misfortunes that have or shall come to the Hurt, Detriment, or Damage of the said Goods and Merchandises, or any part thereof; and in case of any Loss or Misfortune, it shall be lawful for the Assured, his or their Factors, Servants, or Assigns, to sue, labour, and travel for, in and about the Defence, Safeguard and Recovery of the said Goods and Merchandises, or any part thereof, without prejudice to this *Insurance*; to the Charges whereof the said *Company* will contribute. It is expressly declared and agreed that no acts of the *Insurer or Insured* in recovering, saving, or preserving the property insured, shall be considered as a waiver or acceptance of abandonment. AND it is agreed that this Writing or Policy of *Insurance* shall be of as much Force and Virtue as the surest Writing or Policy of *Insurance* made in LONDON. And so the said Nippon Kanzei Marine & Fire Insurance Co., Ltd. are contented, and do hereby promise and bind themselves to the *Assured*, his or their Executors, Administrators, or Assigns, for the true Performance of the Premises; confessing themselves paid the Consideration due unto them for this *Insurance*, at and after the rate of　*as arranged*　*Per Cent.*
∵ Corn, Fish, Salt, Fruit, Flour and Seed are warranted free from Average, unless General, or the Ship be stranded, sunk or burnt; Sugar, Tobacco, Hemp, Flax, Hides and Skins are warranted free from Average under *Five per cent.*, and all other Goods are warranted free from Average under *Three per cent.*, unless General, or the Ship be stranded, sunk or burnt.

This insurance is understood and agreed to be subject to English law and usage as to liability for and settlement of any and all claims.

In witness whereof, I the Undersigned of Nippon Kanzei Marine & Fire Insurance Co., Ltd. on behalf of the said *Company* subscribed My Name in　to　Policies of the same tenor and date, one of which being accomplished, the others to be void, *as of the date specified as above.*

For Nippon Kanzei Marine & Fire Insurance Co., Ltd.

- *Signed* -

AUTHORIZED SIGNATORY

貨物海上保険証券（S.G.フォーム）裏面
Reverse Side of Marine Insurance Policy (S.G. Form)

INSTITUTE CARGO CLAUSES

INSTITUTE WAR CLAUSES (CARGO)

INSTITUTE STRIKES RIOTS AND CIVIL COMMOTIONS CLAUSES

INSTITUTE WAR CLAUSES
For the insurance of sendings by Post

INSTITUTE EXTENDED RADIOACTIVE CONTAMINATION EXCLUSION CLAUSE

INSTITUTE REPLACEMENT CLAUSE

UNDER DECK OR ON DECK CLAUSE

LABEL CLAUSE

DUTY CLAUSE

WILD FAUNA AND FLORA CLAUSE

CO-INSURANCE CLAUSE

MAIL AND PARCEL POST CLAUSES

CARGO ISM ENDORSEMENT

TERMINATION OF TRANSIT CLAUSE (TERRORISM)

IMPORTANT
PROCEDURE IN THE EVENT OF LOSS OR DAMAGE FOR WHICH
UNDERWRITERS MAY BE LIABLE
LIABILITY OF CARRIERS, BAILEES OR OTHER THIRD PARTIES

It is the duty of the Assured and their Agents, in all cases, to take such measures as may be reasonable for the purpose of averting or minimising a loss and to ensure that all rights against Carriers, Bailees or other third parties are properly preserved and exercised. In particular, the Assured or their Agents are required:—

1. To claim immediately on the Carriers, Port Authorities or other Bailees for any missing packages.
2. In no circumstances, except under written protest, to give clean receipts where goods are in doubtful condition.
3. When delivery is made by Container, to ensure that the Container and its seals are examined immediately by their responsible official.
   If the Container is delivered damaged or with seals broken or missing or with seals other than as stated in the shipping documents, to clause the delivery receipt accordingly and retain all defective or broken seals for subsequent identification.
4. To apply immediately for survey by Carriers' or other Bailees' Representatives if any loss or damage be apparent and claim on the Carriers or other Bailees for any actual loss or damage found at such survey.
5. To give notice in writing to the Carriers or other Bailees within 3 days of delivery if the loss or damage was not apparent at the time of taking delivery.

NOTE:— The Consignees or their Agents are recommended to make themselves familiar with the Regulations of the Port Authorities at the port of discharge.

INSTRUCTIONS FOR SURVEY

In the event of loss or damage which may involve a claim under this insurance, immediate notice of such loss or damage should be given to and a Survey Report obtained from this Company's Office or Agents specified in this Policy or Certificate.

DOCUMENTATION OF CLAIMS

To enable claims to be dealt with promptly, the Assured or their Agents are advised to submit all available supporting documents without delay, including when applicable:—

1. Original policy or certificate of insurance.
2. Original or certified copy of shipping invoice, together with shipping specification and/or weight notes.
3. Original or certified copy of Bill of Lading and/or other contract of carriage.
4. Survey report or other documentary evidence to show the extent of the loss or damage.
5. Landing account and weight notes at port of discharge and final destination.
6. Correspondence exchanged with the Carriers and other Parties regarding their liability for the loss or damage.

★An enlarged copy of the clauses printed hereon is available from this Company upon request.
★Only those clauses specified on the front shall apply to this insurance.

第5章　Chap.5

受取船荷証券（Received B/L）

Shipper

B/L No.

FESLINE

FAR EAST SEA

BILL OF LADING

Consignee

RECEIVED by the Carrier from the Shipper in apparent good order and condition unless otherwise indicated herein, the Goods, or the container(s) or package(s) said to contain the cargo herein mentioned, to be carried subject to all the terms and conditions provided for on the face and back of this Bill of Lading by the vessel named herein or any substitute at the Carrier's opinion and / or other means of transport, from the place of receipt or the port of loading to the port of discharge or the place of delivery shown herein and there to be delivered unto order or assigns.

Notify Party

If required by the Carrier, this Bill of Lading duly endorsed must be surrendered in exchange for the Goods or delivery order.

In accepting this Bill of Lading, the Merchant agrees to be bound by all the stipulations, exceptions, terms and conditions on the face and back hereof, whether written, typed, stamped or printed, as fully as if signed by the Merchant, any local custom or privilege to the contrary notwithstanding, and agrees that all agreements or freight engagements for and in connection with the carriage of the Goods are superseded by this Bill of Lading.

In witness whereof, the undersigned, on behalf of Far East Sea Line, the Master and the owner of the Vessel, has signed the number of Bill(s) of Lading stated under, all of this tenor and date, one of which being accomplished, the others to stand void.

Pre-carriage by	Place of Receipt		
Ocean Vessel	Voy.No.	Port of Loading	
Port of Discharge	Place of Delivery		Final Destination(for the Merchant's reference only)

Container No.	Seal No. ;Marks & Nos.	No. of Contain-ers or P'kgs.	Kind of Packages;	Description of Goods	Gross Weight	Measurement

Particulars furnished by the Merchant

TOTAL NUMBER OF CONTAINERS
OR PACKAGES (IN WORDS)

FREIGHT & CHARGES	Revenue Tons	Rate	Per	Prepaid	Collect

TCS

B/L

Ex. Rate	Prepaid at	Payable at	Place of B(s)/L Issue	Dated
@	Total Prepaid in Local Currency	Number of Original B(s)/L	**FAR EAST SEA LINE**	

Laden on Board the Vessel

Date

By

(JSA STANDARD FORM A)
SECOND ORIGINAL

(TERMS CONTINUED ON BACK HEREOF)

船積船荷証券（Shipped B/L）

Shipper	B/L No.
	MACK **MACK SEA LINE LTD.**
	BILL OF LADING
Consignee	
	BILL OF LADING
Notify Party	SHIPPED on board the Goods, or the total number of Containers or other packages or units enumerated below(*) in apparent external good order and condition except as otherwise noted for transportation from the Port of Loading to the Port of Discharge subject to the terms hereof. One of the original Bills of Lading must be surrendered duly endorsed in exchange for the Goods or Delivery Order unless otherwise provided herein. In accepting this Bill of Lading the Merchant expressly accepts and agrees to all its terms whether printed, stamped or written, or otherwise incorporated, notwithstanding the non-signing of this Bill of Lading by the Merchant. IN WITNESS whereof the number of original Bills of Lading stated below have been signed, one of which being accomplished, the other(s) to be void.
*Local Vessel From	**(Terms of Bill of Lading continued on the back hereof)** Declared value USD_____ subject to clause 5 (5) overleaf. If no value declared, liability limit applies as per clause 5 (4) or 32 as applicable.
Ocean Vessel Voy.No. Port of Loading	
Port of Discharge For Transhipment to Final destination (for the shipper's reference only)	

Marks and Numbers	No. of pkgs or Units	Kind of Packages, Description of goods	Gross weight	Measurement
Total Number of packages or units				

Freight and charges	Revenue tons	Rate per	Prepaid	Collect

Exchange rate	Prepaid at	Payable at	Place and date of issue
	Total prepaid in national currency	No. of original B(s)/L	**MACK SEA LINE LTD. as Carrier**

Particulars furnished by shipper

*Applicable if carriage by local vessel to port of loading of ocean vessel arranged by carrier as agent for Merchant in accordance with clause 7.

ICS

FIRST ORIGINAL

B/L   **DB**   JSA STANDARD FORM(B) BL501 PRINTED IN JAPAN

House Air Waybill

Shipper's Name and Address		Shipper's Account Number	Not negotiable
			Air Waybill
			Issued by

Consignee's Name and Address	Consignee's Account Number	Copies 1, 2 and 3 of this Air Waybill are originals and have the same validity.
		It is agreed that the goods described herein are accepted in apparent good order and condition (except as noted) for carriage SUBJECT TO THE CONDITIONS OF CONTRACT ON THE REVERSE HEREOF. ALL GOODS MAY BE CARRIED BY ANY OTHER MEANS INCLUDING ROAD OR ANY OTHER CARRIER UNLESS SPECIFIC CONTRARY INSTRUCTIONS ARE GIVEN HEREON BY THE SHIPPER, AND SHIPPER AGREES THAT THE SHIPMENT MAY BE CARRIED VIA INTERMEDIATE STOPPING PLACES WHICH THE CARRIER DEEMS APPROPRIATE. THE SHIPPER'S ATTENTION IS DRAWN TO THE NOTICE CONCERNING CARRIER'S LIMITATION OF LIABILITY. Shipper may increase such limitation of liability by declaring a higher value for carriage and paying a supplemental charge if required.

Issuing Carrier's Name and City	Accounting Information

Airport of Departure (Addr. of First Carrier) and Requested Routing

To	By First Carrier	Routing and Destination	to	by	to	by	Currency	CHGS Code	WT/VAL PPD COLL	Other PPD COLL	Declared Value for Carriage	Declared Value for Customs

Airport of Destination	Requested Flight/Date	Amount of Insurance	If shipper requests insurance in accordance with the conditions thereof, indicate amount to be insured in figures in box marked "Amount of Insurance".

Handling Information

No. of Pieces RCP	Gross Weight	kg lb	Rate Class / Commodity Item No.	Chargeable Weight	Rate / Charge	Total	Nature and Quantity of Goods (incl. Dimensions or Volume)

Prepaid	Weight Charge	Collect	Other Charges
	Valuation Charge		
	Tax		
	Total other Charges Due Agent		Shipper certifies that the particulars on the face hereof are correct and agrees THE CONDITIONS ON THE REVERSE HEREOF.
	Total other Charges Due Carrier		
			Signature of Shipper or his Agent
Total Prepaid		Total Collect	Carrier certifies that the goods described hereon are accepted for carriage subject to THE CONDITION OF CONTRACT ON THE REVERSE HEREOF, the goods then being in apparent good order and condition except as noted hereon.
Currency Conversion Rates		CC Charges in Dest. Currency	
			Executed on (date) at (place) Signature of Issuing Carrier
For Carriers Use only at Destination	Charges at Destination	Total Collect Charges	

COPY

複合運送証券（Combined Transport B/L）

SHIPPER		B/L No.
CONSIGNEE		**K-LS** **Kanzei Logistics System, Ltd.** COMBINED TRANSPORT BILL OF LADING
NOTIFY PARTY		Received in apparent good order and condition except as otherwise noted the total number of containers or other packages or units shown below for transportation from the place of receipt or the port of loading to the place of destination or the port of discharge subject to the terms hereof. One of this original Combined Transport Bills of Lading must be surrendered duly endorsed in exchange for the Goods or Delivery Order. In accepting this Bill of Lading, the Merchant (as defined by Article 1 on the back hereof) agrees to be bound by all the stipulations, exceptions, terms and conditions on the face and back hereof, whether written, typed, stamped, data processed or printed, as fully as if signed by the Merchant, any local custom or privilege to the contrary notwithstanding, and agrees that all agreements or freight engagements for and in connection with the transport of the Goods are superseded by this Bill of Lading.
PRE-CARRIAGE BY	PLACE OF RECEIPT	Party to contact for cargo release
OCEAN VESSEL VOY. NO.	PORT OF LOADING	
PORT OF DISCHARGE	PLACE OF DELIVERY	FINAL DESTINATION (FOR MERCHANT'S REFERENCE ONLY)

PARTICULARS FURNISHED BY SHIPPER

MARKS AND NUMBERS CONTAINER NO. & SEAL NO.	NO. OF PKGS OR CONTAINERS	DESCRIPTION OF PACKAGES AND GOODS TYPE OR KIND OF — PACKAGES — OR — CONTAINERS	GROSS WEIGHT	MEASUREMENT

COPY

FREIGHT & CHARGES	R/TONS	RATE	PER	PREPAID	COLLECT

EX. RATE @ ¥	PREPAID AT	PAYABLE AT	PLACE OF B(S)/L ISSUE DATED
	TOTAL PREPAID IN YEN	NO. OF ORIGINAL B(S)/L	IN WITNESS WHEREOF three (3) original Bills of Lading have been signed, not otherwise stated above, one of which being accomplished the others shall be void.

LADEN ONBOARD		**Kanzei Logistics System, Ltd.**
DATE : _____	BY : _____	BY : _____
		AS CARRIER

第7章 Chap.7

信用状（郵送）

Letter of Credit (Mail)

①NAME OF ISSUING BANK THE BANK OF AUSTRALIA, LTD. AUCKLAND, NEW ZEALAND	②IRREVOCABLE DOCUMENTARY CREDIT	ORIGINAL ③ Number SG-36-25

⑤Date and Place of Expiry
OCT.30, 20××, TOKYO

④Place and Date of Issue
AUCKLAND, SEP. 25, 20××

⑥Applicant
THE AUCKLAND STEEL, LTD.
100 Pacific St. #206
Newton, Auckland, New Zealand

⑦Beneficiary
THE KATSURAGI CORPORATION
2-8-6 Shiba-Koen, Minato-ku,
TOKYO, JAPAN

⑧Advising Bank
TOKYO CITY BANK, LTD.
2-10-8 Otemachi, Chiyoda-ku, Tokyo

⑨Amount
US$94,054.00
(SAY US DOLLARS NINETY FOUR
THOUSAND AND FIFTY FOUR ONLY)

Dear Sir(s),

⑩ We hereby issue in your favor this documentary credit which is available by negotiation against your draft(s) at sight drawn on us for 100% of the Invoice value, accompanied by the following documents;

⑪ 1 Signed Commercial Invoice in 3 copies

2 Full set of clean On Board Ocean Bills of Lading made out to the order showing FREIGHT PREPAID and marked Notify Applicant.

3 Insurance Policy/Certificate in duplicate for 110% of the invoice value endorsed in blank stipulating claims payable in AUCKLAND, NEW ZEALAND, covering Institute Cargo Clauses (A), Institute War Clauses, Institute Strikes Clauses.

4 Packing List in 3 copies

⑫ Covering : STAINLESS STEEL SHEETS AND COILS
　　　　　 Order No.T6695, 6696, 6697　　CIP AUCKLAND

⑬Shipment from: JAPAN To AUCKLAND Latest Oct.20, 20××	⑭Partial Shipments Prohibited	⑮Transshipment Prohibited

Special Conditions;
⑯ All bank charges outside NEW ZEALAND are for the account of beneficiary.
⑰ Documents must be presented within 10 days after the date of issuance of the Bill of Lading or other shipping documents, but not later than expiry date.

⑱ The negotiations under this credit are strictly restricted to Tokyo City Bank, Ltd.

⑲ For reimbursement, please reimburse yourselves by debiting our A/C with you.

⑳ THE AMOUNT OF ANY DRAFT UNDER THIS CREDIT MUST BE ENDORSED ON THE REVERSE HEREOF.

㉑ WE HEREBY AGREE WITH THE DRAWERS, ENDORSERS AND BONA FIDE HOLDERS OF DRAFTS DRAWN UNDER AND IN COMPLIANCE WITH THE TERMS OF THIS CREDIT THAT THE SAME SHALL BE DULY HONORED ON DUE PRESENTATION TO THE DRAWEES.
YOURS VERY TRULY.

㉒ Signed
AUTHORIZED SIGNATURE

㉓ THIS CREDIT IS SUBJECT TO UNIFORM CUSTOMS AND PRACTICE FOR DOCUMENTARY CREDITS (2007 REVISION), INTERNATIONAL CHAMBER OF COMMERCE PUBLICATION NO.600.

第 7 章　Chap.7

信用状（電信）

Letter of Credit (Cable)

```
         700   ISSUE A DOCUMENTARY CREDIT
               OUTPUT HEADER      F 01 1645 081230ABCJPJTAXXX2836216351
               INPUT HEADER          1345 081230XYZTWTPXXXA5645683153
  ①          SENDER'S BANK       THE BANK OF AUSTRALIA, LTD.

               MESSAGE TYPE, PRIORITY 700 N
          27   *SEQUENCE OF TOTAL               : 1/1
  ②      40A   *FORM OF DOCUMENTARY CREDIT      : IRREVOCABLE
  ③       20   *DOCUMENTARY CREDIT NUMBER       : SG-36-25
  ④      31C   *DATE OF ISSUE                   : XX0925
  ⑤      40E   *APPLICABLE RULES                : UCP LATEST VERSION
  ⑥      31D   *DATE AND PLACE OF EXPIRY        : XX/10/30, JAPAN
  ⑦       50   *APPLICANT                       : THE AUCKLAND STEEL, LTD.
                                                   100 PACIFIC ST. #206 NEWTON, AUCKLAND, NEW ZEALAND
  ⑧       59   *BENEFICIARY                     : THE KATSURAGI CORPORATION
                                                   2-8-9 SHIBA-KOEN, MINATO-KU, TOKYO 123-4567, JAPAN
  ⑨      32B   *AMOUNT                          : USD94,054.00
  ⑩      39A   *PERCENT. LC AMOUNT TOLERANCE    : 5% MORE OR 5% LESS
  ⑪      41A   *AVAILABLE WITH                  : TOKYO CITY BANK, LTD.
                                                   BY NEGOTIATION
  ⑫      42C   *DRAFT AT                        : SIGHT FOR FULL INVOICE VALUE
  ⑬      42A   *DRAWEE                          : THE BANK OF AUSTRALIA, LTD.
  ⑭      43P   *PARTIAL SHIPMENTS               : NOT ALLOWED
  ⑮      43T   *TRANSSHIPMENTS                  : NOT ALLOWED
  ⑯      44E   *PORT OF L/A OF DEPARTURE        : AS FOLLOWS
               JAPANESE PORT
  ⑰      44F   *PORT OF D/A OF DESTINATION      : AS FOLLOWS
               AUCKLAND PORT
  ⑱      44C   *LATEST DATE OF SHIPMENT         : XX/10/20
  ⑲      45A   *SHIPMENT OF GOODS               : AS FOLLOWS
               STAINLESS STEEL SHEETS AND COILS, ORDER NO. T6695, 6696, 6697
               CIP AUCKLAND
  ⑳      46A   *DOCUMENTS REQUIRED              : AS FOLLOWS
  (1)          SIGNED COMMERCIAL INVOICE IN 3 COPIES
  (2)          PACKING LIST IN 3 COPIES
  (3)          FULL SET OF CLEAN ON BOARD OCEAN BILLS OF LADING MADE OUT TO ORDER
               SHOWING 'FREIGHT PREPAID' AND MARKED NOTIFY APPLICANT
  (4)          INSURANCE POLICY OR CERTIFICATE IN DUPLICATE FOR 110% OF THE INVOICE VALUE
               ENDORSED IN BLANK STIPULATING CLAIMS PAYABLE IN AUCKLAND, NEW ZEALAND, COVERING
               INSTITUTE CARGO CLAUSES (A), INSTITUTE WAR CLAUSES, INSTITUTE STRIKES CLAUSES.
  ㉑      47A   *ADDITIONAL CONDITIONS           : AS FOLLOWS
               + HANDLING CHARGE OF USD50.00 WILL BE DEDUCTED FROM THE PROCEEDS OF EACH
               PRESENTATION OF DISCREPANT DOCUMENTS, WHICH HAS TO BE REFERRED TO APPLICANT
               FOR ACCEPTANCE. NOTWITHSTANDING ANY INSTRUCTION TO THE CONTRARY, THIS
               CHARGE SHALL BE FOR ACCOUNT OF BENEFICIARY.
  ㉒      71B   *CHARGES                         : AS FOLLOWS
               ALL BANK CHARGES OUTSIDE NEW ZEALAND ARE FOR THE ACCOUNT OF BENEFICIARY.
  ㉓       48   *PERIOD FOR PRESENTATION         : DOCUMENTS MUST BE PRESENTED WITHIN 10 DAYS AFTER
                                                   THE DATE OF ISSUANCE OF THE BILL OF LADING OR OTHER
                                                   SHIPPING DOCUMENTS, BUT NOT LATER THAN EXPIRY DATE.
  ㉔       49   *CONFIRMATION INSTRUCTION        : WITHOUT
  ㉕       78   *INSTRUCTIONS TO THE PAYING/ACCEPTING/NEGOTIATING BANK : AS FOLLOWS
               + NEGOTIATING BANK MUST FORWARD DRAFTS AND DOCUMENTS TO US IN ONE LOT, WITH
               ADDRESS: 111 XYZ ROAD, AUCKLAND, NEW ZEALAND
               + THE AMOUNT OF EACH DRAFT MUST BE ENDORSED ON THE REVERSE OF THIS CREDIT BY
               THE NEGOTIATING BANK.
               + FOR REIMBURSEMENT, PLEASE REIMBURSE YOURSELVES BY DEBITING OUR A/C WITH YOU.
  ㉖      57a   *'ADVISE THROUGH' BANK           : TOKYO CITY BANK, LTD.
               TRAILER    -CHK:28460513A51C5
                          MAC:00000000
```

第 7 章　Chap.7

荷為替手形
（Bill of Exchange）

BILL OF EXCHANGE　　　NO　1234

FOR　US$94,054.00　　　　　　　　　　　October 22, 20XX

　　AT　XXXX　SIGHT OF THIS SECOND BILL OF EXCHANGE (FIRST OF THE
SAME TENOR AND DATE BEING UNPAID) PAY TO TOKYO CITY BANK, LTD. OR ORDER
THE SUM OF　SAY U.S. DOLLARS NINETY FOUR THOUSAND FIFTY FOUR ONLY.

....
....

VALUE RECEIVED AND CHARGE THE SAME TO ACCOUNT OF　THE AUCKLAND STEEL, LTD.
100 Pacific St. #206, Newton, Auckland, New Zealand
DRAWN UNDER　THE BANK OF AUSTRALIA, LTD.
L/C NO.　SG-36-25　DATED　SEP. 25, 20XX
TO　THE BANK OF AUSTRALIA, LTD.

　　　　　　　　　　　　　　　　　THE KATSURAGI CORPORATION

　　　　　　　　　　　　　　　　　　　-Signed-

　　　　　　　　　　　　　　　　　　F.Nakagawa
　　　　　　　　　　　　　　　　Shipping Manager

第7章　Chap.7

荷為替手形(記載項目の説明)

Bill of Exchange (Instructions in Japanese)

為替手形　　　　**BILL OF EXCHANGE**　　NO. インボイス番号

FOR　L/C 金額　　　　　　　　　　銀行買取り日付

AT　一覧支払い　SIGHT OF THIS SECOND BILL OF EXCHANGE (FIRST OF THE
SAME TENOR AND DATE BEING UNPAID) PAY TO　買取銀行　OR ORDER THE SUM OF

L／Cの金額記入（英語での記入）

SAY U.S. DOLLAR 金額 ONLY.又は SAY JAPANESE YEN 金額 ONLY.と記載

VALUE RECEIVED AND CHARGE THE SAME TO ACCOUNT OF ....輸入業者名 及び 住所の記載

DRAWN UNDER　L/C 発行銀行名 ....

L/C NO.　L/C 番号 ....　DATED L/C 発行日付 ....　　　会 社 名　　収入印紙
TO ....名宛人を記載 ....　　　サ イ ン　　¥200-

　　　　　　　　　　　　　　　　　　　　　　　　名　前

L/C に記載されている
DRAWN ON US と書かれている場合は、名宛人(DRAWEE)は、信用状発行銀行
宛に TO の欄に書きいれます。
DRAWN ON APPLICANT と L/C に記載されている場合は、この APPLICANT
は、L/C 開設依頼人を意味しているので、この開設依頼人の名前を記載します。
又、同時に住所の記載が要求される事がありますので、注意してください。

収入印紙は割印の代わりに自筆英語のサインをして下さい。
特に、誤字などのタイプミスは一字たりとも L/C 買取り銀行で受け付けませんの
で注意して下さい。

Commercial Invoice（商業送り状）（L/C用）

Commercial Invoice (for L/C)

INVOICE

THE KATSURAGI CORPORATION

2-8-6 Shiba-Koen, Minato-ku
Tokyo 123-4567, Japan
Phone: 81(3)3456-7890 Fax:81(3)3456-7893

Date	October 18, 20××
Invoice No.	ASW-102-00
Ref. No.	

Buyer

THE AUCKLAND STEEL, LTD.
100 Pacific St, #206
Newton, Auckland, New Zealand

Payment Terms

IRREVOCABLE L/C AT SIGHT IN OUR FAVOR

L/C No.		Date	
SG-36-25		SEP. 25, 20××	

Vessel or	On or about
FES-GO 43/750	October 20, 20××

From	Via
TOKYO, JAPAN	

Issuing Bank

THE BANK OF AUSTRALIA, LTD.

To	
AUCKLAND	

Remarks

Marks & Nos.	Description of Goods	Quantity	Unit Price	Amount
			CIP AUCKLAND	
	STAINLESS STEEL SHEETS AND COILS		IN US$	
	T6695 STAINLESS STEEL SHEETS 120cm × 150cm	80 SHEETS	US$550.00/SHEET	US$44,000.00
	T6696 STAINLESS STEEL SHEETS 200cm × 200cm	120 SHEETS	US$250.00/SHEET	US$30,000.00
	T6697 STAINLESS COILS	100 PIECES	US$200.00/PIECE	US$20,000.00
	ELEMENT			US$54.00
AUCKLAND STEEL AUCKLAND CTN NO. 1-300 MADE IN JAPAN				
TOTAL	200 SHEETS & 100 Pcs.		CIP US$94,054.00	

THE KATSURAGI CORPORATION

－Signed －

authorized signature

Packing List（梱包明細書）(L/C用)

Packing List (for L/C)

PACKING LIST

THE KATSURAGI CORPORATION

2-8-6 Shiba-Koen, Minato-ku
Tokyo 123-4567, Japan
Phone: 81 (3) 3456-7890 Fax: 81 (3) 3456-7893

Date	October 18, 20××
Invoice No.	ASW-102-00
Ref. No.	

Buyer	Payment Terms
THE AUCKLAND STEEL, LTD. 100 Pacific St, #206 Newton, Auckland, New Zealand	IRREVOCABLE L/C AT SIGHT IN OUR FAVOR

L/C No.	Date
SG-36-25	SEP. 25, 20××

Vessel or	On or about	Issuing Bank
FES-GO 43/750	October 20, 20××	
From	Via	THE BANK OF AUSTRALIA, LTD.
TOKYO, JAPAN		
To		Remarks
AUCKLAND		

Case No.	Description of Goods	Quantity	Net Weight	Gross Weight	Measurement
	STAINLESS STEEL SHEETS AND COILS				
1-80	T6695 STAINLESS STEEL SHEETS 120cm × 150cm	80 Cartons	800kg	850kg	18M3
81-200	T6696 STAINLESS STEEL SHEETS 200cm × 200cm	120 Cartons	1,200kg	1,300kg	30M3
201-300	T6697 STAINLESS COILS ELEMENT	100 Cartons	800kg	850kg	12M3
AUCKLAND STEEL AUCKLAND CTN NO. 1-300 MADE IN JAPAN					
	TOTAL	300 Cartons	2,800kg	3,000kg	60M3

THE KATSURAGI CORPORATION

－Signed －
_____
authorized signature

Bill of Lading (B/L) (船荷証券) (L/C用)

Bill of Lading (B/L) (for L/C)

(Forwarding Agents)

Shipper	B/L No.
THE KATSURAGI CORPORATION	FES-9720

FES LINE

FAR EAST SEA

BILL OF LADING

Consignee	
to the order	

RECEIVED by the Carrier from the Shipper in apparent good order and condition unless otherwise indicated herein, the Goods, or the container(s) or package(s) said to contain the cargo herein mentioned, to be carried subject to all the terms and conditions provided for on the face and back of this Bill of Lading by the vessel named herein or any substitute at the Carrier's opinion and / or other means of transport, from the place of receipt or the port of loading to the port of discharge or the place of delivery shown herein and there to be delivered unto order or assigns.

If required by the Carrier, this Bill of Lading duly endorsed must be surrendered in exchange for the Goods or delivery order.

In accepting this Bill of Lading, the Merchant agrees to be bound by all the stipulations, exceptions, terms and conditions on the face and back hereof, whether written, typed, stamped or printed, as fully as if signed by the Merchant, any local custom or privilege to the contrary notwithstanding, and agrees that all agreements or freight engagements for and in connection with the carriage of the Goods are superseded by this Bill of Lading.

In witness whereof, the undersigned, on behalf of Far East Sea Line, the Master and the owner of the Vessel, has signed the number of Bill(s) of Lading stated under, all of this tenor and date, one of which being accomplished, the others to stand void.

Notify Party	
THE AUCKLAND STEEL, LTD. 100 Pacific St. #206 Newton, Auckland, New Zealand	

Pre-carriage by	Place of Receipt TOKYO CY	
Ocean Vessel "FES-GO"	Voy.No. 43/750	Port of Loading TOKYO
Port of Discharge AUCKLAND	Place of Delivery AUCKLAND CY	Final Destination(for the Merchant's reference only)

Container No.	Seal No. Marks & Nos.	No. of Containers or P'kgs. Kind of Packages	Description of Goods	Gross Weight	Measurement
			"SHIPPER'S LOAD AND COUNT" "SAID TO CONTAIN"	3,000KGS	60.000M3
FES-081946-1	FES-MLB WA 123		200 SHEETS STAINLESS STEEL SHEETS		
			100 PIECES OF STAINLESS COILS		
	300 CARTONS		and ELEMENTS		
			Order No.T6695, 6696, 6697		
AUCKLAND STEEL					
AUCKLAND			" FREIGHT PREPAID "		
CTN NO. 1-300					
MADE IN JAPAN					
			SAY: ONE(1) CONTAINER ONLY.-		
			OR THREE HUNDRED(300) CARTONS ONLY		
TOTAL NUMBER OF CONTAINERS OR PACKAGES (IN WORDS)					

Particulars furnished by the Merchant

FREIGHT & CHARGES	Revenue Tons	Rate	Per	Prepaid	Collect
Ocean Freight	FREIGHT AS ARRANGED			FREIGHT AS ARRANGED	

	Ex. Rate	Prepaid at TOKYO, JAPAN	Payable at	Place of B(s)/L Issue TOKYO, JAPAN OCTOBER 19, 20××	Dated
ICS B/L	@	Total Prepaid in Local Currency	Number of Original B(s)/L THREE (3)	FAR EAST SEA LINE	

Laden on Board the Vessel

Date TOKYO, JAPAN, OCT. 20, 20×× By _Signed_

By _Signed_

(JSA STANDARD FORM A)
SECOND ORIGINAL

(TERMS CONTINUED ON BACK HEREOF)

第8章　Chap.8

B/L Instructions

B/L INSTRUCTIONS (Container Vessel Only)

SHIPPER	BOOKING NO.	B/L NO.
	FORWARDER'S NAME	TEL （市外局番を必ず御記入ください）
	NO. OF BL INSTRUCTIONS **1 OF**	NO. OF ATTACH SHEET
CONSIGNEE	FAX NO.(FAX サービス用) 1)	2)
	WAYB/L ☐　RECEIVED B/L ☐　FREIGHT AS ARRANGED ☐	
NOTIFY PARTY		
	ALSO NOTIFY PARTY	
PRE-CARRIAGE BY	PLACE OF RECEIPT （SERVICE TYPE）	
OCEAN VESSEL　　VOY.NO.	PORT OF LOADING	
PORT OF DISCHARGE	PLACE OF DELIVERY (SERVICE TYPE)	FINAL DESTINATION (for the Merchant's reference only)

PARTICULARS FURNISHED BY SHIPPER

MARKS & NUMBERS	NO. OF CONTAINERS OR PACKAGES	KIND OF PACKAGES　　DESCRIPTION OF GOODS	GROSS WEIGHT	MEASUREMENT

TOTAL NUMBER OF CONTAINERS
OR PACKAGES (IN WORDS)

PREPAID AT	PAYABLE AT	PLACE OF B(S)/L ISSUE	NUMBER OF ORIGINAL B(S)/L

CONTAINER NO.	SEAL NO.	SIZE	TYPE	NO. OF PACKAGE(S)		CARGO WT	TARE WT	GROSS WT (PER CTNR)	M3 (PER CTNR)	TEMP/DANGEROUS
				NUMBER	PKG TYPE					

TYPEは下記から選択願います。
DRY(DRY CTNR) / **REF** (REEFER CTNR) / **TNK** (TANK CTNR) /**OPT**(OPEN TOP CTNR) /**FLT**(FLAT RACK CTNR)
HCD (HIGH CUBE DRY CTNR) / **HCR** (HIGH CUBE REEFER CTNR)

Shipping Instruction

SHIPPING INSTRUCTION

To :   Date :
                                                       Ref No.

Shipper	Invoice No.
	荷物搬入日
Consignee	荷物搬入先
Notify Party	海貨業者
	船会社
Vessel	Sailing Date
Port of Loading	Destination
Description	

○○○○○○○ Company Limited

Name　:
Title　:

第8章　Chap.8

Shipping Instruction（記載項目の説明）

Shipping Instruction(Instructions in Japanese)

SHIPPING INSTRUCTION

To：　海貨業者　宛（海貨業者に業務を委託した場合）　　　　Date：インボイス作成日
又は　船会社／代理店 宛　　　　　　　　　　　　　　　　　Ref No.控え番号

Shipper　荷送人（輸出者） 通常、L/C に記載されている BENEFICIARY（受益者）が Shipper となる	Invoice No. 　インボイス（送り状）番号
	荷物搬入日 海貨業者と打合せて搬入日を決める
Consignee　荷受人 L/C に FULL SET OF CLEAN ON BOARD BILL OF LADING MADE OUT TO ORDER と記載の時 MADE OUT TO ORDER となっているので TO ORDER（指図人宛の D/L を作成するようにとの指示）と記入	荷物搬入先 海貨業者と打合せて搬入場所を決める
Notify Party　着荷通知先 例えば L/C に NOTIFY APPLICANT（L/C 発行依頼人）となっていたら、指示通り発行依頼人である輸入者名を記入	海貨業者 船積前に海貨業者を選定しておく 通常は海貨業者が船会社の手配業務を代行
	船会社 船会社／代理店と連絡を取り船名、出港日の打合せを行う
Vessel 　　"船名"	Sailing Date 　　出港日
Port of Loading 　　船積港	Destination 　　仕向地

Description　　内容
FCA、CPT、CIP など 契約条件の記載 ケースマークの表示　　　　商品の明細 バイヤーからの指定が　　　L/C 取引の場合は L/C 条件どおりに記載する事 あれば、指定通りに記 入しなければならない 指定がない場合は輸出者 が決める 　　　　L/C No.の記載 　　　"FREIGHT PREPAID" 　　　L/C に指示されている場合のみ記載

○○○○○○○ Company Limited

サイン
名　前
役　職

第8章 Chap.8

輸出申告書

Export Declaration Form in Japan

輸 出 申 告 書

税関様式C第5010号

	申 告 番 号

あ て 先 ＿＿＿＿＿＿＿ 長殿

申 告 年 月 日 ＿＿＿＿＿＿＿

積 込 港 ＿＿＿＿＿＿＿

積載船（機）名 ＿＿＿＿＿＿＿

出港予定年月日 ＿＿＿＿＿＿＿

仕 向 地 ＿＿＿＿＿＿＿
（都市） （国）

輸出者住所氏名 ＿＿＿＿＿＿＿

代理人住所氏名 ＿＿＿＿＿＿＿

仕向人住所氏名 ＿＿＿＿＿＿＿

蔵 置 場 所

積 込 港 符 号

船（機）籍 符 号

貿 易 形 態 別 符 号

仕向国（地）符号

輸 出 者 符 号

※ （調査用符号）

本 船 扱		ふ 中 扱	

品 名	統 計 品 目 番 号	単 位	数 量	申 告 価 格 （F.O.B）	※（調査欄）
(1)				千 円	
(2)				千 円	
(3)				千 円	

個数、記号、番号

「外国為替及び外国貿易法」及び「輸出貿易管理令」関係

	（該当）	（非該当）
外国為替及び外国貿易法第48条第1項に基づく輸出貿易管理令第1条第1項別表第1の 項		
輸出貿易管理令第2条第1項第 号別表第2の 項		
輸出貿易管理令第4条第 項第 号の別表第 の 項（号）		
輸出貿易管理令第1条第1項別表第1の 項	（許可要）	（許可不要）

輸出許可証又は輸出承認証の番号

認定製造者（特定製造貨物輸出申告）

運送者（特定委託輸出申告及び特定製造貨物輸出申告）

保税運送区 分	※承認		
	陸路、 海路、 空路		
期 間 年 月 日から 年 月 日まで			

申 告 書 枚 欄

※許可印・許可年月日

添付書類（輸出貿易管理令関係を除く）

仕 入 書	（有）
輸 出 取 引 承 認 書	
その他関税法第70条関係許 可・承 認 書 等（法令名）	

関税定率法、関税暫定措置法第 条第 項第 号関係

内国消費税輸出免税（還付金）関係

※積 込 年 月 日

※ 税関記入欄

1 検査場検査

2 現場検査

※受 理　※審 査

通 関 士 記 名

（注） ※印の欄は記入しないで下さい。

「不服申立てについて」この申告に基づく処分について不服があるときは、その処分があったことを知った日の翌日から起算して3月以内に税関長に対して再調査の請求又は財務大臣に対して審査請求をすることができます。

（規格A4）

税関様式C第5010号-2

輸 出 申 告 書 （つづき）

個数・記号・番号	※税関記入欄	申　告　番　号	
		積 込 港 符 号	
		船（機）籍符号	
		貿易形態別符号	
		仕向国（地）符号	
		輸 出 者 符 号	
		※ （調査用符号）	

品　　　　名	統 計 品 目 番 号	単 位	数　　　　　量	申 告 価 格　（F．O．B）	※ (調査欄)
（　）				千　　　　　円	
（　）				千　　　　　円	
（　）				千　　　　　円	
（　）				千　　　　　円	
（　）				千　　　　　円	

（規格A4）

第9章 Chap.9

輸入（納税）申告書

Import (Customs Duty Payment) Declaration Form in Japan

輸入（納税）申告書
（内国消費税等課税標準数量等申告書兼用）

申告年月日

税関様式 C 第5020号

申告番号

IC	IS	IM	IA	BP
RE-IMP	ISW	IMW	IAC	IBP

あ て 先　　　　　　　　長崎　船（取）卸港

船（取）卸港符号

輸 入 者　　　　　　　積載船（機）名

船（機）籍符号

住所氏名（名
称及び代表者
の氏名）　　　　　　　入 港 年 月 日

貿易形態別符号

電 話 番 号　　　　　　原 産 地

原産国（地）符号

（都市）　　　　（国）

代 理 人　　　　　　　積 出 地

輸 入 者 符 号

住 所 氏 名　　　　　　　　　　　　（都道府県名　　　　）

電 話 番 号　　　　　　船荷証券番号

※
（調査用符号）

仕 出 人

蔵 置 場 所

住 所 氏 名　　　　　　　蔵入、移入又は総保入先

品　名		単位	正 味 数 量	申告価格（CIF）△内国消費税等課税標準額	税　率 △種別等・税率	関 税 額 △内国消費税等税額	減免税条項 適用区分
番　号	統計細分						

貨物の個数・記号・番号

関税法施行令第4条第1項第3号
又は第4号に係る事項　有　無

評価申告書　Ⅰ　Ⅱ　個別　包括

評価
申告

包括申告
受理番号

税　額
合　計
（欄数）　枚

関　税（　欄）
△　税（　欄）
△　税（　欄）
△ 消費税（　欄）
△ 地方消費税（　欄）

添付書類（許可・承認・申請等輸入承認又は契約の許可番号）

納期限の延長に係る事項　延長しない税額

※許可・承認印、許可・承認年月日

				（税額）	円 （特定月）　　月	
関税	包個			（納期限）　年　月　日		
所・地税	包個			（税額）　　　　円 （特定月）　　月		
				（納期限）　年　月　日		円
税	包個			（税額）　　　　円		
				（納期限）　年　月　日		円

仕 入 書

仕入書に代わる書類

原 産 地 証 明 書

本船扱・ふ中扱・
輸 入 前 申 告 扱

（有）税関確認

輸入貿易管理令
別表第1・2第　号

関税法第70条関係許可・承認等

法令名

食品・植物・家畜・薬事・化審

※ 受 理　　　※ 審 査　　　※ 収 納

通 関 士 記 名

（注）　1.　※印の欄は記入しないで下さい。
　　　2.　この申告による課税標準又は納付すべき税額に誤りがあることがわかったときは、修正申告又は更正の請求をすることができます。なお、輸入の許可後、税関長の調査により、この申告による税額等を更正することがあります。
　　　3.　この申告に基づく処分について不服があるときは、その処分があったことを知った日の翌日から起算して3月以内に税関長に対して再調査の請求又は財務大臣に対して審査請求をすることができます。

（規格A4）

税関様式C第5020号-2

輸入（納税）申告書（つづき）
(内国消費税等課税標準数量等申告書兼用)

貨物の個数・記号・番号	条税関記入欄

	申　告　番　号
輸（取）卸港符号	
船（機）籍符号	
貿易形態別符号	
原産国（地）符号	
輸入者符号	
申 （調査別符号）	

品　名 番　号 統計細分	単位	正味数量	申告価格（CIF） △内国消費税等課税標準額	税　率 △種別等・税率	関税額 △内国消費税等税額	減免税条項 適用区分
（　）税表番号細分			千　円 基 筐 特 暫 減免税額	千　円 符号 定率 別表 輸 暫定	条 項 号 条 項 号	
		酒 名 消 地		減免税額	輸 条 項 号	
		酒 名 消 地		減免税額	輸 条 項 号	
		酒 名 消 地		減免税額		
（　）税表番号細分			千　円 基 筐 特 暫 減免税額	千　円 符号 定率 別表 輸 暫定	条 項 号 条 項 号	
		酒 名 消 地		減免税額	輸 条 項 号	
		酒 名 消 地		減免税額	輸 条 項 号	
		酒 名 消 地		減免税額		
（　）税表番号細分			千　円 基 筐 特 暫 減免税額	千　円 符号 定率 別表 輸 暫定	条 項 号 条 項 号	
		酒 名 消 地		減免税額	輸 条 項 号	
		酒 名 消 地		減免税額	輸 条 項 号	
		酒 名 消 地		減免税額		
（　）税表番号細分			千　円 基 筐 特 暫 減免税額	千　円 符号 定率 別表 輸 暫定	条 項 号 条 項 号	
		酒 名 消 地		減免税額	輸 条 項 号	
		酒 名 消 地		減免税額	輸 条 項 号	
		酒 名 消 地		減免税額		

備　考　：　用紙の大きさは縦297ミリメートル、横210ミリメートル（日本工業規格A列4番）とする。

（規格A4）

第9章　Chap.9

輸入許可通知書（NACCS見本　空欄）

Import Declaration (NACCS Sample Blank Copy)

（別紙7－2）　別紙様式M-507号

1 / 2

〈AIR/IMP〉　　　　　　　　　　　　輸入許可通知書

代表税番	申告種別	区分	あて先税関	部門	申告年月日	申告番号

[ ]

申告条件 [ ]　　　　　　　申告予定年月日　　　　　本申告 [ ]

輸　入　者　　－
　住　所

　電　話
輸入取引者　　－
仕　出　人　　－
　住　所

輸出の委託者
　　　　　－

代　理　人　　　　　　　　　　　　　　　　　　　　　通関士コード

AWB番号　　－　　　　　　貨物個数　　　　個　保税地域
MAWB番号　－　　　　　　貨物重量　　　　　　搬入予定
　　　　　　　　　　　　　　　　　　　　　　　　最初蔵入年月日
取　卸　港　　　　　　　　　　　　　　　　　　　貿易形態別符号
積　出　地　　　　　　　　　　　　　　　　　　　調査用符号
積載機名
入港年月日

貿易管理令 [ ]　輸入承認証 [ ]　　仕入書番号　　－
関税法70条関係許可承認　　　　　　　仕入書（電子）　－
共通管理番号　　　　　　　　　　　　仕入書価格　　　－　　－　　－
食品　　　　　　　　　　　－　　　　運賃　　　　　　－　　　　－
植防　　　　　　　　　　　　　　　　保険　　　　　　－　　　　－
動検　　　　　　　　　　　－　　　　通関金額　　　　－
輸入承認証番号等(1)　　　　　　　　　評価　　　　　　　　　　　－
　　　　　　　　(2)　　　　　　　　　補正　　　　　　－　　　　－
　　　　　　　　(3)
　　　　　　　　(4)　　　　　　　　　BPR合計　　　　－　　　　　　　　計算 [ ]
　　　　　　　　(5)　　　　　　　　　原産地証明 [ ]　戻税申告 [ ]　内容点検結果 [ ]

税科目	税額合計	欄数		通貨レート	－
			納税額合計		
			担保額		

納期限延長 [ ]　都道府県　　BP申請事由　　石油承認
口座　　　　　　　　　　　　　　　　　たばこ登録
納付方法 [ ]
　　　　　　　　　　　　　　　　　　　構成　　枚　欄

記事（税関）

記事（通関）　　　　　　　　　　　　利用者整理番号
記事（荷主）　　　　　　　　　　　　社内整理番号

［税関通知欄］

　輸入許可日　　　　　　　審査終了日　　　　　　　　事後審査

　　　　　　　　　　　　　延滞税額合計

（注）この申告による課税標準又は納付すべき税額に誤りがあることがわかったときは、修正申告又は更正の請求をすることができます。なお、輸入の許可後、税関長の調査により、この申告による税額等を更正することがあります。
（注）この申告に基づく処分について不服があるときは、その処分があったことを知った日の翌日から起算して3月以内に税関長に対して再調査の請求又は財務大臣に対して審査請求をすることができます。

<AIR/IMP>

別紙様式M-507号
2 / 2

輸入許可通知書（つづき）

代表税番	申告種別 [ ]	区分	あて先税関	部門	申告年月日	申告番号

< 01 欄 >統合先欄
品名
税表番号
申告価格（ＣＩＦ）

品目番号　　　　　　-　　　　価格再確認 [ ]
数量（1）
数量（2）
課税標準数量

関税率
関税額
減免税額

輸入令別表　　　　　　　　特恵 [ ]
ＢＰＲ按分係数
ＢＰＲ金額　　　-

減免税　　　　　　法
　　　　　　　　　令
　　　　　　　　　別表

欠減控除数量

運賃按分 [ ]　原産地　-　-

― 内国消費税等(1)
　課税標準額

種別
課税標準数量

　税率
　税額
　減免税額

減免税
　条項

― 内国消費税等(2)
　課税標準額

種別
課税標準数量

　税率
　税額
　減免税額

減免税
　条項

― 内国消費税等(3)
　課税標準額

種別
課税標準数量

　税率
　税額
　減免税額

減免税
　条項

― 内国消費税等(4)
　課税標準額

種別
課税標準数量

　税率
　税額
　減免税額

減免税
　条項

― 内国消費税等(5)
　課税標準額

種別
課税標準数量

　税率
　税額
　減免税額

減免税
　条項

― 内国消費税等(6)
　課税標準額

種別
課税標準数量

　税率
　税額
　減免税額

減免税
　条項

第9章　Chap.9

実行関税率表(一部)

An Excerpt from Customs Tariff Schedules of Japan

番 号 No.	統計 細分 Stat. Code No.	NACCS用	品　名	税　率 Rate of Duty 基 本 General	協 定 WTO	特 恵 Preferential	暫 定 Temporary	単位 Unit	Description
(0802.12)	100	3	1 ビターアーモンド	無税 Free	(無税) (Free)			KG	1 Bitter almonds
	200	5	2 スイートアーモンド	4%	2.4%	無税 Free		KG	2 Sweet almonds
			ヘーゼルナット(コリュルス属のもの)						Hazelnuts or filberts (*Corylus spp.*):
0802.21	000	6	殻付きのもの	10%	6%	無税 Free		KG	In shell
0802.22	000	5	殻を除いたもの	10%	6%	無税 Free		KG	Shelled
			くるみ						Walnuts:
0802.31	000	3	殻付きのもの	10%	(10%)	×無税 Free		KG	In shell
0802.32	000	2	殻を除いたもの	10%	(10%)	×無税 Free		KG	Shelled
			くり(カスタネア属のもの)						Chestnuts (*Castanea spp.*):
0802.41	000	0	殻付きのもの	16%	9.6%	×無税 Free		KG	In shell
0802.42	000	6	殻を除いたもの	16%	9.6%	×無税 Free		KG	Shelled
			ピスタチオナット						Pistachios:
0802.51	000	4	殻付きのもの	無税 Free	(無税) (Free)			KG	In shell
0802.52	000	3	殻を除いたもの	無税 Free	(無税) (Free)			KG	Shelled
			マカダミアナット						Macadamia nuts:
0802.61	000	1	殻付きのもの	5%	(5%)	2.5% ×無税 Free		KG	In shell
0802.62	000	0	殻を除いたもの	5%	(5%)	2.5% ×無税 Free		KG	Shelled
0802.70	000	6	コーラナット(コラ属のもの)	20%	12%	×無税 Free		KG	Kola nuts (*Cola spp.*)
0802.80	000	3	びんろう子	無税 Free	(無税) (Free)			KG	Areca nuts
			その他のもの						Other:
0802.91	000	6	殻付きの松の実	20%	12%	×無税 Free		KG	Pine nuts, in shell
0802.92	000	5	殻を除いた松の実	20%	12%	×無税 Free		KG	Pine nuts, shelled
0802.99			その他のもの						Other:
	100	0	1 ペカン	5%	4.5%	無税 Free		KG	1 Pecans
	900	2	2 その他のもの	20%	12%	×無税 Free		KG	2 Other
08.03			バナナ(プランテインを含むものとし、生鮮のもの及び乾燥したものに限る。)						Bananas, including plantains, fresh or dried:
0803.10			プランテイン						Plantains:
			1 生鮮のもの						1 Fresh:

(注) 08.03　植物防疫法　食品衛生法

(Note) 08.03　Plant Quarantine Law　Food Sanitation Law

番 号 No.	統計 細分 Stat. Code No.	NACCS用	品 名	税 率 Rate of Duty				単位 Unit	Description
				基 本 General	協 定 WTO	特 恵 Preferential	暫 定 Temporary		
(0803.10)	100	†₁	(1) 毎年4月1日から同年9月30日までに輸入されるもの	40%	20%	10% ×無税 Free		KG	(1) If imported during the period from 1st April to 30th September
	100	†₂	(2) 毎年10月1日から翌年3月31日までに輸入されるもの	50%	25%	20% ×無税 Free		KG	(2) If imported during the period from 1st October to 31st March
	200	5	2 乾燥したもの	6%	3%	無税 Free		KG	2 Dried
0803.90			その他のもの						Other :
			1 生鮮のもの						1 Fresh.
	100	†₁	(1) 毎年4月1日から同年9月30日までに輸入されるもの	40%	20%	10% ×無税 Free		KG	(1) If imported during the period from 1st April to 30th September
	100	†₂	(2) 毎年10月1日から翌年3月31日までに輸入されるもの	50%	25%	20% ×無税 Free		KG	(2) If imported during the period from 1st October to 31st March
	200	2	2 乾燥したもの	6%	3%	無税 Free		KG	2 Dried
08.04			なつめやしの実、いちじく、パイナップル、アボカドー、グアバ、マンゴー及びマンゴスチン(生鮮のもの及び乾燥したものに限る。)						Dates, figs, pineapples, avocados, guavas, mangoes and mangosteens, fresh or dried :
0804.10	000	6	なつめやしの実	無税 Free	(無税) (Free)			KG	Dates
0804.20			いちじく	10%	6%	3% ×無税 Free			Figs :
	010	6	―生鮮のもの					KG	Fresh
	090	2	―乾燥したもの					KG	Dried
0804.30			パイナップル						Pineapples :
	010	†	1 生鮮のもの	20%	17%	×無税 Free		KG	1 Fresh
	090	6	2 乾燥したもの	12%	7.2%	×無税 Free		KG	2 Dried
0804.40			アボカドー	6%		無税 Free			Avocados :
	010	0	―生鮮のもの		3%			KG	Fresh
	090	3	―乾燥したもの		3%			KG	Dried
0804.50			グアバ、マンゴー及びマンゴスチン	6%	3%	無税 Free			Guavas, mangoes and mangosteens :
			―生鮮のもの						Fresh :
	011	5	――マンゴー					KG	Mangoes
	019	6	――その他のもの					KG	Other
	090	0	―乾燥したもの					KG	Dried
08.05			かんきつ類の果実(生鮮のもの及び乾燥したものに限る。)						Citrus fruit, fresh or dried :
0805.10			オレンジ						Oranges :
	000	†	1 毎年6月1日から同年11月30日までに輸入されるもの	20%	16%	×無税 Free		KG	1 If imported during the period from 1st June to 30th November

(注) 08.04,08.05 　植物防疫法
食品衛生法

(Note) 08.04,08.05 　Plant Quarantine Law
Food Sanitation Law

Letter of Guarantee

Letter of Guarantee

Delivery without Bill of Lading

①To :Macky Japan Co., Ltd.　　　　　　　　Date:　Dec. 10, 20XX

②　M.V. "Korean Pearl"　　　　　　　③ Voy　No. CSF-008

④　　at　　Tokyo　　　　　on　December 10, 20XX

⑤B/L No.	FB-5814	⑥Shipper	Korean Trading Co., Ltd.
⑦Marks	KTC	⑧Port of	Busan
&	Tokyo	Shipment	
Container	C/T No. 1-10	⑨Port of	Tokyo
Nos.	Made in Korea	Delivery	
⑩Description	Plate Heater	⑪Contact	Minato Soko Co., Ltd.
of Goods		乙仲	
⑫Number of	10 cartons	Person Tel	03-1234-5678
Packages	(23,800 pcs)	担当者	Ichirou Yamada
⑬Remarks	Nil		

In consideration of your granting us delivery of the above mentioned goods and consigned to the undersigned, without presentation of Bill of Lading which has not yet been received by us, we hereby agree and undertake to surrender the said Bill of Lading duly immediately on obtaining, or at latest within one month after this date, and further guarantee to indemnify you against all consequences that may arise from your so granting us delivery, and to pay you on demand any freight and/or charges that may be due on the cargo.

We hereby certify that the Bill of Lading covering the above consignment is not hypothecated to any other bank or person. In the event of the said Bill of Lading being hypothecated to any other bank or person, we further guarantee to hold you harmless from all consequences whatever arising thereafter.

Yours faithfully,

⑭ WASEDA TRADING CO., LTD.

Consignee　(Singed)

We, the undersigned, hereby join in the above indemnity and jointly and severally guarantee due performance of the above contract and accept all the liabilities expressed therein.

⑮ The Tokyo-City Bank, Ltd.

Banker　(Singed)

海上運送状（Sea Waybill）

Shipper	WAYBILL No.
	FES LINE
Consignee	FAR EAST SEA
	SEA – WAYBILL
Notify Party	RECEIVED by the Carrier from the Shipper in apparent good order and condition unless otherwise indicated herein, the Goods, or the container(s) or package(s) said to contain the cargo herein mentioned, to be carried subject to all the terms and conditions on the face and back hereof by the vessel named herein or any substitute at the Carrier's opinion and /or other means of transport, from place of receipt or the port of loading to the port of discharge or the place of delivery shown herein and there to be delivered unto the Consignee named herein, or its authorized agents, on production of proof of identity. The carrier to exercise due care ensuring that delivery is made to the proper party. However, in case of incorrect delivery, no responsibility will be accepted unless due to malignant or gross negligence on the part of the Carrier. In witness whereof, the undersigned, on behalf of Far East Sea Line, as Carriers, has signed the number of Waybill(s) stated under, all of this tenor and date.

Pre-carriage by	Place of Receipt	
Ocean Vessel	Voy. No.	Port of Loading
Port of Discharge	Place of Delivery	Final Destination(for the Merchant's reference only)

Container No.	Seal No. :Marks & Nos.	No. of Contain-ers or P' kgs.	Kind of Packages:	Description of Goods	Gross Weight	Measurement

Particulars furnished by the Merchant

TOTAL NUMBER OF CONTAINERS OR PACKAGES (IN WORDS)

NON–NEGOTIABLE

FREIGHT & CHARGES	Revenue Tons	Rate	Per	Prepaid	Collect

TCS
B/L

Ex. Rate	Prepaid at	Payable at	Place and date of issue
@	Total Prepaid in Local Currency	Number of Original Waybill(s)	**FAR EAST SEA LINE**
	Laden on Board the Vessel		
Date		By	

(JSA STANDARD FORM A)
SECOND ORIGINAL

(TERMS CONTINUED ON BACK HEREOF)

事故通知

Notice of Damage

Messrs.　JP Sea Line Co., Ltd.

Tokyo,　April. 11, 20××

Notice of Damage

Please be advised that damage has been found in connection with the following goods, for which we reserve the right to file a claim with you when the details are ascertained.

Condition of Damage　1 Carton Heavy Wet (20 pcs.)

Ship's Name :　M/S "Neptune"　　B/L No.　JP-12345

Arrived at : Tokyo　　　　　　　VOY No.　No.IT-882

Shipped on :　April 8, 20××　　INV.No.　IF03-124

Shipped from :　Busan, Korea　　I/P No.　23-336

Marks & Nos.	Description of Goods	No. of P'kgs	Quantity
KFC Tokyo C/No.1-100 Made in Korea	LEATHER JACKET		
	(1)Model : M-12	36 cartons	720 pcs.
	(2)Model : M-15	50 cartons	1,000 pcs.
	(3)Model : M-23	14 cartons (One carton heavy wet)	280 pcs.
	Total	100 Cartons	2,000 pcs.

You are kindly requested to acknowledge this notice and to inform us in writing of your candid opinion on this matter as soon as possible.

Yours truly,

Japan Trading Co., Ltd.

— Signed —

保険金請求書

Insurance Claim Form

Messrs. The Japan Marine & Fire Insurance Co. Ltd.

Tokyo,   April 11, 20××

Dear Sirs:
  We are presenting to you a claim with the supporting documents as attached and shall be glad of your remittance to our designated bank account in due course.

Yours truly,
Japan Trading Co., Ltd.
— Signed —

Policy No.	23-336
Vessel	"Neptune"
Arrived at	Tokyo Shipped on April 8, 20××
Casualty	Container Broken Cont's 1 Carton Heavy Wet

Calculation :

Cargo Amount Insured   ¥4,153,600
———————————————————————   R = 1.11058823529
Invoice Amount   ¥3,740,000   (US$34,000.00)

Model : M-23   1 Carton × @FOB¥110,000 × R = ¥122,164

Amount of Claim ¥122,164

The following paper to be submitted together :

☒ Insurance policy (Original endorsed)   ☒ Bill of Lading (Signed Copy)

☒ Shipper's signed Invoice   ☒ Cargo Boat Note, Devanning Report

☐ Landing Report   ☐ Survey Report

☒ Notice of Claim to Carriers

☒ Letter from Carrier (Shipping Co.) on rejection of claim

☐ Other Documents

銀行口座	東京シティー銀行 丸の内支店 当座預金 123456
	口座名義 カブ)ニホンボウエキ

索引

Index

索引

【あ】

一覧払手形 150
インコタームズ 060
インコタームズ2020 070
印刷条項 022,028
ウィーン売買条約（CISG）. 030
受取船荷証券 086,092,094,096,178
運送人渡し 070,072
運賃込み 070,076
運賃着払い 064
運賃保険料込み 070,076
運賃前払い 064
FCL貨物 090,174
LCL貨物 090,174
オールリスク 132

【か】

海貨業者 164,170
海上運送状 194
買取銀行 146
確定保険 136
確定申込み 012
課税標準 186
貨物の危険の移転時点 066
為替先物予約 050
為替変動リスク 044,050
関税込持込渡し 070,074
還付 188
勧誘 010
期限付手形 152
旧ICC 112
協会貨物約款（A）. 116
協会貨物約款（B）. 116
協会貨物約款（C）. 116
協会貨物約款（ICC）. 112
協会貨物約款（航空貨物）. 116

協会ストライキ約款 116,124
協会戦争危険担保約款 134
協会戦争約款 116,124
協会同盟ひ業暴動騒乱担保条項 134
共同海損 114,132
クレーム 030
経済連携協定 188
原産地証明書 188
減免税 188
航空運送状 104
工場渡し 070,072
国際航空運送協会 100
国際複合輸送 106
故障付船荷証券 098
個別予定保険 136
コンテナ船 086
コンテナ・ターミナル 170
コンテナ・フレート・ステーション
. 094,170,172
コンテナ・ヤード 094,170,172
混載航空運送状 104
梱包明細書 054

【さ】

サーベイ 204
サーベイ・レポート 204
在来船 086
事故通知 202
市場調査 002
仕向地持込渡し 070,074
重量逓減制 102
重量容積建て 090
商業送り状 054
白地裏書 070
新ICC 112
信用状 142
信用リスク 044
スペース・ブッキング 088
製造物責任 208

船側渡し 070,074
全損 114,132
送金小切手 158
損害鑑定人 204

【た】

代金回収リスク 044
代金取立 156
タイプ条項 022
代理店契約 038
代理人 036
諾成契約 020
タリフ・レート 088
単独海損 114,132
着荷通知先 184
仲裁 222
懲罰的損害賠償金 214
追加被保険者 214
通知銀行 144
定期船 086,088
定型取引条件 062
ディスクレパンシー 148
電信送金 158
独占的代理権 038
独占的販売権 038
特別特恵受益国 188
特恵関税 188
特恵受益国 188

【な】

荷卸込持込渡し 070,074
荷為替手形 142
荷渡指図書 184,190

【は】

バース・ターム 088
バラ荷 088
反対申込み 010,012
販売店契約 038

PL保険 212
引合い 010
引受け 152
ファーム・オファー 012
付加危険 124
不可抗力 030
複合運送人 106
複合運送証券 108
普通送金 158
不定期船 086,088
船積通知 178
船積船荷証券 086,092
船荷証券 054,146
フレート・トン 090
紛争の解決 030
分損 114
分損担保 132
分損不担保 132
貿易条件 060
包括予定保険 138
保険金額 116
保険証券 056
保証 030
保証状荷渡し 192
保税地域 168,186
ボックス・レート 090
本クレーム 202
本船渡し 070,074
本人 036

【ま】

マスター・エア・ウェイビル 102,104
無過失責任 208
無故障船荷証券 098,200
免税 188
申込み 010,012
戻し税 188
元地回収B/L 196

【や】

ユーザンス手形 152
輸出FOB保険 068
輸出許可証 176
輸出実務 164
輸出申告 176
輸出通関 168
輸出手形保険 156
輸出PL保険 212
輸送費込み 070,072
輸送費保険料込み 070,074
輸入許可 192
輸入実務 182
輸入申告 192
輸入PL保険 216
予定保険 136
予備クレーム 202

【ら】

ライナー・ターム 088
リマーク 098,200
利用運送事業者 106
利用航空運送事業者 100,102

【A】

acceptance 153
additional insured 215
advising bank 145
agency agreement 039
agent 037
air cargo consolidator 103
air freight forwarder 101
Air Waybill 102,103,104,105
amount insured 117
A/R（All Risks） 131,132,133
arbitration 223

【B】

BAF → Bunker Adjustment Factor . . . 091

Berth Term 089
bill for collection 157
Bill of Lading → B/L 054,055,146,147
B/L → Bill of Lading 054,055,146,147
B/L instructions 166,167,176,177
blank endorsement 071
bonded area 169,187
Box Rate 091
bulk cargo 089
Bunker Adjustment Factor → BAF . . . 091

【C】

CAF → Currency Adjustment Factor . . 091
Carriage Paid To 071
Carriage and Insurance Paid To 071
Certificate of Origin 189
CFR 064,065
CFR → Cost and Freight . . 070,071,076,077
CFS → container freight station
. . . . 094,095,170,171,172,173
CIF 064,065
CIF → Cost Insurance and Freight
. . . . 070,071,076,077
CIP → Carriage and Insurance Paid To
. . . . 070,071,074,075
CISG → United Nations Convention on
Contracts for the International
Sale of Goods（Vienna, 1980） 031
claim 031
claim notice 203
clean B/L 099,201
collection risk 045
combined transportation 107
Combined Transport Bill of Lading
. 108,109
combined transport operator 107
Commercial Invoice 054,055
consensual contract 021

container freight station → CFS
. . . . 094,095,170,171,172,173
container ship 087
container terminal. 171
container yard → CY
. . . . 094,095,170,171,172,173
conventional vessel 087
Cost and Freight 071
Cost Insurance and Freight 071
counter offer 011,013
CPT → Carriage Paid To. . 070,071,072,073
credit risk 045
Currency Adjustment Factor → CAF . . 091
currency exchange risk 045,051
customs broker. 165,171
CY → container yard
. . . . 094,095,170,171,172,173

【D】

D/A. 154,155
DAP → Delivered at Place
. . . . 070,071,074,075
D/D → Demand Draft 158,159
DDP → Delivered Duty Paid
. . . . 070,071,074,075
definite insurance contract 137
Delivered at Place 071
Delivered at Place Unloaded 071
Delivered Duty Paid 071
Delivery Order → D/O. . . 184,185,190,191
Demand Draft → D/D 158,159
discrepancy 148,149
distributorship agreement. 039
D/O → Delivery Order . . . 184,185,190,191
documentary bill. 143
D/P 154,155
DPU → Delivered at Place Unloaded
. . . . 070,071,074,075

【E】

Economic Partnership Agreement → EPA
. 188,189
E/D → Export Declaration 176,177
E/P → Export Permit. 176,177
EPA → Economic Partnership Agreement
. 188,189
exclusive agency 039
exclusive distributorship. 039
Export Bill Insurance 157
export clearance 169
Export Declaration → E/D 176,177
Export Permit → E/P. 176,177
export practice 165
export PL insurance 213
extraneous risk 125
EXW → Ex Works 070,071,072,073
Ex Works 071

【F】

FAF → Fuel Adjustment Factor 091
FAS → Free Alongside Ship
. . . . 070,071,074,075
FCA → Free Carrier 070,071,072,073
FCL cargo → Full Container Load Cargo
. . . . 091,173,174,175
final claim 203
firm offer. 013
force majeure. 031
forward exchange contract 051
FOB 062,063,064,065
FOB → Free On Board
. . . . 062,070,071,074,075
FOB Attachment Clause 068,069
foul B/L. 099
FPA (Free from Particular Average)
. 131,132,133
Free Alongside Ship 071

Free Carrier 071
Free On Board. 062,063,071
Freight Collect 064,065
freight forwarder. 165,171
Freight Prepaid 064,065
Freight Ton 091
Fuel Adjustment Factor → FAF 091
Full Container Load Cargo → FCL cargo
. . . . 091,173,174,175

【G】
General Average 114,115,133
Generalized System of Preferences → GSP
. . . . 189
GSP beneficiary country 189
GSP → Generalized System of Preferences
. . . . 189

【H】
House Air waybill. 104,105

【I】
IATA → the International Air Transport
Association 100,101
ICC (1963) 113
ICC (1982) 113
ICC(A). 118,119
ICC(B). 118,119
ICC(C). 120,121
I/D → Import Declaration 191
Import Declaration → I/D 191
Import Permit → I/P. 191
import PL insurance. 217
import practice. 183
I/P → Import Permit 191
the International Air Transport Association
→ IATA. 101
Incoterms 060,061
Incoterms 2020. 071

inquiry 011
institute cargo clauses (A) 117
institute cargo clauses (B) 117
institute cargo clauses (C) 117
Institute Cargo Clauses (Air) (excluding
sending by post). 116,117
Institute Strikes Clauses (Cargo)
. . . . 116,117,124,125
institute cargo clauses (ICC). 112,113
Institute Strikes Riots and Civil Commotions
Clauses(S.R.C.C. Clauses) 134,135
Institute War Clauses (Cargo)
. . . . 116,117,124,125,134,135
Insurance Policy 056,057

【L】
L/C → Letter of Credit. 142,143
LCL cargo → Less than Container Load
Cargo 091,173,174,175
LDC → least developed country 189
Letter of Guarantee → L/G 192,193
least developed country → LDC 189
Less than Container Load Cargo
→ LCL cargo 091,173,174,175
Letter of Credit → L/C 142,143
L/G → Letter of Guarantee 192,193
liner. 087,089
Liner Term 089

【M】
MAR Form 112,113
Mail Transfer → M/T 158,159
market research 003
Master Air Waybill 104,105
M/T → Mail Transfer 158,159
Multimodal Transport Bill of Lading
. 108,109

【N】

negotiating bank 147
Non-Vessel Operating Common Carrier
　→ NVOCC 106,107,108,109
notify party 184,185
NVOCC → Non-Vessel Operating Common
　Carrier 106,107,108,109

【O】

offer 011,013
on board notation 098,099
open cover contract 138,139

【P】

Packing list 054,055
Partial Loss 114,115
Particular Average 114,115,133
P/L → Product Liability 208,209
preliminary claim 203
principal 037
printed clause 023,029
Product Liability (P/L) 209
product liability insurance 213
proposal 011
provisional insurance contract . . .136,137
punitive damages 214,215

【R】

Received B/L . . . .
　086,087,092,093,094,095,096,097,178,179
remark 099,201

【S】

Sea Waybill 194,195
settlement of dispute 031
S.G. Form 112,113
Shipped B/L
　. 086,087,092,093,096,097
shipping advice 178,179
shipping instruction 166,167,176,177
sight bill 151

space booking 089
strict liability 209
Surrendered B/L 196,197
survey 204,205
surveyor 204,205
survey report 204,205

【T】

Tariff Rate 089
tax base 187
Telegraphic Transfer → T/T 158,159
Total Loss 114,115
trade terms 060,061,063
tramper 087,089
transfer of risks 067
T/T → Telegraphic Transfer 158,159
typed clause 023

【U】

United Nations Convention on Contracts
　for the International Sale of Goods
　(Vienna, 1980) 031
usance bill 153

【W】

WA (With Average) 131,132,133
warranty 031
W/M 091

【Y】

YAS → Yen Appreciation Surcharge . . 091
Yen Appreciation Surcharge → YAS . . 091

【0〜9】

3Cs 014,015
4Cs 014,015
4P 008
4Ps 009

（著　者）

曽我しのぶ

〔略　歴〕

早稲田大学卒業後、旧富士銀行（現・みずほ銀行）人事
部研修課にて外為研修ほか各種研修に従事。退職後、貿
易実務、国際法務、外国為替、通関士、ビジネス英語等
の講師活動を開始し、現在、ジェトロ認定貿易アドバイ
ザー有資格者としてジェトロ各事務所、商社、人材派遣
会社等の講座で活躍。海外展開を検討している企業への
コンサルタントも行っている。

基礎から学ぶ**貿易実務** 日英対訳（改訂版）
2023年10月2日発行　ISBN 978-4-88895-507-2
発行所　公益財団法人 日本関税協会
〒101-0062 東京都千代田区神田駿河台3-4-2 日専連朝日生命ビル6F
URL https://www.kanzei.or.jp/